THE MEANING OF PHILOSOPHY

THE MEANING

OF

PHILOSOPHY

A Survey of the Problems of Philosophy
and
of the Opinions of the Philosophers

JOSEPH GERARD BRENNAN

BARNARD COLLEGE, COLUMBIA UNIVERSITY

HARPER & BROTHERS

Publishers   New York

THE MEANING OF PHILOSOPHY

To **MARY**

CONTENTS

PREFACE

PHILOSOPHY has not one, but many, meanings. As this book develops its themes from logic to the philosophy of art, some of these meanings may emerge. Here philosophy is presented by an introduction to its problems rather than to its history. Because the liveliest developments in our time have been in the fields of logic and language, these topics are given as a place of honor the opening chapters. Theory of knowledge comes next with new changes rung as well as old. Metaphysics is approached with respect; when all the anti-metaphysical complaints have been heard, the subject is defined in such a way that it need not be identified with nonsense. A chapter each to ethics and aesthetics, and the survey is complete.

Both student and general reader will find in these pages a cheerful assortment of philosophic names: those of contemporaries—Russell, Heidegger, Carnap, Wisdom, Sartre; those of the noble and recently deceased—Whitehead, Dewey, Croce, Santayana; and the grand old ones of the traditions—Plato, Aquinas, Kant, and the rest. In short, something for everybody.

As I wrote this modest introduction to philosophy, I thought constantly of my former teachers—J. H. Woods, A. N. Whitehead, C. I. Lewis, H. A. Wolfson, W. P. Montague. Specific aid came from my present or former colleagues. Professor John E. Smith, now of Yale, read the

larger part of the book in manuscript and contributed helpful criticisms. Professor Gertrude Rich read the book in
proof and made valuable suggestions. Professor Helen Huss
Parkhurst read the chapter on aesthetics. Thanks are also
due for various helpful things to my colleagues Professors
Edgar Lorch, Henry Boorse, Gertrude Hirst, and to Professor Arthur Szathmary of Princeton. My warm thanks go
to Professor William McEwen and to Hofstra College for
placing numerous facilities at my disposal. Thanks, too, to
Irene and Henry Acres for frequent and pleasant intervals
of hospitality during the writing process.

J. G. B.

April, 1953

THE MEANING OF PHILOSOPHY

INTRODUCTION

For philosophy, Socrates, if pursued in moderation and at the proper age, is an elegant accomplishment, but too much philosophy is the ruin of human life.
—CALLICLES, the Sophist

What Is Philosophy?

Everyone knows that "philosophy" comes from Greek words meaning love of wisdom. But since "wisdom" is even harder to define than "philosophy," a definition of our subject as love of wisdom does not tell us very much. It is not easy to define philosophy in such a way as to please everybody. Philosophers of an older day used to define the aim of their study as "the knowledge of things generally, from the point of view of their ultimate causes, so far as natural reason can attain to such knowledge." This definition is now considered too ambitious. Some hold that the most that may safely be said today is that philosophy is a study in which certain very general questions are raised about a number of different things. Perhaps we could go a little further to say that philosophy is that field of inquiry which studies basic assumptions or "first principles," whether those that people take for granted in ordinary life or those assumed in systems of organized knowledge. Professional philosophers sometimes wince when they hear businessmen talk about "the philosophy of advertising,"

or "the philosophy of the suburban home owner." Yet even
this popular usage of the term "philosophy" shows concern
with basic presuppositions or first principles. The common
phrase "philosophy of life" refers to some set of primary
beliefs according to which a man guides his conduct. A
"philosophy of history" proceeds from those basic assumptions upon which a particular historian's interpretation of
history depends. A "philosophy of science" sets forth principles more basic and comprehensive than the conclusions of
the individual sciences.

We have mentioned that philosophy is a subject in which
some very general questions are raised. What sort of questions? There are *logical* or *semantic* questions about inference, symbols, language, and meaning. There are *epistemological* questions about truth and certainty; about human
knowledge, its methods, its reliability, and its limits. There
are *metaphysical* questions about the cosmos and man's
place in it; questions about God, Nature, Mind, and human
existence. There are questions about the foundations of
value; that is, questions about *good,* whether this be the
good in conduct (morality) or the good in art (beauty).
All these are questions which have been raised at one time
or another by philosophers. Now not every philosopher is
interested in *all* these questions. Indeed a given philosopher
or group of philosophers living at a certain time or place
may be so interested in some particular set of problems that
they tend to define philosophy in terms of these problems
which absorb them.

In certain historical periods of culture, the philosophy of
the time is marked by agreement among philosophers as to
just what kind of questions philosophy should deal with.
In other periods (in eras of cultural transition perhaps, such

as our own) the philosophy of the day is scored by strife over what sort of things philosophers have the right to talk about. Today especially there is serious disagreement among professional philosophers as to the meaning of their own subject. This disagreement is not just a difference of opinion about the way in which particular philosophic problems should be solved. It is a quarrel over just what the proper business of philosophy *is*. "The task of philosophy," says one contemporary, "is as it always has been to answer the question 'What is Reality?'" "The business of philosophy today," says another, "is to formulate and to grapple with the moral problems presented to us by our social environment." What philosophy must do today, says a third, is to "confine itself to examination and analysis of the presuppositions of the sciences." Perhaps the confusion over the definition of philosophy might be reduced somewhat if we suggested that there are at least three different *approaches* to philosophy, and that a philosopher's opinion as to what the proper business of his subject may be will depend upon the particular set of interests and motives that brought him to philosophy. These three fundamental approaches to philosophy we may name the *analytic*, the *metaphysical*, and the *valuational*.

The Analytic Approach

Many come to philosophy because they feel it important to subject to analysis and critical reflection notions which are taken for granted by most of us. Such persons are attracted by rigor and precision in thinking; they admire exactness in procedure. The analytic philosopher asks *"How do you know?"* for he is interested in problems concerning the range, methods, and limits of human knowledge. He asks

"What do you mean?" for he is convinced that many
problems of philosophy will be solved if inquiry is made
into the meaning of the terms of the argument. Today the
analytic philosopher uses the highly developed technique
of modern logic to help him in his analysis of philosophical
problems. He may explore the relation between the symbolic structure of logic and the symbolism of language. The
concepts and methodologies of the special sciences interest
him, and he is likely to occupy himself with constructing a
"philosophy of science." If he belongs to an extreme school,
he may say that philosophy should stick to analysis of logical, linguistic, and basic scientific notions; that it no longer
has any business asking questions about God or the soul, or
mind or Nature, or human existence and its place in the
cosmos. Such questions he may tend to dismiss as "metaphysical."

The Metaphysical Approach

"The effort after the general characterization of the world
around us," says the philosopher Alfred North Whitehead,
"is the romance of human thought." Many come to philosophy to find a cosmic vision, a world perspective on
the universal scale; to set forth a systematic account of the
nature of things in terms that go far beyond those of the
special sciences both in generality and in depth. Metaphysics, or speculative philosophy as it is often called, has given
Western thought some of its greatest intellectual landmarks.
In ancient Greece, Plato taught that the world which our
senses disclose to us is but a transient copy of an eternal
realm of forms or "Ideas" to which all individual things
owe what poor measure of stability they have. In the Middle Ages, Aquinas described a hierarchy of Being, arranging

all things in gradations from God down through lower levels of the spiritual world, thence to man and to corporeal Nature. In modern times, Hegel charted the history of Spirit, a force which moves toward self-realization through Nature and through mind, generating along its dialectical course whole series of arts, cultures, religions and philosophies until at length it fulfills itself and becomes the Absolute.

Antimetaphysical philosophers claim that the day of these grand world-perspectives is over. Such visions, they say, are no more than poetry, for they do not describe the world as it is; they are but prescientific speculations, mythopoeic accounts of matters which only physical science is competent to describe. But metaphysically inclined philosophers reply that even today there is a place, and an important place, for speculative philosophy. For the physical scientist by nature of his work is restricted to those aspects of the universe and our experience of it which can be correlated with pointer readings, clocks, and rulers. The philosopher's scope is broader, so inclusive that he takes for his province *all* phases of experience—poetic, religious, moral, and social, as well as scientific. The aim of philosophy, the metaphysician tells us, is to formulate categories which will help us understand the underlying character of this all-inclusive scheme of things we call the world, and to assess with due proportion the role played within it by that tiny yet knowledgeable part if it—man.

The Valuational Approach

There are, among others, two types of values—moral and aesthetic. Moral values have to do with good in human conduct, that is, with what a person does with his life. Aesthetic values refer to good in aesthetic experience, in a word, to beauty whether found in Nature or in art. Many come to philosophy seeking answers to the question "What is the good life for man?" Such a philosopher whose dominant interest is *moral* presents us with a "philosophy of life," a doctrine concerning the nature of man, desirable goals of human life, principles by which we may guide our conduct. The interest of the moral philosopher is often said to be practical, since moral philosophy or "ethics" is more concerned with doing or action than with knowing. From Confucius and Socrates to Nietzsche and John Dewey, moral philosophy has been more strongly marked by interest in standards and values of human action and conduct than by speculative concern with ultimate cosmological factors.

Philosophy, in the sense of traditional metaphysical and moral philosophy, has much in common with religion. It is interesting to note how many of those who teach and write philosophy have had strong religious ties at least during some period of their lives. This should not surprise us, for both philosophy (in the sense above stated) and religion are concerned with the nature and destiny of man. The difference between philosophy and religion is usually explained by saying that religion holds its conclusions on the basis of faith, whereas philosophy establishes its conclusions without any appeal to religious faith, with no attempt to base its teachings on revelation, scriptures, religious doctrine, or tradition. In philosophy, arguments must stand on their own feet. In religious faith, there is no need for argument. If there were such need, it would no longer be religious faith. It would have become philosophy.

Integration of the Three Approaches?

There is an obvious disadvantage in explaining what philosophy is by dividing the approaches to the subject into three—analytic, metaphysical, and valuational. Such a division seems to imply that any given philosophy will fall neatly into one of three compartments. Now in practice this is rarely the case. Of course it is possible to single out individual philosophers whose interests are primarily analytic, and others whose interests are chiefly valuational. But many philosophers combine in their work elements from each of the three approaches. This is particularly true in classical philosophy. Consider Plato. His reliance on philosophical analysis is obvious to anyone who reads him. Whether the topic under discussion be knowledge, virtue, beauty, justice, or piety, philosophy for Plato always begins with an inquiry into the *meaning* of these concepts. This is followed by a closely reasoned analysis of the logical implications of the definitions offered. Plato's fame, however, does not rest on his talents as an analytic philosopher. The world knows him as a moralist and as a political philosopher, as well as a metaphysician on the grand scale. Not only Plato, but also most of the other great classical Western philosophers managed to combine in their thinking all three approaches to philosophy. In Aristotle, in Spinoza, in Kant, and in many others, we find a synthesis of the three approaches, an integration of critical analysis, systematic world perspective, and moral doctrine.

It would seem, therefore, that the philosophy would tend toward a synthesis or integration of the three elements—analysis, metaphysics, and value. But this again is too simple. In contemporary philosophy, the tendency has for some time been definitely away from integration. Philosophy today is polarized. At one pole stand those analytic philosophers who sincerely believe that metaphysics in the classical sense should be dropped from philosophy. These men hold that the job of philosophy is critical analysis, by aid of modern logical and linguistic techniques, of basic concepts employed in human discourse whether ordinary or scientific. At the opposite pole are those philosophers whose conception of the task of their subject is close to that of the classical philosophers. They believe that analysis, however important it may be, is never more than an instrument of philosophy; that the principal task of philosophy is to attempt the achievement of some kind of general world perspective together with some conclusions concerning the nature of man and the moral life. In between the two poles today are certain groups of philosophers trying for a new orientation, seeking a new set of concepts which might put an end to the strife between the scientific analysts and the humanistic traditionalists, thus permitting philosophy to "break through" once more. One such enterprise is Susanne Langer's "philosophy in a new key" in which the idea of the *symbol* is used as a new integrating concept to bridge such different areas of human thought and activity as logic, language, art, and religion.

This at least may be said. Despite their very different and frequently opposing concepts of the meaning of philosophy, nearly all philosophers, ancient and contemporary, are in fundamental agreement on one point. That is, that philosophy is an important enterprise and its business is serious business. Only a few old sophists like Callicles believe it to be a superficial and dilettantish pursuit. It may even be that Callicles himself took philosophy quite as seriously as it deserves, and that he was maliciously misquoted by Plato. For Plato was the pupil of Socrates, and Socrates bore the sophists no love. After all, they were his bitter competitors and took money for their teaching, while Socrates' only fees were the dinners his pupils gave him.

The Division of the Present Survey

The divisions of our survey of philosophy are rather conventional. The inquiry falls into two main parts, the first of which concentrates largely on the analytic side of philosophy, the second on the metaphysical and valuational. The analytic part of the survey is in its turn subdivided into inquiries concerning logic and language on the one hand, and on the other into epistemology or theory of knowledge in which are considered problems concerning the nature, scope, and methods of human knowledge. The second half of our survey proceeds to an examination of metaphysical topics, then enters the field of value with a brief tour of ethics, the science of the good, and concludes with aesthetics or philosophy of art.

PART I

LOGIC AND LANGUAGE

I

LOGIC AND FORMAL SCIENCE

---

*Contrariwise, if it was so it might be;
and if it were so, it would be; but as it
isn't, it ain't. That's logic.*
— Tweedledee in
Through the Looking Glass

What Is Logic?

Logic is a discipline first expounded in systematic form by the ancient Greek philosopher Aristotle. Since Aristotle's time, logic has been more or less closely associated with philosophy, although it has not always been regarded as an integral part of the subject. In our own century, logic has undergone extensive development. Today logic has particular prominence as an instrument of analytic philosophy.

It is not easy to explain just what logic is. Many who teach logic and write logic books have different opinions of the proper business of the subject. Some hold that it is the purpose of logic to teach people how to "think straight." If you take a course in logic, they say, you will learn how to "reason" properly and how to avoid error. This definition is too optimistic. "Thinking" is a word which designates an area of human activity which is very broad and not clearly delimited. Everyone would agree that if people could only learn how to "think correctly" it would be a fine thing. If there were a science which provided remedies for "bad thinking," one would suppose that every man would enroll for a course. But to date no such science has been developed. Logic has been taught as an academic subject in the West for more than two thousand years, and only a comparatively small number of students have taken the trouble to study it. It is well known that logic students, as well as their less industrious fellow men, are not immune to making mistakes in many important types of thinking.

Logic the Science of Inference?

"The province of logic," says the nineteenth-century English philosopher John Stuart Mill, "must be restricted to that portion of our knowledge which consists of inferences from truths previously known."[1] If the subject matter of logic is "restricted" to *inference*, logic is a very inclusive subject indeed, for most of what passes for human knowledge is derived by inference. Mill himself admits that it follows from his definition that the scope of logic must be wide. "By far the greatest portion of our knowledge . . . being avowedly matter of inference," he says, "nearly the whole, not only of science, but of human conduct is amenable to the authority of logic."[2] Although Mill's definition of logic as the *science of inference* is too broad to permit exactness, we may use it as the occasion of asking *what inference is,* and of stating an important distinction between two kinds of inference.

What Is Inference?

Inference, let us say, is *the process in which we pass from what is known to new knowledge.* There is an inference

[1] John Stuart Mill, *A System of Logic,* Longmans, Green and Co., London, 1925, p. 5.
[2] *Ibid.*

situation whenever there is a transition from what is now known to some further knowledge. Consider these examples of simple inference situations:

1. I wake up in the morning and notice that the room is rather gloomy. I see drops of water running down the outside of my windowpane, and I hear a light drumming sound on the roof. This is what I know. I *infer* that it is raining.

2. I am introduced to a gentleman whose name is Pablo Lopez. I *infer* that he is of Spanish ancestry.

3. I put some mercuric oxide in a test tube. Holding the tube over a lighted burner, I thrust a glowing splint of wood in the open end of the tube. The splint flares up in flame. I *infer* that oxygen is being liberated from the mercuric oxide.

4. The geometry teacher points out that angle A is equal to angle B, and that angle C is equal to angle B. I *infer* that angle A is equal to angle C.

Of course, not every inference is a sound one. Despite his name, Pablo Lopez may just possibly be of Irish ancestry, and, appearances to the contrary, it may not actually be raining. In such cases, the inference leads to "apparent" knowledge only. But at this point we are not concerned with the complex question of how to distinguish sound from unsound inferences. For the moment, we shall be content to consider some more examples of inference:

What Is Known	What Is Inferred
5. My friend, usually ruddy and good-natured, is pale and irritable today.	Either he did not have enough sleep last night or he is not feeling well.
6. Treason is a capital offense; to libel the king is treason.	To libel the king is a capital offense.

What Is Known	What Is Inferred
7. A kettle of water is being heated on the stove.	The water will boil at 212 degrees F.
8. Two parallel lines are cut by a transversal.	The alternate interior angles are equal.
9. My hostess yawns and glances at the clock.	She would like me to go home.
10. The number of New Yorkers who have hair on their heads is greater than the number of hairs any one New Yorker has on his head.[3]	There are at least two New Yorkers with the same number of hairs on their heads.
11. After I have placed a certain mineral specimen on an exposed photographic plate, a dark area forms on the plate.	The mineral contains a radioactive element.
12. Whatever is an element of A is also an element of B, and X is an element of A.	X is an element of B.
13. The prisoner was in the victim's apartment at the time of the murder, and his fingerprints were found on the gun.	He is guilty of the crime.

Formal and Empirical Inference

Let us now divide these random examples of inference into two kinds. Examples 4, 6, 8, 10, and 12 are of the sort known as *formal* or *deductive* inferences. In these instances, if you take "What Is Known" as true, then it follows, on no

---

[3] Cited by Morris Cohen and Ernest Nagel, *An Introduction to Logic and Scientific Method*, Harcourt, Brace and Co., 1934, pp. 5–7.

basis other than that of the statements alone, that "What Is Inferred" is also true. If two parallel lines are cut by a transversal, then it does not merely happen to be so that the alternate interior angles are equal. Within the framework of Euclidean geometry, it is so beyond question. Similarly, if the sentences "Treason is a capital offense" and "To libel the king is treason" are taken as true without reference to anything beyond the meaning of the sentences themselves, then the sentence "To libel the king is a capital offense" is certainly true. The reason formal inferences have this peculiar "certainty" will become apparent if we compare them with inferences of the *second* type (examples 1, 2, 3, 5, 7, 9, 11, 13). Miscellaneous though they be, inferences of the second variety have this in common: they all concern the character or behavior of things and events that make up the world around us. Most of the inferences we draw every day are of this type; they are known as *empirical* or *factual* inferences.

Empirical Inference and Scientific Method

The daily run of our empirical inferences includes many that are careless and random and some that are foolish. If we see a man display fondness for children and dogs, we may infer that he is a man of good character. This is an inference about the behavior of a human being, a very variable item of the world about us, and it is obviously not a careful inference. We frequently call this kind of inference "jumping to conclusions," because the inference process is attended by little reflection upon the nature of the evidence (if any) which supports it. We make more careful inferences about the empirical world when we *reflect* upon the data we know, pausing to consider whether these data afford sufficient grounds for justifying the conclusions we have reached. A conscientious citizen in the jury box will heed the judge's instruction to "weigh the evidence carefully" before he proceeds to the conclusion that the prisoner is guilty.

A very careful type of empirical inference procedure may be found in the methods of the physical sciences. Upon the basis of certain data (*what is known*), a bacteriologist may state provisionally that a given disease is caused by a certain virus (*what is inferred*). The latter statement—conventionally called a hypothesis—is tested experimentally under numerous and varied empirical conditions. The testing is an important part of the *verification* of the statement. We should not think, however, that "scientific method" concerns a special kind of inference which is wholly empirical and which is analyzable solely in terms of categories like "hypothesis" and "verification." "Scientific method" is a name we give to a careful and reflective form of the ordinary thinking we use in everyday life. Moreover, scientific method includes complex patterns of thought which employ formal as well as empirical or factual inference.

Broad and Narrow Senses of "Logic"

Taken in a very comprehensive sense, logic is the study of inference in general. Any systematic explanation of how conclusions are drawn from various types of evidence may be called logic. More precisely, logic refers to the study of *formal* inference. Ever since the rise of the physical sciences after the Renaissance, analysts of knowledge have tried to formulate a "logic" of scientific method which would rival, in its precision, the logic of formal inference. To date, however, these attempts have not been wholly successful. Methodologies of empirical science have failed to achieve the systematic character of formal logic chiefly because empirical inference is *not* formal inference. The latter, as we shall see, by its very nature lends itself to exactness and system.

Formal or Deductive Inference

Formal inferences do not appear to be inferences about things present to sense observation. They are of the kind found in the operations of arithmetic, geometry, and other mathematical disciplines. These sciences are called *formal* sciences to distinguish them from the *empirical* sciences, which include astronomy, physics, chemistry, etc. While the empirical sciences *employ* formal science (as in the case of physics, where mathematics is an indispensable instrument), they are ultimately concerned with the behavior of Nature.

The mode of inference employed in formal science is called *deduction*. Now there are at least three senses in which the word "deduction" may be taken. The term is popularly used simply as a *synonym for "inference,"* particularly the kind of inference detectives are supposed to rely upon. Admirers of Sherlock Holmes will remember that Holmes wrote a paper about "Deduction" which his newly met acquaintance Dr. Watson criticized as "ineffable twaddle." Whereupon the sleuth proceeded to explain how he "deduced" that Watson was a medical man and former army officer invalided out of the service after wounds received in Afghanistan.[4] Throughout his career, Holmes continued to astonish his ingenuous companion by such *tours de force* of "deduction." Brilliant as Holmes' deduc-

[4] A. Conan Doyle, *A Study in Scarlet*, chap. 1.

tions were, however, they were but miscellaneous kinds of inferences about very variable components of the empirical world. There was nothing especially "deductive" about them, if the term is taken in a strict sense.

A narrower usage of the term "deduction" identifies it with *that kind of inference we use in predicting an event by reference to a general empirical law.* From this sense of "deduction" is derived the frequent definition of the term as inference which proceeds from the general to the particular. From knowledge of a general pattern of events in Nature, I may infer that some particular state exists. Knowing that mammals suckle their young, I may infer deductively that a whale will nourish its offspring in this way. Recalling the law that gases expand when heated will cause me hurriedly to punch a hole in a can of beans I am heating in a saucepan over a fire. The fact that we can refer to general empirical laws in order to predict the behavior of particular cases is of enormous importance in the investigations of the physical sciences. The term "deduction" is frequently used in this sense in contrast to *induction*—a mode of empirical inference in which examination of particular instances leads us to formulate a general law. The generalization "Infants which are frequently cuddled thrive better than those which are not" is *inductively* established on the basis of examination of particular instances of babies. If, recollecting this generalization, a mother hastens to give her baby a little extra loving, she is proceeding via *deductive* inference.

The strictest sense of "deduction" is that generally employed in logic and formal science. Strict deduction may be defined thus: *When from a given statement or statements another statement or statements necessarily follows, the first is said to imply the second, and inference from the first to the second is said to be deductive.*[5] From the statements (1) "Danbury is north of Stamford" and (2) "Stamford is west of New London" we may infer deductively that (3) "Danbury is north of west of (northwest of) New London." Similarly, from the statement $2x + 5 = x + 10$, we may deduce that $x = 5$. It does not just *happen* that x equals 5. Granted the first equation, the second must follow by virtue of the formal scheme (algebra) of which these expressions are parts.

Meaning of "Formal"; Truth and Validity

We have referred to inferences of strict deductive type as *formal.* Generally speaking, a *form* is something that remains the same while that which is put into it may change. Federal Income Tax Form 5040 is the same for all who receive it from the Bureau of Internal Revenue, but the content filled in will vary with the individual taxpayer. So, in logic, inferences of strictly deductive character have nothing to do with any particular subject matter, even though the statements used in the inference process may refer to subject matter that is factual. The formal logician is concerned only with the *pattern*, with the *structure* of the relationship between the statements. Take, for instance, the example of strict deductive inference previously cited:

Danbury is north of Stamford.
Stamford is west of New London.

[5] Note the distinction between "infer" and "imply." The statements "X is twice Y" and "Y is twice Z" *imply* that "X is four times Z." The relationship of *implication* exists between the first two statements and the third whether anyone "draws the conclusion" or not. But when someone perceives the relationship of implication, and "draws the conclusion," then and not until then do we have *inference.* Inference has an element of psychological activity in it that implication lacks.

Therefore, Danbury is north of west of (northwest of) New London.

As formal logicians we are not concerned with the question of whether or not these statements are factually true. If we substitute "Buenos Aires" for "Danbury" in the first statement, the conclusion "Buenos Aires is northwest of New London" will follow. The deductive inference will still be formally sound although the conclusion happens as a matter of empirical fact to be false. Here we meet the distinction between *truth* and *validity*. Our deduction with the modified subject matter will be *valid*, even though the conclusion is not factually *true*. As formal logicians, we are not concerned with whether there are actual things named Buenos Aires or Danbury. What we are concerned with is the *form*, the deductive *pattern* upon which the subject matter is imposed:

A certain factor (A) is related in a certain way (r_1) to a second factor (B).

Factor B is related in a certain way (r_2) to a third factor (C).

Therefore, A's relationship to C is the product of relations r_1 and r_2, that is, R.

More precisely, this may be noted:

$$\frac{\begin{array}{l} A \ r_1 \ B \\ B \ r_2 \ C \end{array}}{A \ R \ C}$$

The Syllogism

Consider the classic syllogism, a deductive pattern first systematized by Aristotle. A valid syllogism provides us with two statements, called *premises*, from which a third statement, the *conclusion*, necessarily follows. Let us examine the syllogism:

> All marsupials carry their babies in their pockets.
> All wallabies are marsupials.
> Therefore, all wallabies carry their babies in their pockets.

A quick inspection of this syllogism will convince us that the conclusion follows necessarily, if the premises are taken as true. Now consider this syllogism:

> All angels have wings.
> All amoebas are angels.
> Therefore, all amoebas have wings.

Again, the conclusion follows, if the first two statements are taken as true, and the deduction is valid. It might be objected that there may be no such things as angels, and that amoebas are not angels but unicellular animals. But this objection is irrelevant, because the soundness of the deduction lies not in the factual truth of the statements but in the way the pattern is put together:

> All *a*'s are *b*'s.
> All *c*'s are *a*'s.
> Therefore, all *c*'s are *b*'s.

Now consider the following syllogism:

> New Englanders are Americans.
> Bostonians are Americans.
> Therefore, Bostonians are New Englanders.

This is clearly not a valid deduction, even though the conclusion may happen to be an empirically true statement. The fact that two subclasses happen to fall within the same class is no reason for asserting that therefore one subclass contains the other. Fish swim and so does Jane, but it does not *therefore* follow that Jane is a fish. Nor is the following syllogism valid:

> Philanthropists are generous.
> No beggars are philanthropists.
> Therefore, no beggars are generous.

Because a class K has a property P, it does not necessarily follow that a class outside of K does not have the property P.

LOGIC AND FORMAL SCIENCE

Modern Generalized Logic

Aristotle's brilliant treatment of logic was limited to analysis of the syllogism and its constituent parts. For over two thousand years the development of formal logic moved almost wholly along lines Aristotle had staked out. Medieval logicians devised remarkable analytic techniques in logic and analysis of language. They did not succeed, however, in widening appreciably the borders of purely formal logic beyond the limits of the syllogism. In the seventeenth century, the German philosopher-mathematician Leibniz envisioned a universal symbolic language based on mathematical concepts. The work of Boole, Frege, and others initiated in the nineteenth century a revolutionary expansion of logic beyond the classical Aristotelian boundaries. In our own century there has been tremendous development of logic. The publication in 1910 of the monumental *Principia Mathematica* of Whitehead and Russell is the great initial landmark of this development.

It is now known that logic can be set forth as a purely formal and deductive science with a breadth and inclusiveness far beyond bounds ever dreamed of by Aristotle. This new extended logic is popularly referred to as *symbolic logic*. In some respects this is a misleading name. Modern generalized logic is not a logic *different* from the classical system founded by Aristotle in the sense that it treats of a wholly separate order of concepts. The new logic is, however, far more inclusive, and its basic concepts are far more generic than are those of classical logic.

Logic and Mathematics

Contemporary experts generally agree that formal logic, conceived in the extended modern sense, is the science of the general structure of deduction or formal inference. It is further generally held that mathematical disciplines such as arithmetic, algebra, and geometry are *particular cases* of the amalgamation of certain general logical concepts with concepts peculiar to the special formal discipline in question (as "number" in the case of arithmetic). In other words, the various mathematical disciplines *presuppose* or assume the principles of logic and are therefore related to logic as the particular is related to the general.

Moreover, it is widely agreed that "logic" is not the name of any *single* formal deductive system. Rather "logic" is the name we give to all possible sets of systems of a purely formal deductive character.

The Structure of Formal Science

Logic, then, is a formal or deductive science of very general character. The propositions of logic are not derived from sense observation but "follow" from other previously established statements. Arithmetic and algebra are deductive disciplines, too, but they are not usually presented to us *as such.* Our first arithmetic teacher did not approach the subject by saying, "Now children, we shall begin the study of arithmetic with a definition of number. We will then list the primary axioms and rules of arithmetic, and proceed to deduce some interesting theorems, among them '2 + 2 = 4.'" In learning arithmetic, we plunge into the middle of it. In secondary school, however, we do encounter an example of a deductive system *presented in strict form.* This is plane geometry, which for most of us represents our first acquaintance with a deductive system presented *as such.* Although geometry can give us a good idea of what a logical system is like, the classical system of Euclid is less generic than logic, for it supports a specifically geometrical subject matter.

A formal or deductive system is built up in the following way. Certain undefined notions are put forward, together with a set of statements which are admitted without proof. The latter are the *axioms* or *postulates* of the system. Selected *definitions* are set forth, and specific *rules* are laid down which allow us to perform certain operations upon the postulates. Using the postulates, definitions, and rules, we are able to show that certain *statements* necessarily follow. These statements are called *theorems* in the system. In the demonstration of a theorem, previously demonstrated theorems may be used as well as the basic postulates and definitions.

Analytic and Synthetic Statements

What are analytic statements, and how do they differ from *synthetic* statements? Classical logic tells us that a statement or *proposition* is composed of two *terms*, subject and predicate. In the proposition "Gold is a heavy metal" *gold* is the subject term, *heavy metal* the predicate term. Now in analytic propositions, the predicate term is *equivalent* to, though not necessarily identical in form with, the subject term. That is, in analytic propositions, the predicate is something like a *definition* of the subject. Consider the sentence: *Bachelors are unmarried men.* If we analyze the subject term, "bachelor," by asking what are the attributes of a bachelor, we quickly come upon the properties "man" and "unmarried." But in the sentence we are considering, these attributes are explicitly stated by the predicate term. Since, upon analysis of the subject term of the statement, we found the predicate *implicit* in it, the statement "Bachelors are unmarried men" is *analytic*.

Suppose someone should tell you that recently he came upon a bachelor who was married, you would not say, "What an interesting exception to the general rule—something like a white kangaroo!" Rather you would say, "You are not using the word 'bachelor' in the way I am using it." Your reply would show that you recognized the proposition "Bachelors are unmarried men" to be analytic, and that such statements are not established by empirical observation but by certain rules governing the proper use of language.

Now contrast with the statement "Bachelors are unmarried men" the following sentence: *The box fell down stairs.* Once more, let us analyze the subject term, in this case "the box." We set down the attributes "container," "wooden," "red," "dimensions six feet by eight by four," etc. But we do not find anything in the *definition* of "the box" that means the same as "falling down stairs." So we classify this statement as *synthetic*, that is, one whose subject term does not in any way "contain" the predicate. Those sentences which describe situations or "goings-on" in the empirical world are synthetic or factual statements and present a contrast to the sentences found in formal science which are analytic.

Formal Science Composed of Analytic Statements

It is commonly held by logical analysts today that all statements of formal science, whether logic or mathematics, are analytic. Thus, "$2 + 2 = 4$" is an analytic statement. It does not describe an empirical situation like a bird flying or a cork popping. "Four" is *another way* of saying "two plus two," just as "unmarried man" is another way of saying "bachelor." Now if the statements of formal science are analytic, then any theorem of formal science, however complex it may be, can only make explicit what is implicit in the basic equipment of the system of which it is a part. The moves in chess, like many theorems of mathematics, can be very complicated. Yet they all derive ultimately from certain assumptions about the pieces and the rules for moving them. The statement "$2 + 2 = 4$" is often cited as an example of an obvious *truth*. But what does it mean to say that this statement is true? Strictly speaking, it means that this is a theorem of arithmetic, that is, a statement which follows from certain prior theorems, which in turn derive ultimately from certain basic notions, postulates, and rules. Now what holds for "$2 + 2 = 4$" holds as well for more complex mathematical and logical statements. They too are "true" in that they are theorems which draw their truth from the structure of the scheme which contains them.

The Nature of Logical Axioms

We have stated that logic, in its modern generalized sense, is considered to be the basic formal science. The other formal disciplines, like those of mathematics, must *presuppose* the rules of logic in carrying out their operations. We have also noted that the statements which compose formal science are considered to be analytic statements. Now, what about the *first principles* upon which logic itself rests? Aristotle tells us that first principles cannot be demonstrated and that those people who demand such demonstration show a "want of education."[6] For if we demonstrate first principles, we must do so by reference to other principles. But these other principles would then be more primary than the first set. Granted that the first principles of logic cannot be demonstrated, where do they come from? How do we get them?

First, it should be noted that modern logicians generally agree that there is no unique set of logical axioms or postulates which must be taken as fundamental. In classical logic, the following principles were considered to be the "primary laws of thought":

> Identity: If a statement is true, it is true.
> Noncontradiction: It is not the case that the same statement is true and false.
> Excluded Middle: Either a statement is true or it is false.

But it can easily be shown that these particular logical axioms are no more fundamental than others. In fact, a deductive system based on them would be less compact than one which took different (though analogous) postulates as a starting point. Modern generalized logic includes a very large number of deductive systems, and the character of the postulates will vary according to the needs of each system. Yet the question remains: how are these axioms obtained?

[6] Aristotle, *Metaphysics*, W. D. Ross (trans.), Book 4, 1006a4.

This question is of considerable theoretical interest, and not all logicians are in agreement on the subject. "Formalists" hold that the choice of postulates is purely a matter of convention. On the other hand, "intuitionists" maintain that certain logical axioms possess a basic character in their own right, the nature of which we recognize immediately upon understanding them. C. G. Hempel says that the first principles of logic and mathematics are simply rules which determine the meaning of the concepts of these sciences, and that the theorems of logic and mathematics are therefore true "by definition."[7] But A. P. Ushenko denies that the primary laws of logic are "true by convention," and insists that they are "principles about form which are recognized to be true by logical intuition, i.e., by direct inspection and without regard to empirical matters."[8]

Certain traditional philosophers, among them Leibniz, have held that the primary axioms of logic, such as the principle of noncontradiction, are a priori principles of thought, that is, principles according to which we must think about things, but which cannot be demonstrated. Others, following Aristotle, have held that we perceive the primacy of these axioms upon examination of Nature, that these "laws

[7] C. G. Hempel, "The Nature of Mathematical Truth," *Readings in Philosophical Analysis*, H. Feigl and W. Sellars (eds.), Appleton-Century-Crofts, Inc., 1949, p. 225. Hempel does not hold, nor do most logicians today, the oversimple "formalist" view that logic consists of collections of mutually consistent theorems which are in turn consistent with postulates arbitrarily chosen. Many paradoxes or apparent contradictions have been discovered in logical systems which cannot adequately be accounted for in terms of such a conception of the nature of logic or mathematics. K. Gödel has shown, in the case of certain logico-mathematical deductive systems, that it is impossible to demonstrate the mutual consistency of all the propositions of such systems, because the proof would show that they are inconsistent!

[8] A. P. Ushenko, *The Problems of Logic*, Allen and Unwin, London, 1941, p. 26.

of thought" are derived from certain first principles of being or reality. In our next chapter we shall have occasion to examine the question whether the law of noncontradiction is a principle governing the *nature of things* or simply a basic rule for the use of *language*.

ILLUSTRATION OF THE SYMBOLIC CHARACTER OF MODERN LOGIC

Just what is the difference between classical or Aristotelian logic and modern generalized or "symbolic" logic? We have spoken very generally about the two systems, stating that logic is today considered to be the foundation of all formal science, including mathematics, and that the concepts of modern logic are far more inclusive than those of classical logic. But is it not possible to be more specific about the differences between the two systems? Unfortunately, we cannot offer such clarification without turning our book into a logic text. We can, however, show something of the "symbolic" character of modern logic by simple illustrations of types of notation used in the construction of deductive systems.

Notations for Classes

The classical Aristotelian syllogism, traditionally regarded as the culmination of formal logic, is accommodated in modern logic within a more general deductive system known as the *calculus of classes*. Suppose we wish to construct a deductive system involving classes. There is the class "cat," the class "fat man," the class "automobile." We need not use *words* to designate particular classes. Symbols, such as a, b, c, etc., will stand for *any* class. Here is a class, the class of "all cats" if you like:

$$a$$

Here is another class—the class of "all who are polite":

$$b$$

Now here is the class of all those things that are not cats:

$$\overline{a} \text{ (not-}a\text{)}$$

And here is the class of all those things which are not polite:

$$\overline{b} \text{ (not-}b\text{)}$$

Now consider the following two symbolic notations:

$$a \times b \qquad\qquad a + b$$

The first expression designates the *product* of classes *a* and *b*. In this class product or combined class are contained the members of both class *a* and class *b*. In terms of our subject matter, $a \times b$ represents "polite cats." The second expression designates the *sum* of the classes *a* and *b*. The class sum contains those things which are either in class *a* or in class *b* or in both. In terms of our subject matter, $a + b$ represents a class which contains all the cats and all those who are polite, a much larger group than $a \times b$ which holds only polite cats.

If we wish to represent symbolically that one class is included or contained in another class, we write:

$$a \subset b \text{ (}a \text{ is included in } b\text{)}$$

In terms of our subject matter, $a \subset b$ stands for "cats are members of the polite class."

There is a symbol used for a class that has no members. This is called the *null* class, and it is represented by the symbol:

$$0$$

The class which contains everything is called the *universal* class and is noted as:

$$1$$

For a simple illustration of some of these symbolic class notations, consider how they would work out in the case of the following four standard Aristotelian types of propositions:

1. All Italians are music lovers.

$$a\overline{b} = 0$$

The class product or combined class "Italians who are non-music lovers" is a class of no members.

2. No Spartans are cowards.

$$ab = 0$$

The class product "Spartans who are cowards" is a class of no members.

3. Some cassowaries are vicious.

$ab \neq o$

The class product "vicious cassowaries" is *not* a class of no members. That is, there is at least one vicious cassowary.

4. Some choirboys are not mischievous.

$a\overline{b} \neq o$

The class product "nonmischievous choirboys" is *not* a class of no members. That is, there is at least one nonmischievous choirboy.

A deductive system of classes can be constructed by forming postulates containing these and other class notions and developing theorems from these postulates in quasi-algebraic form.

Notation for Sentences

If we wish to construct a deductive system of propositions or *sentential calculus*, we use other basic notions, represented symbolically in the following way:

In place of a sentence with definite subject matter, like "Koalas like eucalyptus leaves," we simply use a letter symbol to stand for any sentence at all:

$$p$$

For another sentence, we use a different letter symbol. "It is cold in Greenland" may be represented by

$$q$$

Suppose we wish to represent a sentence which is to be taken as *false*. We note the sentence "It is not the case that bats are birds" as:

$$\sim p \quad (\text{not-}p)$$

If we wish to show the relation of *conjunction* or "and-ness," as in the compound sentence "America is my country and heaven is my destination," we note:

$$p \bullet q \quad (p \text{ and } q, \text{ or } p \text{ is true and } q \text{ is true.})$$

Suppose we want to show the relation of *implication* (if . . . then) as in the sentence "If you marry me, I shall be eternally happy," we set down:

$$p \supset q \quad (\text{If } p \text{ is true, } q \text{ is true.})$$

If we wish to show the relation of *alternation*, as in the sentence "Either Sue will help or Pat will help," we write:

$$p \lor q \quad \text{(Either } p \text{ is true or } q \text{ is true.)}$$

Recapitulating, our basic notions include:

p, q, r, etc.	sentence symbols
$\sim$	"not"
$\cdot$	"and"
$\supset$	"implies" or "if . . . then"
$\lor$	"either . . . or"

Accepting these basic notions, we can proceed to form certain postulates of such a general character that theorems may be deduced from them. For example, here are three axioms singled out by classical logicians as basic:

IDENTITY: $p \supset p$
If p is true, p is true.

NONCONTRADICTION: $\sim (p \cdot \sim p)$
It is not the case that p is true and p is false.

EXCLUDED MIDDLE: $p \lor \sim p$
Either p is true or p is false.

Postulates used in modern logic are even more generic. Here are three used by Whitehead and Russell in the *Principia:*

TAUTOLOGY: $p \lor p \cdot \supset \cdot p$
If either p is true or p is true, then p is true.

ADDITION: $q \cdot \supset \cdot p \lor q$
If q is true, then p or q is true.

PERMUTATION: $p \lor q \cdot \supset \cdot q \lor p$
If p implies q, then q implies p.

FURTHER READINGS

Ambrose, A., and Lazerowitz, M., *Symbolic Logic*, Rinehart and Co., 1948.

Aristotle, *Prior Analytics*.

Aristotle, *Posterior Analytics*.

Cohen, M., and Nagel, E., *An Introduction to Logic and Scientific Method*, Harcourt, Brace and Co., 1934.

Dewey, John, *Logic: a Theory of Inquiry*, Henry Holt and Co., 1938.

Hempel, C. G., "On the Nature of Mathematical Truth" and "Geometry and Empirical Science," in H. Feigl and W. Sellars (eds.), *Readings in Philosophical Analysis*, Appleton-Century-Crofts, Inc., 1949.

Jevons, W. S., *Elementary Lessons in Logic* (London, 1870), The Macmillan Company, 1948.

Kapp, E., *Greek Foundations of Traditional Logic*, Columbia University Press, 1942.

Joseph, H. W. B., *Introduction to Logic*, Oxford University Press, 1942.

Mace, C. A., *The Principles of Logic*, Longmans, Green and Co., London, 1933.

Mill, J. S., *A System of Logic*, Longmans, Green and Co., 1925, Books 1 and 2.

Quine, W. V., *Methods of Logic*, Henry Holt and Co., 1950.

Stebbing, L. S., *A Modern Introduction to Logic* (rev. ed.), Methuen and Co., Ltd., London, 1933.

Stebbing, L. S., *Thinking to Some Purpose*, Penguin Books, 1939.

Tarski, A., *Introduction to Logic*, Oxford University Press, 1941.

Ushenko, A. P., *The Theory of Logic*, Harper & Brothers, 1936.

2

LANGUAGE

---

*We must speak by the card,
or equivocation will undo us.*
—*Hamlet,* V, i

NEW developments in logic in our time have been paralleled by increasing critical interest in the role played by *language* in philosophy. The word "language" here refers not to specific tongues like French or English but to language in general.

Critical awareness of the relation between philosophy and language is by no means new. The quip to the effect that philosophers' arguments are no more than *disputes about words* is of ancient origin. In the seventeenth century the philosopher Francis Bacon compiled a list of *Idols* or obstacles to the advancement of human knowledge. The "Idols of the Market-place" refers to the habit of men to use words carelessly and to mistake words for things. Says Bacon: ". . . The ill and unfit choice of words wonderfully obstructs the understanding. Nor do the definitions or explanations wherewith in some things learned men are wont to guard and defend themselves by any means set the matter right. But all words plainly force and overrule the understanding, and throw all into confusion, and lead men away into numberless empty controversies and idle fancies."[1]

[1] *Novum Organum,* xliii.

36

In recent years, however, critical inquiry into the relation between language and philosophy has gone far beyond warnings of a general nature concerning obscurities inherent in words and pitfalls of language which beset even the most learned men. Today, technical analysis of the structure of language together with the development of artificial languages like symbolic logic have produced batteries of new techniques for the investigation of problems of language and philosophy. Since most of these devices for the analysis and construction of language are technically difficult, we shall not examine them in detail. We must be content with a few general observations and useful distinctions concerning the nature of language and its relation to philosophy.

Semantics; Syntactics; Semiotic

In the analysis of language, *semantics* refers to that discipline in which we study the relation between *words* and that which is *meant* by words. For instance, if we ask about the relation between the word "cat" or the word "blue" and the objects or properties these words stand for, this is a semantic inquiry. When we raise questions about the rules which prescribe how a language is to be used, this is a matter of *syntactics*. In grammar, *syntax* refers to the rules for putting sentences together. For example, in English and in many other particular languages it is a rule of syntax that a pronoun may be substituted for a noun. Analogously, when we treat of language *generally*, and inquire into the rules which govern the use of *any* language, ordinary or artificial, we are moving in the field of syntactics. This discipline is sometimes called the study of *logical syntax* in order to distinguish it from the study of grammatical syntax. Both semantics and syntactics are today considered as *parts* of the general discipline of *semiotic*. The name for this study was introduced into general usage by Charles Morris. *Semiotic* is defined as the general theory of signs and languages.

Words as Linguistic Signs

Words belong to the general class of signs or symbols.[2] Not all signs are words, however. Flags, lodge pins, traffic lights, emblems of political parties, as well as tears, blushes, and sneezes may all be classed as signs, although none of them are words. What is the function of a sign? A sign *stands for something*. It leads us beyond itself to the thought of something other than itself. The hammer and sickle stands for the Communist party, the cross for Christianity, a skull and crossed bones for pirates or poison, depending on the context.

The classification of signs is a very ticklish business, but there is a rather obvious breakdown of signs into two subclasses, *natural* signs and *conventional* signs. In natural signs, the connection between sign and thing signified is a connection "of nature" rather than one which is arbitrary, conventional, and man-made. In natural signs, the sign is *part* of the thing signified. A blush and a rapidly falling barometer are natural signs. The blush is a sign of embarrassment because it is part of the total complex we call "embarrassment." The rapidly falling barometer is related to the storm as *effect* to natural *cause*.

In *conventional* signs, there is no connection "of nature" between sign and thing signified, although there may be one of *appropriateness*. The figure of a lion would have done as

[2] Many philosophers, e.g., Kant, Hegel, W. M. Urban, make a distinction between "sign" and "symbol." Here, for reasons of simplicity, we take them as synonyms.

well as that of an elephant for the symbol of the Republican party, although the image of a pterodactyl would not. A fish was once the symbol of Christianity, and a rattlesnake was proposed, though not accepted, as an emblem for the flag of the United States.

Words are *linguistic* signs. As such, they form a subclass of conventional rather than of natural signs. There is no connection "of nature" between a word and the thing signified by the word, although the peasant who said "The pig is rightly so called, for it is a very dirty animal" doubtless thought there was. If words were natural signs, the French word for "house" would be the same as the English word. It is said that primitive people commonly believe that a word *is* naturally connected with what it stands for. Hence the widespread conviction among primitives that possession of the *name* of a man or a god gives the possessor some magical control over the owner of the name. But even though we classify words as conventional rather than arbitrary signs, we should not think that all words have been chosen by some process of conscious agreement. As Bertrand Russell remarks, it is hard to imagine a scene from some bygone day in which a council of hitherto speechless elders sat down to agree to call a cow a cow and a wolf a wolf.[3] Only small classes of words—such as scientific terms like "radium" or "Parkinson's disease"—are chosen by parliamentary procedure.

Ways of Using Words

Some words form names or *terms*, like "duck-billed platypus," "hot," or "jumping." Known as *categorematic* words,

---

[3] Bertrand Russell, *The Analysis of Mind*, Allen and Unwin, London, 1921, p. 190.

names or term words can stand alone as subject or predicate of propositions (declarative sentences). *Syncategorematic* words, like prepositions, conjunctions, adverbs, etc., must be used *with* other words to form names or terms.

Words are combined to form sentences. Sentences may make assertions, or they may be questions, commands, or expressions of a wish. The grammatical classification of sentences as declarative, interrogative, optative, etc., reminds us that we use language in many different ways. Some sentences are *informative*. They point out certain situations that exist, and they may describe those situations. They are generally declarative sentences, such as "It is raining," "Tibetans drink buttered tea," and "Silver is a good conductor of electricity."

A basic function of language is to produce appropriate *action* on the part of the hearer. "Look out!" and "By the left flank, march!" are action signals. There is also the *ceremonial* use of language. "How do you do" and "I'm very glad to have met you" are simple examples from everyday discourse. More complex instances of the ceremonial usage of language may be found in religious ceremonies. Language is often used to express our *feelings* or *wishes*, as in the sentences "I despise that man" and "Would to God I were a tender apple blossom!"

Descriptive and Emotive Use of Language

Contemporary philosophers of language have made much of the distinction between the employment of words to inform or describe and their use to convey the state of our feelings or emotions. This distinction is frequently supported by reference to the contrast between *science* and *poetry*. Science is said to be made up of informative sentences which describe states of affairs in the actual world. Poetry is asserted to consist of statements about the poet's emotions, composed for the purpose of arousing similar emotions in us. Distinguishing between what he terms the representative and the expressive functions of language, Carnap says: "Many linguistic utterances are analogous to laughing in that they have only an expressive function, no representative function. Examples of this are cries like 'Oh, Oh' or, on a higher level, lyrical verses. The aim of a lyrical poem in which occur the words 'sunshine' and 'clouds' is not to inform us of certain meteorological facts, but to express certain feelings of the poet and to excite similar feelings in us. A lyrical poem has no assertional sense, no theoretical sense, it does not contain knowledge."[4]

While it is important to perceive the distinction between descriptive and emotive usage of words, and to recognize that scientists and poets use language in different ways, there is some danger in pushing the distinction too far. In the first place, the word "emotive" has acquired a subtly derogatory flavor. In a discussion of this kind, the words "emotive" and "emotions" are frequently used to make a covert value judgment in which descriptive or scientific language is implicitly accorded a high status, with "emotional" or "poetic" language relegated to inferior rank. Secondly, it is not certain that poetry (even lyric poetry) is completely defined as the expression of certain feelings on the part of the poet with the purpose of stimulating similar feelings in others. There may be implicit in such a definition the assumption that questions of poetry are nothing but questions of somebody's "feelings," and that such "feel-

[4] Rudolf Carnap, *Philosophy and Logical Syntax*, Kegan Paul, London, 1935, p. 28.

ings" are out of place in science and philosophy. It is possible that poetry may go beyond mere expression of feelings. It may even be the case that poets *in their way* attempt to describe "the nature of things," and that the description of "reality" is not an exclusive prerogative of empirical science.

Ambiguity, Vagueness, and Metaphor

Words that have one meaning only are traditionally called *univocal*. There are very few such words, and illustrations of them may be drawn only from a limited number of categories, such as household words ("egg beater," "teakettle") or scientific terms ("vanadium," "cyclotron"). Most words have more than one meaning, and these are conventionally labeled *equivocal*. In many equivocal words we can clearly distinguish the separate meanings without much trouble, as in the case of "box," "bear," "note," and the like. But there is a large class of equivocal words in which various levels of meaning have become fused. In these *ambiguous* words, the multiple meanings shade over into one another and are difficult to distinguish. When such words are employed in argument, we cannot be sure, short of a definition of terms, in just what sense the words are being used. Ambiguous words are frequently heavy with emotional content. In poetry such terms add to the richness of the poetic material and may serve to invoke a host of associations. A less admirable usage of ambiguous words charged with emotion is frequently encountered in public discussion. Such "loaded" words as "democracy," "socialism," and "Americanism" are often used to prejudice the argument in favor of the speaker rather than to enlighten his audience. The role of question-begging words in everyday discourse is amusingly illustrated in Bertrand Russell's well-known conjugation:

I am firm.
You are obstinate.
He is a pig-headed fool.

It is possible to distinguish between ambiguity and *vagueness*. The word "liberal" is *ambiguous*, because we are not sure which of the various shades of meaning is intended. The word "dead," on the other hand, is *vague*, because there are borderline cases—such as that of a man whose heart has ceased to beat—to which we are not sure whether to apply the word "dead" or not. The words "knowledge" and "science" are vague. We use them appropriately, but we are not sure of the limits of their application. Does "knowledge," for example, include simple sense perception; does "science" apply to philosophy?

Scientists and philosophers have long pursued the idea of a *precise* language in which there would be neither ambiguity nor vagueness. Contemporary achievements in the construction of artificial languages such as symbolic logic or "model" linguistic systems represent a partial fulfillment of this ideal. But, precise as these symbolic languages may be, they all have the limitation of lacking *content*. While neither vague nor ambiguous, they are *vacuous*. It is Max Black's opinion that vagueness in ordinary and even in scientific language is unavoidable. But, since symbolic systems are available, he says, "the need is removed for regarding vagueness as a defect of language."[5]

[5] Max Black, "Vagueness," *Language and Philosophy*, Cornell University Press, 1949, p. 27.

The part played in language by *metaphor* is very great. A metaphor is a figure of speech which embodies a transfer of meaning by analogy or likeness, as in the expressions "a barrage of questions" or "a ship plowing the sea." Poetic language is high metaphorical:

> O the mind, mind has mountains; cliffs of fall
> Frightful, sheer, no-man-fathomed.

Not only in poetry but in every type of ordinary language metaphor abounds—although this is not always obvious. The basic meaning of the word "foot" refers to the parts of our legs we walk on. By transfer of meaning, we speak of the foot of a bed and the foot of a hill. Language has grown by metaphor. The root meaning of "governor" is steersman, of "character," an engraving tool, of "spirit," breath. We speak even of scientific matters in metaphor.[6] When we explain the tides by the "pull" of the moon or the motion of iron filings by the "attraction" of the magnet, we are unconsciously using analogy words the meanings of which derive from human behavior and experience. Philosophical language, even of the soberest variety, owes much to metaphor. For example, contemporary philosophers are quite fond of the word "structure." Such expressions as "the structure of language," "the structure of personality," and "the structure of experience" are common today in philosophical discussions. A little reflection reveals the metaphorical character of the word "structure," the primary meaning of which concerns the building of houses, dams, and bridges.

Many philosophers of language warn us that indiscrimi-

[6] See chap. 6, "The Growth of Language," in W. S. Jevons, *Elementary Lessons in Logic* (London, 1870), The Macmillan Company, 1948.

nate use of metaphors and analogies leads us into error by providing us with apparent solutions or "pseudo explanations" of certain problems. Plato's explanation of the genesis of the physical universe as the production of a "Maker" or Artificer-God is sometimes given as an example of a pseudo explanation derived from uncritical use of metaphorical language.[7] Hans Reichenbach takes classical philosophers severely to task for their "pseudo explanations" based on naïve parallelisms. "Pernicious errors through false analogies," he says, "have been the philosopher's disease at all times."[8] It is doubtless impossible (and probably unnecessary) to purge philosophical language entirely of metaphor. The use of metaphor and analogy is not *in itself* objectionable. These linguistic devices can be dispensed with only in artificial and symbolic language systems. The danger lies in the *uncritical* use of metaphor, in the *undiscriminating* employment of analogical expressions without realizing the limitations of analogy.

Connotation and Denotation; Definition

Two senses in which those words we call terms or names may be taken are *connotation* (or "intension") and *denotation* ("extension"). The connotation of a term refers to the attributes, essential properties, or characteristics of that which the term stands for. Denotation refers to the individuals to which the name applies. For example, the connotation of *chair* is "separate seat for one." The denotation of *chair* is this chair, that chair, and each and every other individual chair. The connotation of *bassoon* is "bass member

[7] Plato, *Timaeus*, 28 et seq. In this instance Plato warns his readers that his account of the creation of the world is no more than a "likely tale."

[8] Hans Reichenbach, *The Rise of Scientific Philosophy*, University of California Press, 1951, p. 11.

of the double-reeded woodwind instruments." The denotation of *bassoon* is each and every bassoon. Proper names have a denotation of 1, but logicians and analysts of language disagree as to whether proper names have any connotation at all.[9]

The distinction between connotation and denotation carries over into *definition*. When we define a word, we indicate in some way the appropriate use of the word. We try to raise thoughts in the mind of another person which he will associate with things familiar to him. Now there is more than one way of defining. We may explain what we mean by a word with a set of words whose meanings are presumed to be known. This is formal or *verbal* definition of a word and may be identified with its connotation: "A squirrel is a small animal, a rodent with a bushy tail. Squirrels live in trees, eat nuts, etc." Or we may explain what we mean by pointing to an example of that to which the word applies. This is known as *ostensive* definition, and obviously relates to the *denotation* of the term: "*That's* a squirrel." Parents of small children often rely on ostensive definition. As a rule, however, it is impractical to define ostensively since the objects to which many words refer are not of a directly observable kind or, if they are observable, are rarely at hand.

Meaning

In definition, whether verbal or ostensive, we try to make clear what we *mean* by a word. We will all concede that

[9] John Stuart Mill denies that proper names have connotation. In order that an object may properly be called "tree," it must have certain attributes—woody, plant, etc. But in order for an object to be named "Laura Banks," no such set of specifications need be met. "Laura Banks" could be the name of a race horse, a pet turtle, a private estate, as well as the name of a woman.

words with which we are familiar *mean* something, but it is not easy to explain just what *meaning* is.

Meaning involves a three-part or *triadic* relationship, that is, a relation between (1) a *sign*, (2) that which the sign stands for (*referent*), and (3) the *interpreter* of the sign. A meaning situation exists whenever a sign produces in the person perceiving the sign a connection or association between the sign and that which the sign stands for. This will hold whether the connection or association exists (a) directly, between the sign and the physical response or action, or (b) indirectly, between the sign and referent through the medium of a mental response—a thought, idea, or concept. Rapid ringing of the ship's bells produces in the sailor on a warship the immediate physical reaction of running to his battle station. The sight of the Crescent and Star stimulates in the interpreter the thought or concept of Islam which in turn relates to that particular culture as ultimate referent. This explanation also holds for both natural and conventional signs:

	Sign		Referent
A. Natural	Red sky at night	means	fair weather next day.
B. Conventional			
1. Non-linguistic	Green light	means	go.
2. Linguistic	"Sanskrit"	means	ancient language of India.

Words are linguistic signs. Their meaning involves the production in a person of some kind of connection between the word and the referent. If no such connection is produced, the word is *meaningless* to the person hearing it or reading it. If a boy, playing his first sand-lot baseball game, does not know the meaning of "Bunt!" he cannot respond to the coach's cry with appropriate physical action. If I do not know Italian, the word "*ragazza*" has no meaning for me. A nonsense word like "blol" has no meaning for anybody. It is touching to see the entrapped victim of a "double-talk" artist try to respond to a question such as: "Don't you think the chufer should be biased on the framis?"

The Status of Referents

The referents of words have a bewildering variety of status or "modes of being." Recollection of the rules of grammar may prompt us to say that nouns refer to things, adjectives to properties, and verbs to actions. But what manner of existence do these things, properties, and actions have? The referent of a word like "cat" seems to offer no difficulty. "Cat" refers to *observable objects* which mew, purr, scratch, etc. The referent of a word like "atom" is not observable directly, yet it is assumed on the basis of a long chain of inferences to have some sort of physical existence. The name "goblin" designates things which are not natural objects at all. Some critics have poked fun at the German philosopher Heidegger because he has written at length and very seriously about Nothing. According to religious people and theologians, the referent of the word "God" is an actual though ordinarily unobservable object. But according to many naturalistic philosophers, the referent of "God" is not an actual object but an idea or concept only.

The Referents of Syntax Words

There is an important class of words used in discourse the status of whose referents is interesting, although difficult to analyze. These are *logical* or *syntax* words. They are syn-categorematic, and include words like "if," "and," "not," and "or." Unlike *descriptive* words, such as "house," "unicorn," "blue," and "running," syntax words do not appear to refer to any state of affairs, actual or fictitious. They seem rather to designate logical or linguistic *attitudes*. That is, syntax words are signs of ways in which we are to "take" the words or sentences with which they are associated. For example, in the sentence "Whales are not fish," the word "not" is a sign of *rejection* of the sentence "Whales are fish." In the conjunctive sentence "Bats are mammals and they fly," the word "and" is a sign of *acceptance* of both conjuncts.

The Material Mode of Speech

In the sentence "There is a cow in that field," the referent of the word "cow" is a *physical object* that moos, gives milk, etc. But in the sentence " 'Cow' is a short word," the referent of "cow" is not the object cow but the *word* "cow." These two senses of "cow" illustrate the classical distinction between the *objective* ("real") and *material* modes of speech. In the syllogism:

> The emu lays large eggs.
> Emu is a three-letter word.
> At least one three-letter word lays large eggs.

the absurdity is the result of confusion between objective and material *suppositions* of the word "emu." Not all confusions between the objective and material suppositions of words and sentences are as obvious as that in the example just given. Contemporary philosophers of language tell us that it is easy to fall into the habit of talking about the syntactical properties of *sentences* while under the impression that we are talking about *things*. (We shall see a possible example of this confusion in the case of the principle of noncontradiction discussed below.) According to Carnap, a great many problems of traditional philosophy have been generated by philosophers' confounding of the objective and material modes of speech.[10] Taken broadly, this amounts to a claim that philosophers have disputed about *words* while convinced they have been disputing about *things*—a charge against philosophy about as old as philosophy itself.

Object-Language and Meta-Language

Contemporary analysts distinguish between *object-language* and *meta-language*. This distinction helps to separate talking about objects or events and talking about the properties of a language. The referents of the sentences of a meta-language are not things or events but the properties or rules of a language. An object-language is that language to which the meta-language refers. If we wish to talk about the properties of a *special* language, we may use English as a meta-language, thus: "There are no articles in the Chinese language." Here the object-language is Chinese. If we wish to talk about the properties or rules of *language in general*, we may use the concepts and vocabulary of semantics or syntactics: "Words are linguistic signs." Shakespeare's unhappy Ophelia is speaking metalinguistically and her object-language is the language of flowers when she says: "There's rosemary, that's for remembrance; . . . and there is pansies, that's for thoughts."

[10] Rudolf Carnap, *op. cit.*, p. 58 et seq. *The Logical Syntax of Language*, Kegan Paul, London, 1937, pp. 298–315.

We shall see, in the next chapter, that if *truth* is taken as a property of sentences rather than of things, then "truth" is not an object-word but a metalinguistic word.[11]

REFERENTS OF LOGICAL AXIOMS AND GENERAL NAMES

The Principle of Noncontradiction

In an earlier discussion of the foundations of logical laws we said that there are different points of view as to the status or mode of being of the primary laws of logic. Some philosophers hold that these laws have *ontological* status— that is, the laws of logic have their foundation in Nature. Others (among whom may be numbered many contemporary philosophers of language) claim that the laws of logic are like the laws of any language system; they are simply *rules* which determine how we are to use language, taken generally. The difference of opinion here is a difference over the *mode of being possessed by the referents of those sentences which set forth the laws of logic.*

The problem may be illustrated by reference to the classical law of logic known as the *principle of noncontradiction.* This law was first formulated by Aristotle: "There is a principle in things about which we cannot be deceived, but must always, on the contrary, recognize the truth. It is that the same thing cannot at one and the same time be and not be."[12] That is, a door cannot be open and shut at the same time, nor can a shoe be black and white in the same

[11] "Meta-language" is sometimes used as a synonym for syntactics or logical syntax of language (see above p. 37). A distinction similar to that between object-language and meta-language is common in discussions of logic. Manipulation of syllogisms or of the various calculi in generalized logic is *logic*, while discussion of the nature of logical systems, their basic notions, postulates, rules, etc., is *meta-logic.*

[12] Aristotle, *Metaphysics*, W. D. Ross (trans.), Book 11, 1061b34.

place. For, says Aristotle, "the same attribute cannot at the same time belong and not belong to the same subject and in the same respect."[13] Aristotle believed that the law of non-contradiction was both a fundamental axiom of logic and of human discourse, and a first principle of Nature or *being*. That is, Aristotle was convinced that this fundamental law holds not only in the realm of logic and language but in the *natural order* as well. Indeed, according to Aristotle, it is the natural order that is the foundation and source of the principle of noncontradiction.

For more than two thousand years philosophers generally held that the principle of noncontradiction was, as Aristotle said, a fundamental law to which *things* as well as *sentences* were subject. At first sight, it does seem that natural objects "obey" this law. Dogs don't bark and "not bark" at the same time, and it is impossible for a man to be dead and not dead "in the same respect." Today, however, many logicians and analytic philosophers deny that the principle of non-contradiction is a fundamental law which all natural objects and events obey. Rather, they hold that the law is no more than a basic *rule of language*. It is a presupposition of human communication, a first principle of syntax, a basic rule for putting sentences together. Aristotle was right, these analysts maintain, in holding that the law of noncontradiction is a primary principle of *discourse*. But he was wrong in assuming that what is undeniably a basic rule of *language* is also a first principle of *Nature*. The reason natural objects like shoes and doors seem to "obey" the law of non-contradiction is that we cannot talk about these things without using language in which the law of noncontradiction is ingrained.

[13] *Ibid.*, Book 4, 1005b18.

Some philosophers who maintain the traditional view that laws such as the principle of noncontradiction have *ontological* as well as logical or linguistic status reply that it is all very well to say that the principle of noncontradiction is a primary rule of language; but why is *this* rule primary rather than another? Is it chosen arbitrarily in preference to some other logical law which could do just as well? A better reason why the principle of noncontradiction is a fundamental rule of logic and language is that the structure of human communication is to some extent influenced by the nature of the world in which we live. It may well be the case that the principle of noncontradiction is a primary law of language simply because it reflects a certain basic and all-pervasive character of things.

To this point of view critics of the traditional view answer: The doctrine that the principle of noncontradiction is a law of Nature or being arises from confusing a rule of sentence structure with a property of the empirical world. But, says Ernest Nagel, while the principle of noncontradiction is a rule of language rather than a description of Nature, nevertheless this law is not arbitrarily chosen. Our language system is based upon certain primary logical rules. This language is (to a degree) adequate to the task of describing the events of the world in which we live. The value of logical laws like the principle of noncontradiction is to be gauged in terms of the way language based on these logical laws measures up to the task of describing the world. The law of noncontradiction is not something laid up in heaven, holding good for all eternity. If it should one day turn out that the behavior of certain particles within the nucleus of the atom can more adequately be described in terms of a language which is based on some primary laws *other than* the law of noncontradiction, then the structure of our communication rules would, under that pressure, be modified to the extent necessary to provide for this special situation.[14]

Referents of General Names; the "Problem of Universals"

Earlier we remarked that the status or mode of being of the referent of a word like "cat" seems to offer no difficulty. Cats are observable physical objects. But we should note that the word "cat" is a *general* word or name, since it applies to *all* cats. Thus the general name "cat" stands in contrast to *singular* terms like "Purrcilla Mewriel" (a proper name) or "this cat" which apply only to one individual cat.

Now one of the most complicated problems in classical philosophy is connected with this simple classification of words as *general* and *singular*. The "problem of universals" concerns the *status or mode of being of the referents of general words*. Since the problem of universals strikingly illustrates the importance of the relation between language and philosophy, it may be useful to spend a little time on it.

Singular names refer to specific objects, events, or instances of qualities. "Dwight Eisenhower," "Boulder Dam," "that ball-playing," "this blue here" are singular terms. General names refer to *classes* or *kinds* of objects, events, or qualities. "Man," "suspension bridge," "swimming," and "yellow" are examples of general words. General names apply to each member of the class or kind. "Mouse" applies to every individual mouse, "hard" to every

---

[14] Ernest Nagel, "Logic Without Ontology," *Readings in Philosophical Analysis*, H. Feigl and W. Sellars (eds.), Appleton-Century-Crofts, Inc., 1949, p. 209.

occurrence of that property, and "singing" to every instance of song. That general words are indispensable in human communication may be proved by the simple experiment of trying to say a few sentences without them.

Now, what kind of objects, if any, do general words refer to? Unlike singular terms, general names, *taken as such*, do not designate observable objects. Consider the sentence "The pig is a domestic animal." No one has ever observed "the pig," but only this pig, that pig, and many other individual pigs. Take the sentence "Tom is a man." We can talk to Tom and shake hands with him. Not so with man. No one has ever seen man walking down the street. What we do see are individual men.

The ancient Greek philosopher Plato drew some remarkable conclusions upon the basis of this and certain other considerations. Since general names stand for universal properties which cannot be observed *as such* by our senses, these general terms must *designate things which exist on some higher plane of being*. There do exist, independently of human thought and language, certain originals or prototypes which correspond to general words. These universal objects or Ideas, as Plato calls them, exist in a world which transcends the world of ordinary experience, a mode of being to which thought alone can penetrate. That is why these universal Forms are not observable by sense perception. Each individual thing, Plato tells us, is a *copy* (εἰκών) of one of the divine originals. Every single man— Socrates, Agathon, Callicles, etc.—derives what measure of reality he has from the *Idea of Man*. Every noble character, each honorable deed "participates" in the *Idea of Good*. Moreover, unlike mortal men and the transient goods of earth, the Universal Man and the Universal Good are imperishable and eternal. Such is Plato's theory of Ideas, which we shall meet again in our discussion of metaphysics.

Aristotle, who was Plato's pupil, thought his master's answer to the question "What sort of objects, if any, are designated by general names?" unnecessarily complicated. The referents of general words like "man" and "tree," thought Aristotle, are *classes* or *kinds* which actually exist in the natural world. These "natural kinds," however, are never experienced *as such*. For the *universal* properties of things are so inextricably mingled with *specific* features that it is impossible to observe the universal in isolation from the particular. "Man" designates an objectively existing feature of Nature which is actually present in Socrates, Agathon, etc. Nevertheless, while *humanity* exists in Nature independently of human thought or language, this property does not exist as a separate entity apart from individual men.

In the twelfth century, European universities resounded with hot debate on the question of universals. According to Abélard, the *realists* (e.g., William of Champeaux) held that there exist in Nature actual entities corresponding to general words. Man is something which exists outside the mind. It is not just a collective word for individual men. In opposition to the realists, the *nominalists* (e.g., Roscelinus) maintained that universals were nothing but *names*. "Man" is just a word, and does not designate anything in Nature, where there are only individuals, Socrates, etc.

Abélard himself taught that the referents of universals are neither mere words (*voces*) nor things (*res*). General words are *signs*, the referents of which are concepts (*sermones*) or thoughts in the mind. These concepts in turn represent to us certain actual situations outside the mind under the mode of generality. The followers of Abélard developed the position of *conceptualism*. Conceptualists held that the referents of general names are concepts only; they are mental constructs rather than actual entities in Nature. Says conceptualist Peter Auriol: "It is clear that the notion of man and of animal in so far as it is distinguished from Socrates is a fabrication of the intellect and is nothing but a concept; for nature has not formed distinct principles of this kind as actual existences."[15]

Philosophers of the fourteenth century, keenly interested in the analysis of logic and language, tended toward the conceptualist or nominalist positions. According to William of Ockham, the referents of general words have no "ontological status"; they are logical or linguistic entities only. Nothing, says Ockham, exists in Nature outside the mind but individual things. (*Nihil est in rerum natura extra animam nisi singulare*.)[16]

A dominant tradition in modern British and American philosophy, known as *empiricism*, holds that the basis of reliable knowledge (other than formal science) lies in *sense experience*, and that true knowledge is concerned directly or indirectly with *observable things*. Now sense experience and observation present us with things which are many, separate, and individual. We should therefore rightly expect that modern empiricists take a *nominalist* position on the problem of universals. Contemporary philosophers of language, of the empiricist school, say that the *realist* doctrine of universals—i.e., that there are actual situations in Nature corresponding to general names—arises from a confusion of the order of *language* and the order of *things*. General

[15] Cited by M. H. Carré, *Nominalists and Realists*, Oxford University Press, London, 1946, pp. 106, 107.
[16] *Ibid.*, p. 112. See also S. C. Tornay, *Ockham: Studies and Selections*, Open Court Publishing Co., La Salle, Ill., 1938, p. 128.

words are *abstract*. All men resemble each other in certain respects. For purposes of communication, we need a word which will apply equally to all of them. Hence the general name "man." The error of the realists, say these critics, consists in the assumption (common in traditional philosophy) that to abstract words there correspond thing-like objects.

The following dialogue supports the realist position in regard to general names. The reader is invited to try his hand at logical and linguistic analysis by evaluating the argument:

Q. Is "measles" a general word?

A. Yes, because it designates a class of events—individual cases of measles.

Q. Do individual cases of measles have any feature in common?

A. Yes. It is in terms of these common features that measles is described in medical textbooks.

Q. Now, do these characteristics which individual cases of measles have in common, and which the medical books describe, exist independently of human thought, "outside the mind," or are they subjective notions only?

A. They exist outside the mind.

Q. It follows then that realism is the correct view, and that nominalism is to be rejected. For if that which all cases of measles have in common has objective existence, then the general word "measles" designates a state of affairs in Nature.

EMPIRICIST THEORIES OF MEANING

We recall that the empiricist position in philosophy is one which may roughly be described as the doctrine that the foundation of reliable knowledge (apart from logic and mathematics) lies in *sense experience*, that true knowledge deals with things directly or indirectly *observable*. Contemporary philosophers of language inclined toward empiricism have developed a *theory of meaning* consistent with this position. It is that words and sentences (and the concepts or thoughts they express) which purport to describe facts have meaning only in so far as they are related, directly or indirectly, to observable things.

Peirce's Doctrine of Meaning

Charles Peirce, an American philosopher once neglected and now renowned, was an early advocate of such a theory of meaning. Peirce held that a term has meaning if it can be explained by other terms which *describe sensible properties*. For example, the word "hard" is meaningful because it can be replaced by the phrase "not scratchable by many other substances."[17] According to Peirce, if a term has meaning, the meaning should be capable of being set forth in such a way as to tell you *what you can do* in order to *observe* the object (referent) of that word or the object's *sensible effects*. Sentences are meaningful if they are experimentally verifiable, that is, if their truth can be tested by some kind of *publicly observable procedure*. The propositions of empirical *science* are notable examples of statements verifiable in such a way. But a large part of the propositions of traditional *philosophy*, particularly those of that part of philosophy known as *metaphysics*, are meaningless, because no public and open procedures exist for testing their truth. When the mass of meaningless propositions which constitute the bulk of traditional metaphysical philosophy is dis-

[17] Charles Hartshorne and Paul Weiss (eds.), *The Collected Papers of Charles Sanders Peirce*, Harvard University Press, 1931–1935, vol. 5, paragraph 403.

carded, says Peirce, "what will remain of philosophy will
be a series of problems capable of investigation by the ob-
servational methods of the true sciences."[18]

Logical Positivism and Logical Empiricism

There is a very popular and influential school of contemporary analytic philosophers known as *logical empiricists*.
Their philosophical ancestry is both British and Continental. On the British side, the line of descent may be traced
back through Bertrand Russell (twentieth century) and
John Stuart Mill (nineteenth century) to the Scottish philosopher David Hume (eighteenth century). The more immediate heritage of logical empiricism is from the Continental side and stems from the doctrines of a group of
twentieth-century philosophers known in the years before
World War II as "the Vienna Circle." This group included
Ludwig Wittgenstein, Morris Schlick, and Rudolf Carnap.
The leaders of the Vienna Circle and their disciples were
known as *logical positivists*—"logical" because their con-
structive work concerned the analysis of logic and language; "positivist" because of the kinship of the spirit of
their enterprise to that of the nineteenth-century French
philosopher Auguste Comte, an admirer of the sciences,
who believed that significant knowledge concerns only that
which is open to "positive" observation. Cross-fertilization
took place between these kindred British and Continental
philosophic strains. The contemporary English logical empiricist A. J. Ayer acknowledges his debt to both Russell
and Wittgenstein, who themselves influenced each other.
Ayer's famous little book *Language, Truth, and Logic*

[18] *Ibid.*, paragraph 423. See Justus Buchler, *Charles Peirce's Empiricism*,
Kegan Paul, London, 1939, pp. 112–120, 149.

(1936) popularized the tenets of the logical positivists. According to C. E. M. Joad, Ayer's book "has in Oxford since the end of the war acquired almost the status of a philosophic Bible."[19]

The general tone of the early logical positivists was harsh and dogmatic. They maintained that nearly all of traditional philosophy, and a great deal else besides, was *nonsense*, and that future philosophers would confine themselves to logical analysis. Some of the extremes to which the earlier logical positivists pushed their doctrines seem today rather amusing to the critics of the movement. For example, Wittgenstein's *Tractatus Logico-Philosophicus* demonstrates that a staggering quantity of what normally passes for meaningful statements is in fact nonsense. Then, at the conclusion of the *Tractatus*, Wittgenstein makes the startling announcement that his own book is nonsense too. But, he reassures his readers, it is *useful* nonsense; it is like a ladder one climbs over, then pushes away because it is no longer needed.[20] *Logical empiricism* is the name given to the doctrines of a school of analytic philosophy, popular today in England and America, which has developed the methods of logical positivism within a broader framework.[21]

[19] C. E. M. Joad, *A Critique of Logical Positivism*, University of Chicago Press, 1950, p. 9.
[20] Ludwig Wittgenstein, *Tractatus Logico-Philosophicus*, Harcourt, Brace and Co., 1922, p. 189.
[21] A variety of the positivist-empiricist approach, with particular reference to the methods of physical science, is known as operationalism, a term introduced by P. W. Bridgman. According to Bridgman, the meaning of a scientific concept is set forth in terms of the *operations* we use to define it. For example, the meaning of the word "foot" as a unit of length, is equivalent to the measuring *operation* we perform when we want to find out whether something is a foot long. Sentences which assert scientific hypotheses are meaningful only if the nature of those operations which could test them can be specified. See P. W. Bridgman, *The Logic of Modern Physics*, The Macmillan Company, 1927.

The Verification Theory of Meaning; A. J. Ayer

A basic tenet of logical empiricism concerns *meaning*. It is maintained that sentences intended to describe facts have meaning only if it is possible to verify them. In his *Language, Truth and Logic* A. J. Ayer divides sentences into (1) those which convey *information* and (2) those which convey or describe *emotions*. Of the sentences which convey information he distinguishes (following Hume) two kinds: (a) statements about formal concepts and relations, such as the propositions of logic or mathematics, and statements about linguistic matters, and (b) statements about matters of fact. Now sentences which are supposed to be statements about matters of fact are significant or *meaningful* only if they are capable of being *verified*. That is, a statement which purports to describe some factual situation has *meaning* only if we are able to specify some way or ways in which the question of its truth or falsity could be settled. According to Ayer: "The criterion which we use to test the genuineness of apparent statements of fact is the criterion of verifiability. We say that a sentence is factually significant to any given person, if, and only if, he knows how to verify the proposition which it purports to express —that is, if he knows what observations would lead him under certain conditions, to accept the proposition as being true, or reject it as being false."[22]

The statement "There are mountains on the other side of the moon" is significant, although no means exist at present for settling the question of its truth or falsity. Since one side of the moon is always turned away from us, we can-

[22] A. J. Ayer, *Language, Truth and Logic* (rev. ed.), Victor Gollancz Ltd., London, 1946, p. 35.

not observe it with our telescopes. Yet such a statement is *in principle* verifiable, since we can specify in a general way the kind of procedure which *would* settle the question, if the means for such procedure were available. In the case of the moon, the procedure would involve the construction of a space ship of sufficiently long range.

Ayer then invites us to consider a typical meaningless statement. Consider the proposition "There is a God," taken as asserting the existence of an actual being who created and who sustains the world. This statement *appears* to be a factual statement—i.e., one which is either true or false—but it is actually *meaningless*. Since we cannot specify, even *in principle*, what procedures would lead us to observations relevant to the truth or falsity of the sentence "God exists," it is a nonsense statement. Now what holds for the statement "There is a God" also holds for the entire class of metaphysical statements. Since these propositions make assertions about things and events which have no connection, direct or indirect, with sense observation, there is no way of determining whether they are true or false. Hence, they are meaningless.

Criticism of the Verification Theory of Meaning

The verification theory of meaning has been the subject of considerable criticism. The following are some of the objections brought against the logical empiricist's claim that "To be meaningful, a sentence must be verifiable."

1. This doctrine lays down an arbitrary and narrow definition of "meaning" in *advance of the argument* and therefore begs the question. What gives the logical empiricist the right to decide that the meaning of a sentence is equivalent to its verifiability by experimental observation? If a man

says, "God made the world," I may find this statement un-
clear. Yet this statement has meaning in a way that the
statement "The torkin jerped boofaz" does not. To this objection, logical empiricists reply by distinguishing various
kinds of meaning.[23] The statement "God made the world"
may have *pictorial* or even *poetic* meaning, but it has no
factual meaning.

2. Another objection concerns the vagueness of the
word "verifiable." It is not at all clear just what specifica-
tion must be met in order that a sentence may be considered
"verified." For example, it is impossible to "verify" inductive general statements such as "Metals melt when heated"
in the sense that we can examine and test every instance of
metal. Many logical empiricists take account of this objection by distinguishing between (a) conclusive or complete
and (b) partial or weak verification. For a factual proposition to be meaningful, say the logical empiricists, it must at
least be *partly* verifiable. That is, there should exist (if only
"in principle") *some* experiments involving sense observation which are relevant to deciding whether the proposition
in question is true or false. Nevertheless, the problem of the
meaning of "verify" and "verifiability" remains a question
which logical empiricists have not resolved.

3. Consider once more the proposition "To be meaningful, a sentence must be verifiable." But, A. C. Ewing points
out, *this statement itself is not verifiable.*[24] It is not an *analytic* statement or tautology like "7 plus 5 equals 12," for, if
it were, no one who *understood* it could fail to see that it
was true. But neither is it a *factual* statement, for the propo-

[23] *Ibid.*, p. 15. H. Feigl, "Logical Empiricism," in H. Feigl and W. Sellars (eds.), *op. cit.*, p. 7.
[24] A. C. Ewing, "Meaninglessness," *Mind*, 1937, p. 349.

sition is making an assertion about sentences, not about empirical facts. Further, what kind of empirical evidence could possibly support it? To answer the objection, logical empiricists frequently invoke a dictum associated with Bertrand Russell's theory of types: *No meaningful statement should ever be taken as making assertions about itself.* The proposition "To be meaningful, a sentence must be verifiable" is of a "higher logical type" than the sentences it talks about. It should not be taken as if it were talking about *itself.* To interpret the proposition thus is to confuse two different logical types or "orders" of sentences.[25]

4. Finally, the following general criticism has been urged against the verification theory of meaning, as well as against the philosophy of logical empiricism taken as a whole. The doctrine of logical empiricism is tied to a classification of sentences that is too simple and sharp-cut. The theory is based on the assumption that propositions fall into two clearly separated classes of *emotive* and *informative* statements, the latter category itself divided into two sharp-cut subclasses, *formal* and *factual.* Such precise compartmentalization of propositions may be useful to us in making certain important elementary distinctions in the usage of logic and language. But these dichotomies should not be taken as ultimates. The world we experience is a very complex situation—very much mixed up with the operations of human thought. It is an error of oversimplification to isolate a single set of propositions, called "factual" (the word "fact" is vague), and to assign to these propositions the

[25] Russell's theory of types was devised to solve technical problems which arise from the existence of certain bothersome *paradoxes* or apparent contradictions in logic. A well-known example is the Antinomy of the Liar, in which Epimenides, the Cretan, says, "All Cretans are liars."

exclusive mission of "describing" the world. Those properties of Nature we describe in informative statements may shade over without a sharp break into those features of experience we speak of in emotive (poetic, pictorial) language. For purposes of formal logic, it is necessary to draw a sharp distinction between formal and factual sentences. But the general character of the world may be such that the "formal" properties of abstract relations are not split completely apart from "factual" situations. The logical empiricist's classification of statements with reference to meaning has the virtues of simplicity and clarity. But there is a danger in such clarity, the danger of reducing to a flat base the complex levels of Nature and experience.

Non-Positivist Critiques of Language

From the foregoing pages we may have gained the impression that criticism of language has been the monopoly of logical analysts hostile to metaphysics like Carnap, Wittgenstein, and Ayer. But this is not the case. Two distinguished metaphysical philosophers of our century—the English philosopher-mathematician A. N. Whitehead and the French metaphysician Henri Bergson—have stressed through their writings the importance of philosophy's relation to language.

Whitehead holds that one of the main errors to which philosophic method is liable is "uncritical trust in the adequacy of language."[26] To illustrate how the limitations of language may warp philosophic and scientific thought, Whitehead invites us to consider the basic structure of sentences we use to describe things. They are divided into subjects and predicates. It is natural for us to use sentences composed of these elements. It is natural to speak of the world as if it were made up of things and qualities of things. Upon this obvious distinction Aristotle

[26] A. N. Whitehead, *Adventures of Ideas,* The Macmillan Company, 1933, p. 293.

built up his logic, a logic based upon the analysis of propositions into subject and predicate terms.

The development of Aristotelian logic over a period of two thousand years fixed the subject-predicate distinction deeply in scientific thought and philosophic language. This subject-predicate distinction is adequate for interpreting the prominent, gross features of experience. But exclusive attention to obvious features of experience may lead to interpreting everything according to an oversimple pattern. It may lead, in this case, to the habit of thinking that the world is simply a large collection of isolated things or substances, and their qualities. "The disease of philosophy," says Whitehead, "is its itch to express itself in the forms, 'Some S is P,' or 'All S is P.' "[27] In another place he says, "The taint of Aristotelian Logic has thrown the whole emphasis of metaphysical thought upon substantives and adjectives to the neglect of prepositions and conjunctions."[28]

The fundamental character of the world, says Whitehead, is *process*. That is to say, the world is a constantly changing, shifting system of transitory events. These events shade over into one another. If these basic features of the world flux are to be described, the language we use must be modified so that it will to some degree be adequate to the task of description. In conformity with his own precepts, Whitehead sets forth his world perspective in a language so full of technical difficulties and novel terminology that many of his readers complain of obscurity.

Bergson, like Whitehead, holds that the basic character of the world is dynamic process. Reality is an ever developing creative flow analogous to organic life and growth. The human intellect arose in the course of evolution primarily as a practical instrument or tool which equips us to handle and to control material things. Our intellects have acquired the useful habit of

[27] A. N. Whitehead, *Modes of Thought*, The Macmillan Company, 1938, p. 194.
[28] A. N. Whitehead, *Adventures of Ideas*, p. 356.

representing our natural environment in terms of stable physical objects. Our language developed its structure in conformity with the practical needs of human beings to deal with a world of material bodies. Hence the structure of language tends to lead us to think of the world as if it were composed exclusively of static objects.

The purely practical need to deal with our material environment *mechanically* produces in us habits of thinking and talking of the world as a whole as if it were a mechanism composed of movable parts. But, says Bergson, our deepest and most compelling intuitions tell us that the all-pervasive and underlying character of things is not analogous to the properties of a machine. It more nearly resembles the inner unbroken flow of life, whose pulse, at critical moments of our experience, we can detect welling up within us. For these reasons Bergson thinks that philosophers and scientists must be on their guard lest a language designed for manipulations of physical bodies, for the handling of the *static*, trick them into misrepresenting a reality whose most generic features are life, growth, development, creative process.

FURTHER READINGS

Aristotle, *De Interpretatione.*

Ayer, A. J., *Language, Truth and Logic* (rev. ed.), Victor Golancz Ltd., London, 1948.

Aristotle, *Metaphysics*, Book 4.

Black, Max, *Language and Philosophy*, Cornell University Press, 1949, chaps. 2, 6, 7.

Carnap, Rudolf, *Philosophy and Logical Syntax*, Kegan Paul, London, 1937.

Carré, M. H., *Nominalists and Realists*, Oxford University Press, London, 1946.

Foss, Martin, *Symbol and Metaphor in Human Experience*, Princeton University Press, 1949.

Hayakawa, S. I., *Language in Action*, Harcourt, Brace and Co., 1941.

Jevons, W. S., *Elementary Lessons in Logic* (London, 1870), The Macmillan Company, 1948, chap. 6.

Joad, C. E. M., *A Critique of Logical Positivism*, University of Chicago Press, 1950.

Langer, Susanne K., *Philosophy in a New Key*, A Mentor Book, The New American Library, 1948, chap. 5.

Morris, Charles, *Signs, Language and Behavior*, Prentice-Hall, Inc., 1946.

Nagel, Ernest, "Logic Without Ontology," in H. Feigl and W. Sellars (eds.), *Readings in Philosophical Analysis*, Appleton-Century-Crofts, Inc., 1949.

Ogden, C. K., and Richards, I. A., *The Meaning of Meaning*, Harcourt, Brace and Co., 1925.

Plato, *Cratylus*.

Reichenbach, H., "Logic and Language," in *Elements of Symbolic Logic*, The Macmillan Company, 1948.

Russell, Bertrand, *The Analysis of Mind*, Allen and Unwin, London, 1921, chaps. 10, 11.

Russell, Bertrand, *Human Knowledge*, Simon and Schuster, 1948, Part 2.

Tornay, S. C., *Ockham: Studies and Selections*, Open Court Publishing Co., 1938.

Urban, W. M., *Language and Reality*, George Allen and Unwin, Ltd., London, 1939.

Urban, W. M., "Whitehead's Philosophy of Language," in P. A. Schilpp (ed.), *The Philosophy of Alfred North Whitehead*, Northwestern University, 1941.

Walpole, Hugh R., *Semantics*, W. W. Norton and Co., 1941.

Wittgenstein, Ludwig, *Tractatus Logico-Philosophicus*, Harcourt, Brace and Co., 1922.

PART II

PROBLEMS OF KNOWLEDGE

3

TRUTH AND CERTAINTY

Pilate saith unto him, what is truth?
—John 18:38

WHETHER we can have trustworthy knowledge is an ancient question of philosophy. Plato divided human knowledge into two classes (1) *true knowledge* and (2) *belief* or *opinion.* He thought that the first kind only was reliable but that it was difficult for anyone but a mathematician or philosopher to obtain.[1] The second kind, he believed, was the equipment of the ordinary man; it was quite unreliable and the ultimate source of all error. The ancient Skeptics, struck by the frequency and ease with which men fall into error, challenged the possibility of obtaining *certainty* in any branch of human knowledge. With the development of modern philosophy after the Renaissance, the problem of what kinds of knowledge are "true" or "certain" became particularly acute. Since the seventeenth century the attention of a distinguished line of philosophers, from Descartes to Bertrand Russell, has been concentrated on the question whether we can have reliable knowledge about anything. It is only very recently that

---

[1] The Greek word for true knowledge ἐπιστήμη (epistemé) is the principal root of the term *epistemology,* a name given to the philosophic inquiry into knowledge.

73

the question "What do we *mean?*" has disputed the place of "How do we *know?*" as the most popular query in philosophy.

Questions about true or certain knowledge raise a number of problems which are rather difficult to disentangle. For the present we shall confine ourselves to an analysis of the meaning of truth and certainty, supplementing this with a glance at some of the problems generated by these notions and the theories of philosophers concerning them.

Truth

Meanings of "Truth"

The words "truth" and "true" are used by people in a number of ways. We frequently speak of the duty of the scholar or scientist to "seek the truth." The shield of Harvard University bears the single word *Veritas.* "To thine own self be true," counsels Polonius, and the poet Keats says, "Beauty is truth, truth beauty. . . ." Sometimes we use "true" in the sense of conforming to a certain standard and "false" when we mean the absence of this conformity, as, for instance, when we say of a member of an animal species, "It is a true goat," or of a man, "He wears false teeth." A true wife is one who is faithful to her husband, and a false friend shows only the appearances of friendship.

Philosophers have much to say about truth. Some hold that truth has *ontological* status, that is, truth is a property of the nature of things. The medievals distinguished between logical truth and ontological truth. The latter, they taught, is one of three "transcendental attributes of being," the other two being unity and goodness. Whitehead says,

"Truth is the conformation of Appearance and Reality."[2] Other philosophers, notably contemporary anti-metaphysical analysts, hold that truth has *metalinguistic* status only, that is, truth is not a property of things but of sentences. To speak of truth as if it were an ingredient in the nature of things, they say, is to commit the metaphysician's error of treating an abstract noun as if it referred to some thing-like entity.

Truth as a Property of Sentences

Now there may well be a perfectly proper *metaphysical* sense of "truth." It would certainly be imprudent for us to assert categorically that "truth" cannot possibly refer to some generic property of the nature of things. But it will be more useful to restrict our present attention to truth taken as a property of *sentences* or of the *beliefs* or *judgments* these sentences express. There is nothing peculiarly modern about this way of handling the word "true." Aristotle held that truth and falsity are properties of statements. "Assertion," he says, "is the saying of something concerning something . . . and is in every case either true or false."[3]

When we say truth is a quality of sentences or propositions we have in mind *statements* or declarative sentences, those which assert something to be so or not to be so. The sentence "The George Washington Bridge crosses the Hudson River" is true, and the sentence "Delius was an Italian composer" is false. Truth and falsity are not properties of interrogative, imperative, or optative sentences. Nor do we apply the words "true" and "false" to *terms* or

[2] A. N. Whitehead, *Adventures of Ideas*, The Macmillan Company, 1933, p. 309.
[3] Aristotle, *De Anima*, J. A. Smith (trans.), 430b27.

names. A person who says "horse" cannot properly be said to speak truly or falsely, except in the case of a child or a foreigner who points to a horse or a cow. In such cases "horse" is a shortened form of the statement "That is a horse." We do not usually attribute truth and falsity to things or happenings in the empirical world, that is, we do not say that Sweden is true or that elephants are false. *Facts* are neither true nor false. They simply *are.*

Normal linguistic usage, then, justifies the claim that truth and falsity are properties of sentences of a certain class. We should note, however, that "true" and "false" are sometimes said to be properties of *beliefs* or *judgments,* on the ground that sentences are expressions of such beliefs. "Truth is a property of beliefs," says Bertrand Russell, "and derivatively of sentences which express beliefs."[4]

Theories of Truth

Just what is it that makes true sentences true? Philosophers have different theories as to just what sort of situation exists when we have true sentences or beliefs. Three well-known doctrines of what truth means are the correspondence theory, the coherence theory, and the pragmatic theory. We can give the gist of these doctrines only by over-simplification. The *correspondence* theory maintains that a sentence or belief is true if it conforms to the facts. The *coherence* theory holds that our beliefs or judgments derive their truth from their coherence or consistency with the system of human beliefs or judgments taken as a whole. The *pragmatic* theory claims that the truth of sentences or beliefs cannot be distinguished from their success as instru-

[4] Bertrand Russell, *Human Knowledge,* Simon and Schuster, 1948, p. 148.

ments of action. Let us examine each of these theories more closely.

THE CORRESPONDENCE THEORY OF TRUTH

The classic formulation of the correspondence theory of truth is that of Aristotle. "To say of what is not that it is," says the Greek philosopher, "is false, while to say of what is that it is, or of what is not that it is not, is true."[5] Applying this formula of Aristotle, we conclude that the sentence "It is raining" is true if it is raining, and the sentence "The house next door is being painted" is true if the house next door is being painted.

A more modern statement of the correspondence theory is: "Truth is the correspondence of our ideas and reality." This formula has serious defects. The terms "idea" and "reality" are so ambiguous that their usage may lead to irrelevant problems. "Idea" can mean (1) a *belief* or opinion, (2) a *concept* or notion of what a thing is, or (3) a sensory *perception* or memory image. "Reality" can mean, among other things, (1) that which is most important or ultimate, (2) that which lasts or endures, (3) that which can be seen and held in the hands, (4) that which exists independently of our perception of it.

Suppose we take "idea" as perception or memory image and "reality" as that which exists independently of our perception of it. Is our idea of "cat" a true idea? If it is, and we use the formula "Truth is the correspondence of our ideas with reality," we shall be compelled to claim that our

[5] Aristotle, *Metaphysics*, Book 4, 1011b26. A highly sophisticated contemporary analysis of the meaning of truth is Alfred Tarski's "Semantic Theory of Truth," which is represented by its author as a modernized version of Aristotle's classic formula. See Alfred Tarski, "The Semantic Conception of Truth," in *Readings in Philosophical Analysis*, H. Feigl and W. Sellars (eds.), Appleton-Century-Crofts, Inc., 1949, p. 52.

sensory image of cat corresponds to the "real" cat as it exists independently of our perception of it. But, as we shall see in our next chapter, such an assertion could not possibly be verified.

A less ambiguous formulation of the correspondence theory is: "A sentence is true if there are such facts as it designates." To be sure, the word "facts" is somewhat vague, but we may take it roughly to mean things or events in the empirical world. The word "correspond" is also troublesome. There cannot be an exact correspondence between a sentence and a situation in the empirical world, for there are no sentences in Nature. These niceties aside, however, we may represent correspondence in the following way:

Sentence ————————————————————————➤ Fact

Relationship of Correspondence

In the case of a false sentence, there is no fact to which the sentence is related, and thus no correspondence relationship. If I say, "There is a checkbook in that drawer," my sentence "corresponds" to the fact. If there is no checkbook in the drawer, there cannot be a correspondence between my sentence and fact, for there is no such fact.

The correspondence theory tries to explain *what is the case* when a sentence is true. It says nothing about how we *discover* or how we *prove* that a sentence corresponds to the facts. The procedure we employ in order to find out whether a statement is true is called *verification*. In regard to a great number of everyday sentences, there is no particular difficulty in specifying what methods are used in verifying correspondence between sentence and fact. If I say, "It is raining," you may verify the correspondence between sentence and fact by stepping outside the door to observe. If I say, "There is a kangaroo in your bathroom," you will hardly require details as to what procedure to adopt in order to check the correspondence between my statement and the fact. Procedures for verification of sentences about less obvious matters may be more complicated.

Proponents of the correspondence theory urge us to keep in mind the distinction between (1) what sort of situation exists when a sentence is true and (2) how we *come to know* a sentence is true. A physician may discover that his belief "This patient has tuberculosis" is true with the aid of x-ray pictures. But this *confirmation* of the truth of the proposition did not make the proposition true. The doctor's belief "This patient has tuberculosis" was true before he examined the radiologist's photographs.

THE COHERENCE THEORY OF TRUTH

Consistency

Logic tells us that it is a mark of a true statement to be consistent with itself and with other true statements. A proposition which contradicts itself, like "This square has five sides," is false. A proposition which contradicts a true statement is also false. In practice, we constantly *test* the truth of empirical statements by investigating their consistency with other propositions we know to be true. If a witness states in one part of his testimony that he was born in 1910 and in another that he was a veteran of the First World War, we would say that these two statements are inconsistent. A man who was born in 1910 would be about eight years old at the time of the Armistice, and we have good reason to believe that no children eight years old or under were soldiers of any army engaged in that war. In Pasteur's time it was thought that putrefaction occurs whenever meat is left standing at ordinary temperatures. Exposing meat in vials, the mouths of which were covered with gauze, Pasteur was able to counter with the statement: There are n instances in which meat does *not* putrefy when left standing at ordinary temperatures. The logical structures of the statements are related thus:

x is y.
Some x is not y.

In practical inquiry, then, whether it be ordinary or scientific, testing of statements for consistency with other statements is an indispensable means of finding out whether they are true. Consistency is thus a valuable *criterion* of truth.

The Coherence Theory Stated

Suppose we grant that consistency is a test of truth and that consistency is a property of all true propositions. Could we go further and say that not only is consistency a *criterion* of truth but it is also the *meaning* of truth? That is, a proposition is true *by virtue of* its consistency with other propositions; it is the proposition's consistency with others that constitutes or "makes" its truth? Now holders of the coherence theory of truth subscribe to something similar to but not exactly like this conclusion. They say that a judgment is true in virtue of its *coherence* with the *total aggregate* of all true judgments. "Any judgment is true," says E. S. Brightman, "if it is both self-consistent and coherently connected with our system of judgments as a whole."[6]

[6] E. S. Brightman, *An Introduction to Philosophy*, Henry Holt and Co., 1925, p. 61.

It is very difficult to make clear just what the proponents of the coherence theory are trying to get at without some familiarity with one particular variety of a certain metaphysical doctrine we call *idealism*. This type of idealism is supported by many coherence advocates, who regard the coherence theory as an integral part of their general world perspective. Briefly, this metaphysical doctrine holds that the world is basically of the nature of mind or thought; that human knowledge is a system of interrelated judgments (appearance) constantly advancing toward a union with an absolute (reality). The metaphysical teaching of the German philosopher Hegel is a source of this doctrine. Hegel taught that the world of our experience is a necessary sequence of processes analogous to thought, and that the multiple interconnections of these processes are united with God or Absolute Spirit to form an organic whole. "In common life," says Hegel, "truth means the agreement of an object with our conception of it. . . . In the philosophical sense of the word . . . truth may be described in general abstract terms, as the agreement of a thought content with itself. . . . God alone is thorough harmony of notion and reality."[7] Reading the following passage from Brand Blanshard, a contemporary and able defender of the coherence theory of truth, we see that it is impossible to separate his coherence theory from his metaphysics:

. . . Reality is a system, completely ordered and fully intelligible with which thought in its advance is more and more identifying itself. We may look at the growth of knowledge, individual or social, either as an attempt by our own minds to return to union with things as they are in their ordered whole-

[7] G. Hegel, *Logic*, W. Wallace (trans.), Oxford University Press, London, Humphrey Milford, 1892, pp. 51–52.

ness, or the affirmation through our minds of the ordered whole itself. And if we take this view, our notion of truth is marked out for us. Truth is the approximation of thought to reality. It is thought on its way home. Its measure is the distance thought has travelled, under guidance of its inner compass, toward that intelligible system which unites its ultimate object with its ultimate end. Hence at any given time the degree of truth in our experience as a whole is the degree of system it has achieved. The degree of truth of a particular proposition is to be judged in the first instance by its coherence with experience as a whole, ultimately by its coherence with that further whole, all-comprehensive and fully articulated, in which thought can come to rest.[8]

Criticism of the Coherence Theory

Critics of the coherence theory of truth are most often those who object to the special metaphysical doctrine involved. The coherence theory, they say, cannot be defended without falling back on some variety of idealism. Moreover, this type of idealism itself ultimately relies for its definition of truth on the concept of correspondence. Suppose we grant that a certain judgment *a* is true because it "coheres" with the total system of true judgments *b*, *c*, *d*, etc. Let the accompanying diagram, then, represent the situation. If it is claimed that *a*, *b*, *c*, etc., being true judgments, are thoughts, and that these thoughts are true in that they are coherent parts of a "whole" which is itself of the nature of thought, then the soundness of the coherence theory of truth must depend on the doctrine that the world is essentially a process analogous to thought. Now, on the

[8] B. Blanshard, *The Nature of Thought*, The Macmillan Company, 1940, vol. 2, p. 264.

coherence assumption, truth is a matter of coherence between individual judgments and the system of our judgments taken as a whole. But by virtue of *what* is this aggregate of judgments true? The whole system of true
judgments supports the truth of each judgment, taken in-

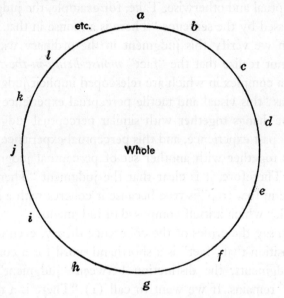

dividually. But what supports the whole system? The
answer is usually given that the system of judgments approximates to or is in the processing of approximating to
"reality." But this means that the coherence theory is itself
based on the assumption of a grand-scale ontological correspondence.

Facts Are Judgments?

Advocates of the coherence theory sometimes argue that
the correspondence doctrine, upon analysis, reduces itself

to a coherence theory. Consider, they say, the claim of correspondence theorists: a sentence is true if it corresponds to the facts. Let us agree that a sentence expresses a judgment or belief. Now the word "fact," says the coherence advocates, is a shorthand word for a complex of judgments, perceptual and otherwise. Take, for example, the judgment expressed by the sentence "There is a mouse in that trap." When we verify this judgment in the ordinary way, we may not realize that the "fact" *mouse-being-in-the-trap* is itself a complex in which are telescoped implicit judgments such as "this visual and tactile perceptual experience I call 'mouse' hangs together with similar perceptual judgments of my past experience, and this perceptual experience 'trap' hangs together with another set of perceptual judgments, etc." Therefore, it is clear that the judgment "There is a mouse in that trap" is true because it coheres with a larger complex which it itself composed of judgments.

But, say the critics of the coherence theory, even on the supposition that "fact" is a shorthand word for a complex of judgments, the distinction between "judgment" and "fact" remains. If we want to call (1) "There is a mouse in that trap" a judgment and (2) the perceptual experience *mouse-being-in-the-trap* a complex of present and past judgments, we may do so. But we can hardly maintain that judgments of type (1) and the judgments in the complex (2) are *of the same order*. The latter are more usually labeled "facts," and, because they have a way of being stubborn, we distinguish them from judgments or *beliefs about facts*. Now whether we say the relation between (1) and (2) is one of "correspondence" or "coherence" is almost a matter of indifference, since both vague words convey the sense of some kind of agreement.

Coherence in Formal Science

There is a class of statements whose truth is, in a broad sense, constituted by their mutual consistency or coherence. These are the sentences of formal science. We have already observed that a simple arithmetical statement like "$7 + 5 = 12$" is true, not because it conforms to a set of empirical facts but because it is a theorem of arithmetic which is deducible from certain prior theorems which in turn derive from the postulates, rules, and basic concepts of that system. The truth of statements of formal science is indistinguishable from their membership or "group coherence" in a system of basic notions and derivative statements. "The laws of mathematics and logic," says W. V. Quine, "are true simply by virtue of our conceptual scheme."[9]

THE PRAGMATIC THEORY OF TRUTH

Origin of "Pragmatism"

"Pragmatism" is a word which is used rather loosely to label the teachings of certain philosophers, most of them Americans, whose major writings were published during or shortly before the present century. The term "pragmatism" was introduced by C. S. Peirce in reference to a theory of *meaning* we have mentioned earlier. The word "pragmatism," however, seems to have been publicly used first in 1898 by Peirce's friend William James, whose subsequent lectures and writings made pragmatism an object of popular interest. The works of F. C. S. Schiller in England and of the late John Dewey in America are also associated with pragmatism. Because of the misunderstandings

[9] W. V. Quine, *Methods of Logic*, Henry Holt and Co., 1950, p. xiv.

and controversies that centered around the term "pragmatism," Dewey adopted the word "instrumentalism" as a label for an aspect of his own doctrine.

James' Theory of Truth

Taken generally, pragmatism is a theory of knowledge. It is that knowledge is made for action, for *doing* something about the problems that face us, for *meeting* the endless succession of obstacles and perplexities which is the condition of human existence. In his pragmatic theory of truth, James tells us that truth is an empty compliment to pay to a proposition in "cold storage." A belief *becomes* true when it is put into action. Its truth is inseparable from its successful engagement in the world of experience.

According to James, truth is an attribute of beliefs upon which we are prepared to *act*. True beliefs are those which are "successful," "expedient," "satisfactory," "useful." A true belief, if acted upon, *works*. In the long run, it is bound to produce satisfactory *results*. A false belief, put into practice, leads ultimately to failure. If a belief cannot be acted upon, or if it makes no difference one way or the other whether it is true or not, such a belief is neither true nor false; it is only meaningless and empty. Says James: "Grant an idea or belief to be true, what concrete difference will its being true make in any one's actual life? How will the truth be realized? What experiences will be different from those which would obtain if the belief were false? What, in short, is the truth's cash-value in experiential terms?"[10]

True beliefs, then, are useful beliefs. But James goes further. Truth and utility are one and the same. Comparing

[10] William James, *Pragmatism*, Longmans, Green and Co., 1928, p. 200.

the statements "it is useful because it is true" and "it is true because it is useful," James says, "Both these phrases mean exactly the same thing."[11] The truth of a belief is not only *discovered* by testing the belief. The verification of a belief *is* its truth.

Criticism of James' Theory of Truth

The pragmatic theory of truth, as set forth by William James, has been charged with *ambiguity*. James' enthusiastic but loose handling of words like "expedient" and "useful" in connection with truth convinced many that he was denying the "objectivity" of truth, offering in its place a subjective criterion, to the effect that the true was whatever it pleased us to think. By literal interpretations of such Jamesian remarks as "We have to live today by what truth we can get today, and be ready tomorrow to call it falsehood,"[12] critics of pragmatism support their charges of *relativism*. They denounce pragmatism as a modern version of the old Sophist doctrine that every man determines his own truth. James, of course, did not for a moment intend that his doctrine be interpreted in this way.

A more specific criticism of the pragmatic theory of truth asserts that it confuses the question *what truth is* with *how we find it out*. There is no doubt that utility or workability is a valuable *test* of the truth of a sentence. In our common reliance upon observation of *results* to guide us in inquiry, we are all pragmatists, including him who said "By their fruits ye shall know them." If we are working over an automobile engine, and you say, "The dirt on the points of your spark plugs makes the engine misfire. Clean

[11] *Ibid.*, p. 204.
[12] *Ibid.*, p. 200.

points will give you a smooth-running engine," it is obvious that pragmatic procedure is in order. I clean the points, and start the engine, which now runs smoothly. Testing the hypothesis by putting it into action solved the problem. It produced satisfying results. It *worked*.

Now we employ variations of this testing procedure as a matter of course not only in problems of everyday life but also in the special sciences. The pragmatic method in inquiry, taken as a test of truth, is not something peculiar or specifically American. It is simply a variety of empirical verification, the general procedure we follow whenever we check the truth of a hypothesis by test and experiment.

The Instrumental Conception of Truth; Dewey

Man, says Dewey, is an organism moving within a natural and a social environment. The interaction between man and Nature, between man and society produces *experience*, which is what we philosophize about. Our dual environment raises problems; it presents difficulties and obstacles which the human organism endeavors to overcome. Now man is able to *control* to an important extent both his natural and his social environment. By controlling his environment, man can *change* it. The relation between man and Nature should not be thought of as a relation between a spectator and an aggregate of fixed and eternal facts. The correspondence theory of truth is inadequate because it covertly assumes this false, static view of man's relation to Nature and to society. The correspondence theory implies that the world is a series of fixed facts. A proposition is true if it agrees with them, false if it does not. But, objects Dewey, facts are not fixed. Man, by virtue of his intelligence, can control and modify his environment. Thus, facts can be *made*. And if facts can be made, *truth* can be made. Verification, then, is not just a way of arriving at truth. It *is* truth. "Verification and truth are two names for the same thing. We call it 'verification' when we regard it as process . . . we call it 'truth' when we take it as product."[13]

Critics of pragmatism readily admit, says Dewey, that the fact that a proposition *works* may lead us to know that it is true. But, they insist, that it works is not the same thing as its truth. The proposition was true all along. The artificiality of this position, says Dewey, may be illustrated by the following example: Suppose a man has just been rescued from drowning. Someone says to him that he is now a saved man. What would we think of a bystander who said, "Yes, but he was a saved man all the time. The process of rescuing, while it gives evidence of that fact, does not constitute it"? It is just as absurd, Dewey maintains, to hold that every proposition verified in experience has antecedent truth.[14] Suppose a man is lost in the woods, and he says to himself, "Acting in such and such a way will bring me safely out." He acts upon the proposition and is successful in reaching a settled area. The truth of this proposition and its success cannot be distinguished without involving oneself in triviality. There is a trap, says Dewey, in the very word "truth"; its traditional overtones of something fixed, eternal, and separated from man are so persistent that when we use the word we tend unconsciously to assume the worn-out metaphysics with which it is associated. For this reason Dewey prefers the phrase "warranted assertibility" to "truth."

[13] John Dewey, *The Influence of Darwin on Philosophy*, Henry Holt and Co., 1910, pp. 139–140.
[14] *Ibid.*, p. 142.

Criticism of the Instrumental Theory

In certain areas of human affairs the tendency to think of truth always as something *fixed in advance* has blocked experiment, and in his criticism of this tendency most contemporary philosophers would agree that Dewey is in the right. When he says, as James did, that "the true means the verified," we can readily agree that in the case of many true propositions it is difficult to separate the "state of affairs" they designate from their actual verification. Such statements as "Minnesota will beat Michigan this year" *become* true only at the moment of their verification. There are no present facts for the correspondence theory to point to as agreeing with the sentence. Similarly, the proposition "Democracy is the best form of government" *becomes* true as it is verified by centuries of trial, error, adjustment, and compromise. For this reason the truth of the proposition and its verification are inextricable.

Nevertheless, Dewey's critics maintain that if we say, as Dewey does, "the true means the verified and means nothing else,"[15] there are situations where this identification simply does not hold. Some situations are *indeterminate*, and here Dewey's theory of truth as verification is applicable. An example of an indeterminate situation is that which precedes the election of a President of the United States. The truth of the proposition "Eisenhower is President" *becomes* true when the intrinsic doubtfulness of the situation is resolved by action of the voters. On election day, truth and verification are the same. Here truth is *made*. But other situations are *determinate*. When I open my pig bank to see

---

[15] John Dewey, *Reconstruction in Philosophy*, Henry Holt and Co., 1920, p. 160.

if there is a dollar in it, my doing so does not constitute the truth of the proposition "There is a dollar in the pig bank." There was a dollar in it all the time. Would we be willing to say that prior to its verification the proposition "The earth is round" was neither true nor false?

The character of a philosopher's theory of truth will depend to a considerable extent upon the kinds of situations that interest him. Thus Dewey is not primarily interested in propositions about determinate situations like dollars in pig banks or the roundness of the earth. James is absorbed with situations in the moral realm—where conflict can be resolved by resolute will, where faith can bring about facts. Dewey sees the problems of philosophy in terms of problematic situations like men lost in forests, scientists searching for a working hypothesis, citizens trying to resolve a social conflict. But there are also philosophers like Bertrand Russell who are interested in propositions about determinate situations, such as the moons of Jupiter, the rate of vibration of red light, the presence of mammoths in North America. Russell is convinced that some type of correspondence theory is needed to deal with these propositions and denies that the pragmatic theory can provide an adequate explanation of the meaning of their truth.

Certainty

Meanings of "Certainty"

Like "truth," "certainty" is a shifty word. Sometimes we use it to describe a *state of mind*. As such, certainty is the opposite of *doubt*. When we are certain, we assent without hesitation to a statement. When we doubt, we withhold our assent. As a state of mind, certainty is often called *subjective* or *psychological* certainty. Now subjective certainty is no guarantee of truth. When I say, "I am certain I saw Jane at Jones Beach," I may have an unshakable conviction that this proposition is true. Yet, as we know too well from experience, we may have such a strong conviction at the time, yet later be forced to admit that we were mistaken. For many centuries a large number of educated men were strongly convinced that the earth was immovable and that there were unicorns. Conviction that something is so does not mean that it is so.

Sometimes we apply certainty to *propositions*. We may say that the statements "I have two legs" and "$2 + 2 = 4$" are certain. Such propositions are certain, we say, because there is no reason whatever to doubt them and there is incontrovertible evidence of an objective character to support them. Certainty used in this sense is frequently called *objective* certainty.

In their quest for certainty, philosophers have often asked what kinds of propositions are certain. The ancient Skeptics believed there were no such propositions. Descartes, the father of modern philosophy, believed there were and recommended a remarkable method for discovering them.

Descartes's Method

The distinguished seventeenth-century French philosopher was disturbed by the fact that learned men disagreed upon every subject. Were there no propositions above dispute? he asked. If there were such, we should find them and build our knowledge upon them. Descartes believed he had a sound method for discovering propositions that were certain. He would consider all the propositions it was possible to think of and see whether it was possible to *doubt* them all. Descartes then proceeded to apply his methodic doubt to all propositions, including those drawn from ordinary experience and from the learned disciplines. He found that it was possible to doubt them all. He was able even to question the objective existence of the world of his experience, for this world *could* be a phantasm induced in him by some powerful malignant demon. But at length Descartes came upon a proposition of such a nature that he could not possibly doubt it. This was the proposition *I exist*. I know that I exist, says Descartes, for I am thinking. Even if there should be an evil genius deceiving me concerning the whole world, at least there exists a René Descartes who is being deceived. He tells us: "As I observed that this truth, I THINK, HENCE I AM, was so certain and of such evidence, that no ground of doubt, however extravagant, could be alleged by the Sceptics capable of shaking it, I concluded that I might, without scruple, accept it as the first principle of the Philosophy of which I was in search."[16]

Descartes then proceeds to search for other certain propositions. The judgment "I exist" has such peculiar *clarity* and *distinctness*, he says, that it is impossible to doubt it. Are there any other judgments similarly clear and distinct? Descartes was convinced that the judgment "A perfect Being exists" had the requisite clarity and distinctness, and that the proposition expressing it was certain. Descartes claims that the truth of the proposition "God exists" is *self-evident*. Once we understand what this proposition means, we cannot possibly doubt it. Having to his own satisfaction established the certainty of "God exists," Descartes concludes that human knowledge is fundamentally reliable,

[16] R. Descartes, *Discourse on Method*, J. Veitch (trans.), M. Walter Dunne, 1901, p. 171.

provided that we use it properly. For God, being good, would not endow us with a faculty inherently deceptive.

Meaning of Self-Evidence

The reader will probably object to the soundness of the chain of inferences by means of which Descartes establishes the existence of God and the comparative reliability of human knowledge. One of the defects of Descartes's procedure arises from his use of clarity and distinctness or *self-evidence* to support the certainty of propositions. Now there are at least two senses in which a proposition may be said to be self-evident. A proposition is sometimes said to be self-evident in the sense that it is *indemonstrable*, that is, we cannot infer it from other propositions. In a second sense, a proposition is self-evident if it is *completely clear to me* that it is so. To those familiar with arithmetic, the proposition "$3 + 3 = 6$" is self-evident in the second sense. But not in the first, for it can be deduced from other more primitive arithmetical statements.

Now self-evidence, in the sense of "completely clear to me," may be a dangerously subjective criterion of certainty. What one man perceives clearly and distinctly another may not. The proposition "God exists" was self-evident to Descartes, but it is not at all self-evident to the majority of philosophers. "The utmost clarity in our thoughts," says Bertrand Russell, "would not enable us to demonstrate the existence of Cape Horn." The proposition "All men are created equal" was self-evident to our founding fathers, but not to the Bourbon kings.

Logical Certainty

Descartes was a mathematician, the discoverer of analytic geometry. As a geometer, he knew he could carry on a complex series of inferences and draw it to a conclusion of unquestionable certainty. For the propositions of formal science *are* certain. It would be silly to say that "$3 + 3 = 6$" is merely *probable*. An analytic statement cannot be denied without involving the denier in a *contradiction*. But the evidence which guarantees the certainty of analytic statements is of a purely formal kind. The evidence for the certainty of "$3 + 3 = 6$" is drawn from the structure of the formal system which contains it. This proposition fits in or "coheres" with the way in which we use notions like "3," "6," "plus," and "equals" in arithmetic.

The peculiar certainty of mathematical conclusions, which philosophers have so much admired, may be classed as *logical* certainty. But we must not expect logical certainty of propositions which make assertions about matters of fact. It is a characteristic of empirical statements that their opposites may be asserted in statements which contain no internal contradiction. I have not the slightest doubt that I have a nose. Yet the proposition "I do not have a nose" does not contradict itself as does the statement "This Euclidean triangle has four sides." What detracts from the excellence of Descartes's method is his apparent conviction that something like logical certainty may be found in some propositions which have nothing to do with formal science. He tried to discover in propositions about God and the world a "clarity and distinctness" found only in mathematics and logic. "In our search for the direct road toward truth," he tells us, "we should busy ourselves with no object about which we cannot attain a certainty equal to that of the demonstrations of Arithmetic and Geometry."[17]

[17] R. Descartes, "Rules for the Direction of the Mind," in *The Philosophical Works of Descartes*, E. S. Haldane and G. R. T. Ross (trans.), Cambridge University Press, 1931, pp. 43-44.

"Incorrigible" Propositions

Are there any *empirical* propositions which may be said to be certain? Consider those statements which refer to simple sensations, such as "I have a pain," or "I see something red." Such statements are sometimes called *incorrigible* (uncorrectable) propositions. Although it is logically possible to doubt such statements (since their opposites do not involve internal contradictions), it seems impossible to question their certainty in any other way. If we are aboard ship and you say, "I feel ill," I may doubt your statement, despite the existence of objective empirical evidence (the rough sea, your pale face, etc.) from which I may *infer* the proposition "You feel ill." But if it is *I* who feel ill, and I say, "I feel ill," *I* at least am certain of this statement. For the evidence which supports it is immediate, sensational, internal, and—as far as I am concerned—beyond question. I do not have to *infer* the proposition. I know it directly. If Descartes's celebrated *Cogito* ("I think") is paraphrased as "I am experiencing," such a proposition may be classified as incorrigible.

Not all philosophers are in agreement about the certainty of incorrigible propositions. Some point out that, while certainty exists in such situations, the certainty is subjective and psychological only. Others say that such statements do not, properly speaking, express knowledge at all, since they are merely reports of *sensations* and do not represent any kind of inference. A few analysts, extreme perhaps in their caution, may go so far as to claim that in the proposition "I feel warm" there may lurk behind the pronoun "I" the covert and unproved metaphysical assumption of a personal unity enduring through change. It would be more exact, they may say, to replace the statement "I feel warm" with the expression "There is a feeling of warmth now."[18]

Particular Empirical Propositions

Apart from incorrigible propositions, are there any statements about matters of fact which may properly be called certain? There is a very large class of nonformal statements which we may call particular *empirical propositions*. They are of this type:

> There is a dictionary on the table.
> Al is playing ball.
> There is a dead mouse under the refrigerator.
> The library is open now.
> I am writing with a pen.
> Etc.

May such propositions be said to be certain? They are not *logically* certain, for their opposites may be supposed true without fear of formal contradiction. Nor is the evidence which supports them of the "incorrigible" type as in the case of propositions like "I feel hungry." Nevertheless it seems that such propositions may be called certain in the sense that (1) there is no reason to doubt them and (2) there is evidence to support them which is adequate.

The evidence which warrants the certainty of particular empirical propositions is based on sense perception and is of a kind that can be corroborated by simple and public procedures. Suppose you approach an object which looks like a table, feels like a table, and functions as a table, and upon

---

[18] Philosophic caution may sometimes be carried to exaggerated lengths. A story is told of a well-known German professor of philosophy who was so fearful of assigning to objects attributes which the objects might not in fact possess that he habitually addressed his wife only as "Being" or "Thing"!

it you find an object which looks like a dictionary, reads like a dictionary, and functions as a dictionary. Suppose further that other members of your family behave as if they were having the same experience. Now what possible reason would there be for questioning the certainty of the proposition "There is a dictionary on the table"? What more could one ask by way of verification? What further procedures could be specified which would measurably increase the certainty of the proposition? To be sure, it *might* be, as Descartes suggests, that a malignant demon with nothing better to do is causing something which is *not* a dictionary to appear as if it *were* a dictionary. But, although this is possible, there is not the slightest reason to suppose it to be true.

Arguments of the type above have been put forward by the English analytic philosopher G. E. Moore in support of the certainty of particular empirical propositions. To insist, says Moore, that the proposition "I am holding a pen" is not *certain* but only *probable* is to use language in a way in which people do not employ it. The pressure exerted in this direction by Moore and his followers has forced most contemporary analysts to concede that particular empirical propositions may correctly be said to be certain, if certainty is used *in the ordinary sense*. Some philosophers, however, still have reservations about this type of proposition. Admitting ordinary certainty, they say, we may wish to use the word "certain" in special philosophic inquiry in some stricter sense.[19]

General Empirical Statements; Induction

The capacity to form general judgments is a characteristic mark of human knowledge. Without general statements

[19] See A. J. Ayer, "Basic Propositions," in *Philosophical Analysis*, Max Black (ed.), Cornell University Press, 1950.

there could be no science. For the essence of scientific explanation is fitting a particular observed fact into a general description or "law." Here are some samples of general statements drawn at random both from science and from ordinary discourse:

> Leaves contain chlorophyll.
> The subway is always crowded at five-thirty on weekdays.
> The specific gravity of gold is 19.3.
> Thin people tend to be nervous.
> Cows get up back end first.
> Human blood falls into four major groupings.
> Once a thief, always a thief.
> The female praying mantis, after mating, decapitates, then eats the male.
> Spinach is good for you.

Suppose we note some elements common to all these general statements: (1) The statements are conclusions of *inferences*. (2) The data on which the inferences are based are *particular instances*. (3) The number of individual instances examined is *less* than the number covered by the general statement. In other words, on the basis of an examination of *some*, we have made a general statement concerning *all*.

The type of inference by which we establish such general statements is called *induction*. Induction may be defined as a mode of inference in which, upon the basis of some examples of an occurrence, a conclusion is drawn concerning *all* such occurrences. Not every general statement or scientific law is established by induction. Scientists frequently derive general statements by *deduction* from other general statements. The same proposition may be derived inductively and deductively. I may base "The sun always rises" on induction, by referring to past instances of the sun's rising. Or I may deduce it by showing that this prop- osition follows from certain general laws of motion in their application to the earth.

The role of inductive inference in science and practical life is very important. The practical utility of inductive generalizations is that they enable us to predict *future* oc- currences. If a copper alloy melts whenever I heat it to a certain temperature, I can form a general description or "law" which I can then apply to future instances of that alloy. Our present inquiry concerns the *certainty* of general empirical propositions. A very large number of such prop- ositions are established inductively. Hence, the question of the certainty of general empirical statements is closely re- lated to the question of the *validity* of induction as a mode of inference.

THE PROBLEM OF INDUCTION

Sound and Unsound Inductions

The problem of induction may be put in this way: What gives us the right, in certain circumstances, to make general statements when we have only examined *some* of the in- stances? Formal logic tells us that the inference "Some *A* is *B*; therefore, all *A* is *B*" is *invalid*. In the course of daily life we meet many examples of inductive generalizations which we quickly recognize as dubious, such as "Japanese are treacherous" and "Pickles and ice cream will make you sick." On the other hand, it would never occur to us to question such statements as "Fire will heat water" and "We shall all one day die." Yet both types of general statements are established by induction. Is it possible to distinguish be- tween a sound induction and an unsound one?

Take the statement "Japanese are treacherous." On what grounds do we question it? Apart from the ambiguity of the word "treacherous," we may challenge this induction on the following points: (1) *insufficient number of instances examined:* the person making the assertion has based his generalization on a small number of experiences with Japanese people; (2) *existence of contrary instances:* we ourselves know of several instances of Japanese who are *not* treacherous; (3) *variable character of that which the generalization concerns:* human behavior is very variable, and experience tells us that general statements about human traits are frequently unreliable. (Note that here we counter with a couple of inductions of our own.)

Contrast with the weak induction "Japanese are treacherous" the strong one "We shall all one day die." What is the nature of the evidence which supports the second statement? (1) A very large number of instances of men's deaths have been examined. (2) We know of no authenticated instance in the past of a man who has failed to die. (3) Mortality is not a variable characteristic of humans, like color of hair. (4) In addition, the statement draws independent strength from that fact that it can be *deduced* from biological laws concerning higher organisms generally.

Number of Instances Examined

We should note that *a large number of instances examined* is not *in itself* a safe criterion of the soundness of an inductive generalization. We may be tempted to say that the strength of an inductive generalization increases in proportion to the increase in the number of instances examined; that the more instances of *A* I find to be *B*, the more likely it is that any future *A* will also be *B*. Now, we *do* employ the criterion of number of instances examined to a considerable extent in ordinary life and in science. After each of a number of bad dinners at a certain restaurant, my conviction increases that any future dinner I am forced to eat there will also be bad. In medicine, in social research, in many other fields of study, the number of instances examined is frequently of great importance to the soundness of inferences drawn.

But there are large areas in both practical life and scientific investigation where the criterion of large number of instances examined does not hold. Consider the inductive statement "The density of argon is about 20." Rayleigh and Ramsay, who discovered the gas, weighed a sample or two and found the density to be 20. This figure was accepted as the measure of argon's density generally.

We need only burn our fingers once to convince ourselves of the certainty of "Fire burns painfully," but inspection of several hundred crows, each of which is black, will not persuade us that "All crows are black." In science, the strength of some general statements may be increased by testing a larger number of cases. But there are countless situations where the testing of further instances would be an obvious waste of time. In his treatise on induction, John Stuart Mill asks: "Why is a single instance, in some cases, sufficient for a complete induction, while in others myriads of concurring instances, without a single exception known or presumed, go such a very little way toward establishing a universal proposition? Whoever can answer this question knows more of the philosophy of logic than the wisest of the ancients, and has solved the problem of Induction."[20]

[20] J. S. Mill, *A System of Logic*, Longmans, Green and Co., London, 1925, p. 201.

Induction by Analogy

J. M. Keynes has pointed out that inductive arguments based upon the number of instances examined is only one kind of induction—induction by *simple enumeration*. Inductive arguments may also be based on *analogy*.[21] Suppose I have examined an instance of A in which the properties of P, Q, R, S, etc., are conjoined. I have been particularly impressed by property X. Now when I come upon another instance of A together with its properties P, Q, R, S, etc., I infer that this instance of A will also have the property X.

> I met a collie dog once, and it bit me.
> Here is another collie dog.
> It might bite me.

A sociologist notices a high incidence of emotional disturbance in children of families marked by certain characteristics—parental conflict, overconcern, etc. When he studies a set of families with analogous characteristics, he expects to find a similar incidence of disturbances in the children.

We argue from analogy, says Keynes, in so far as we depend upon the *likeness* of the instances; from simple enumeration or "pure induction" when we trust the *number* of the instances. In inductive argument, the value of increasing the number of cases examined lies not in the mere multiplication of instances. Increasing the number of instances may either confirm analogy or show up differences which observation of a smaller number of cases did not reveal.

[21] See J. M. Keynes, *A Treatise on Probability*, Macmillan and Co., London, 1921, Part 3.

Intuitive Induction; Aristotle

The obvious uselessness of searching for a large number of examples to support certain classes of general statements (such as "A body tends to fall toward the center of the earth" and "Fish have backbones") convinced Aristotle long ago that the function of induction in such cases is not to *prove* anything, but rather to *call our attention* to the existence of certain general patterns in Nature.[22] The role of induction is to nudge us into awareness of the existence of these general natural features, statements about which form the primary premises of the sciences. Aristotle did not believe that there was any need to prove by extended nose counting (simple enumeration) that which any reasonable man could see for himself after he had observed a few cases. Because of Aristotle's belief that the role of induction in human knowledge is to enable us to "see" the universal pattern manifest in the particular case, his conception of induction is sometimes described as *intuitive* induction. Many analysts do not regard this as a genuine form of inference.

Hume's Criticism of Induction

The explanation we have given above of the difference between sound and unsound inductions would not satisfy the skeptical Scottish philosopher David Hume. Hume called into question the validity of induction generally, and the justice of his criticism is still a matter of debate among philosophers. Hume was an empiricist of an extreme type. As such, he believed that our most reliable knowledge comes from sense experience. According to Hume, experience brings us in contact with particular and individual occur-

[22] Aristotle, *Posterior Analytics*, 99b15 et seq.

rences only. Experience never presents us with general or universal situations.

Hume claims that when we make an inductive statement like "All men are mortal" or "Sodium ignites on contact with water" we are stating something *more* than experience warrants. What experience tells us is that *in the past* men have invariably died and sodium has ignited whenever it was brought in contact with water. Experience does not tell us, however, that those men now living will die; as far as experience is concerned, we know nothing whatever about the deaths of those still living. Nor does past experience of sodium have anything to do with instances of sodium which have not yet been observed. Because something has been observed to behave in a certain way in the past is no guarantee that it will continue to behave that way. On the basis of the properties of instances observed in the past, we *assume* that the same properties will occur in the future. But this assumption is not justified by experience, since its justification would require observation of instances not yet observed. "It is impossible," says Hume, "that any arguments from experience can prove this resemblance of the past to the future; since all these arguments are founded on the supposition of that resemblance."[23]

According to Hume, then, experience gives us no warrant of certainty for inductive statements. Why then do we make them and use them so confidently to support our predictions? We make inductive generalizations, says Hume, through force of *habit*. That things have turned out in a certain way in the past *accustoms* us to believe that they will turn out that way in the future. But for this belief there is neither logical nor factual justification.

[23] D. Hume, *An Enquiry Concerning Human Understanding*, Open Court Publishing Co., 1935, p. 37.

Philosophers have gone to considerable trouble to answer
Hume (we shall in our next chapter see something of Kant's
reply) and to find some kind of principle or "ground" upon
which valid induction rests. One of these is the principle of
the uniformity of Nature.

The Uniformity of Nature

"The proposition that the course of nature is uniform,"
says John Stuart Mill, "is the fundamental principle, or general axiom of Induction."[24] Natural events are not isolated
bits of a miscellaneous jumble. They are part of a vast process of sequences of cause and effect. The principle of uniformity involves the *law of causation.* "The cause of a
phenomenon," Mill tells us, is "the antecedent, or the con-
currence of antecedents, on which it is invariably and *unconditionally* consequent."[25] Observation of a very few
instances of fire and water convinces us that fire will heat
water. For we perceive that fire and the heating of water
are causally connected. They are elements in a causal sequence. Now Nature is a system of such causal sequences,
a grand pattern of events which are not merely haphazardly
associated but necessarily connected with one another.

The principle of the uniformity of Nature, says Mill, is
the ultimate major premise of every inductive argument. It
is the most general empirical proposition. Upon this principle depends not only scientific investigation, which presupposes it, but all conduct of practical affairs. Untold numbers
of instances confirm this general principle, while none, of
which we have reliable knowledge, runs counter to it. This
most general of natural descriptions or "laws of Nature"
communicates its certainty to the inductive statements of

[24] J. S. Mill, *op. cit.,* p. 201.
[25] *Ibid.,* p. 222.

the several sciences. For the causal sequences investigated by these special sciences are particular exemplifications of the principle of uniformity.

It has been objected that Mill's argument is circular. For the principle "Nature is uniform" is *itself* established by induction. Mill, however, thought that his principle of uniformity was exceptional among inductive statements. He did not think that the usual challenge offered to inductive arguments could be brought against this single, all-embracing principle, unique in its comprehensive generality, verified by evidence from all possible quarters, with no known case to the contrary.

Nevertheless, many philosophers have found Mill's principle of uniformity an unsatisfactory explanation either of induction or of causality. It is objected that the principle is too vague; that it does not help us to distinguish between *sound* and *unsound* inductions, between those connections between phenomena which are *causal* and those which are merely *casual*.[26] "The doctrine of the Uniformity of Nature," says Whitehead, "is to be ranked with the contrasted doctrine of magic and miracle, as an expression of a partial truth, unguarded and uncoordinated with the immensities of the Universe."[27] Despite these criticisms of the principle of uniformity, many philosophers think that some principle analogous to the uniformity of Nature may exist, even though it has not yet successfully been formulated.[28]

Inductive Statements as Probable

Many recent philosophers have felt that the quest for certainty in the case of general empirical statements should

[26] See M. Cohen and E. Nagel, *An Introduction to Logic and Scientific Method*, Harcourt, Brace and Co., 1934, pp. 267–269.

[27] A. N. Whitehead, *op. cit.*, p. 99.

[28] More specific than Mill's principle of uniformity is J. M. Keynes' *postulate of limited variety*. See Keynes, *op. cit.*, p. 258 et seq.

be abandoned as hopeless, and that we should be content with the conclusion that inductive statements can at best be considered *probable*. Since all instances (including future occurrences) comprehended within an inductive generalization clearly *cannot* be examined, it is obvious that we cannot be certain about them. What we *can* say is that statements like "All men are mortal" and "Falling bodies accelerate at the rate of 32 feet per second per second" possess, by virtue of the evidence supporting them, a high degree of probability. This view of general empirical statements as probable rather than certain draws strength from the fact that historically a great number of inductive statements taken by scientists as descriptive laws have later required correction. For example, it has been discovered that Boyle's law—which states that the volume of a gas varies inversely with the pressure—is inexact, and that it requires modification if it is applied in certain circumstances. Newton's laws, once considered absolute, have had to be modified to account for certain properties of space subsequently observed.

Now there are two senses of "probable." One is the precise sense of *mathematical probability*. In this context of meaning, probability is represented as a fraction between 0 and 1. If we assume that it is equally likely that a coin will turn up either heads or tails, the probability of obtaining heads on any one throw is ½, in two successive throws, ¼, etc. Life insurance companies use complex probability calculi to predict life expectation within large statistical groups.

A less exact sense of "probable" means a certain degree of *credibility*. When I say, "It is probable that Jones will be elected," I mean that there are good reasons to believe that this will be so, although these reasons are not enough to *compel* my belief. A higher degree of credibility may attach to scientific statements which are supported by evidence subject to test and experiment. It is in the sense of a high degree of credibility that "probability" is most often suggested by philosophers as a means of resolving the problem of the certainty of general empirical statements. Inductive generalizations can never be said to be "certain" because there is always the chance that a contrary instance might turn up. If, however, a given case of induction is supported by tested evidence and independently corroborated, we may say that the general statement has a high degree of probability. We should not, however, regard the statement as closed to correction.

The Problem of Induction; Conclusion

A certain number of instances of *A* have been found to be *B*.

Therefore, all future instances of *A* will be *B*.

As it stands above, schematically represented and taken abstractly, the principle of induction has no justification. There is nothing about induction *as such* which guarantees its soundness. This we know by the enormous number of unsound inductions which follow the pattern above. We cannot formulate induction as a formal logical principle which, when applied, will provide reliable security in inference. Induction is concerned with *empirical* inference; therefore we can never expect it to have *formal* or *deductive* certainty. We draw inductions concerning a huge variety of matters, ranging from the freezing point of mercury to the dispositions of red-headed girls. We cannot discuss the soundness of induction in the abstract *without reference to the nature of the particular evidence which supports a given induction.*

As to the question whether any general empirical propositions may correctly be described as *certain*, the answer will depend upon the meaning assigned to the word "certain." If "certain" is to be used in the sense of *ordinary* or *practical* certainty, then the answer will be yes. Whatever our theoretical doubts, we *behave* as if unexamined instances of fire will burn us and kisses of our loved ones will comfort us. But if by "certain" is meant *logical* certainty, the certainty which attends the inferences of formal science when correctly drawn, the answer will be no. Nor can general empirical statements properly be called certain if by "certainty" is meant *incorrigibility.* We cannot claim that any inductive statement is beyond the possibility of correction or revision, or that the behavior of future unobserved instances can in any case of induction be unconditionally guaranteed in advance.

FURTHER READINGS

Truth

Aquinas, Thomas, *Truth (De Veritate)*, R. W. Mulligan, S.J. (trans.), Henry Regnery Co., 1952, vol. 1, Question 1.

Blanshard, Brand, *The Nature of Thought*, The Macmillan Company, 1940.

Dewey, John, *The Philosophy of John Dewey*, Joseph Ratner (ed.), Henry Holt and Co., 1928, chap. 7.

Dewey, John, "Propositions, Warranted Assertibility, and Truth," *The Journal of Philosophy*, March 27, 1941.

James, William, *The Meaning of Truth*, Longmans, Green and Co., 1909.

James, William, *Pragmatism*, Longmans, Green and Co., 1928, chap. 6.

Joachim, H. H., *The Nature of Truth*, Clarendon Press, Oxford, 1906.

Pap, Arthur, *Elements of Analytic Philosophy*, The Macmillan Company, 1949, chap. 14.

Russell, Bertrand, *An Inquiry into Meaning and Truth*, W. W. Norton and Co., 1940.

Tarski, Alfred, "The Semantic Conception of Truth," in H. Feigl and W. Sellars (eds.), *Readings in Philosophical Analysis*, Appleton-Century-Crofts, Inc., 1949.

Ushenko, Paul Andrew, "Truth," in *Power and Events*, Princeton University Press, 1946.

Whitehead, Alfred North, *Adventures of Ideas*, The Macmillan Company, 1933, chap. 16.

Certainty

Black, Max, "The Justification of Induction," in *Language and Philosophy*, Cornell University Press, 1949.

Cohen, Morris, and Nagel, Ernest, *An Introduction to Logic and Scientific Method*, Harcourt, Brace and Co., 1934, chap. 14.

Descartes, René, *Discourse on Method*, J. Veitch (trans.), M. Walter Dunne, 1901.

Dewey, John, *The Quest for Certainty*, Minton, Balch and Company, 1929.

Hume, David, *An Enquiry Concerning Human Understanding*, Open Court Publishing Co., 1935, Section 3.

Keynes, John Maynard, *A Treatise on Probability*, Macmillan and Co., London, 1921.

Mill, John Stuart, *A System of Logic*, Longmans, Green and Co., 1925, Book III.

Pap, Arthur, *Elements of Analytic Philosophy*, The Macmillan Company, 1949, chap. 8.

Reichenbach, Hans, "The Logical Character of the Principle of Induction" and "The Logical Foundations of Probability," in H. Feigl and W. Sellars (eds.), *Readings in Philosophical Analysis*, Appleton-Century-Crofts, Inc., 1949.

Russell, Bertrand, *Human Knowledge*, Simon and Schuster, 1948, Part 6.

4

OUR KNOWLEDGE OF THE WORLD
OUTSIDE US

> *Wherein, he resembled my Right Reverend friend, Bishop Berkeley—truly, one of your lords spiritual—who, metaphysically speaking, holding all objects to be mere optical delusions, was, notwithstanding, extremely matter-of-fact in all matters touching matter itself. Besides being pervious to the points of pins, and possessing a palate capable of appreciating plum-puddings.*
> —*Mardi*, HERMAN MELVILLE

IN THE preceding chapter it was suggested that some types of propositions may be correctly described as *certain* in the ordinary sense of the word. Among these propositions we included the type based on simple perceptual judgments like "There is a black cat on that chair." Since the evidence supporting such propositions is our sense observation which can be corroborated by similar observations by others, it seemed that there is no reason to doubt them.

But suppose the following questions are raised: What evidence do we have that there exists a cat and a chair *independently* of me and other percipients? What evidence is there that these objects (assuming that they do exist "out there") actually possess in their own right the properties they appear to have? If no such evidence exists, or if the evidence is questionable, it would seem that the certainty of the proposition "There is a black cat on that chair" is, after all, a rather dubious matter. In the external world we distinguish innumerable objects such as cats, trees, tables, houses, and rivers. Common sense tells us that these things exist independently of us and that they themselves possess the properties they seem to have. But suppose it were argued that there is no guarantee whatever that the character of the external world as it is given to us through sense perception is reliably reported.

Now human knowledge goes far beyond particular sense observations. The nature of knowledge is *generalization*. We cannot describe the external world solely in terms of individual *percepts*, of colored shapes that feel hard or soft and move this way and that. We must use general notions, ideas, *concepts* to tie our scattered percepts together, to *interpret* our sense observation, and thus bring order, system, and explanation into knowledge. No man has ever *perceived* an atom, yet the concept of "atom" holds up the world of modern physics and enables us to control mighty forces of Nature.

But if the reliability of sense perception can be questioned, so can the reliability of conceptual knowledge. Our perceptions, at least, are affairs of present sense experience. But concepts go *beyond* sense experience. They deal with what is not immediately present to sense observation. They are abstract. They are general. That one event is the *cause* of another is not seen but inferred. No one perceives "heat" or "electricity" or "gravity" as such. "Evolution" and the "subconscious" are not matters given directly in sense experience. General notions such as these are indispensable to science. But is there any assurance that there actually exists in the external world such situations as they purport to describe?

In modern times philosophers have raised many questions concerning the reliability of perception and the validity of concepts. These problems are conventionally called *epistemological*, that is, problems concerned with the trustworthiness of human knowledge. We shall first examine the problem of perception and then consider some questions relating to conceptual knowledge.

THE PROBLEM OF PERCEPTION

Sense Percepts and Objects

Sense percepts are the simplest elements of human knowledge. They are the reports given to us by the senses of sight, hearing, taste, touch, etc. On the basis of sense perception, we assume the independent existence of objects, such as trees and cats. Now common sense tells us that there is a basic distinction between the perceiver of an object (myself) and the object perceived (the black cat). The question is: what is the nature of the relationship between the perceiver and the perceived object? We shall see that there is more than one way of analyzing this relationship.

Common-Sense Realism or Objectivism

The doctrine of perception which makes the most immediate appeal to common sense may be expressed in the following three propositions: (1) We perceive physical objects *directly*. (2) These objects exist independently of ourselves and occupy a definite position in space. (3) The character of these objects is such as we perceive them to be. In sum, when I see a black cat, I perceive directly and without intermediary a physical body in space which exists independently of me and which in its own right possesses the properties it appears to possess. This theory we may call *common-sense realism* or *objectivism*. Its account of perception may be represented by the accompanying diagram.

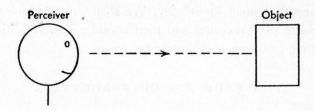

While the common-sense realist holds that we perceive physical objects, he would not claim that everything we perceive is a physical object. In dreams and illusions we have perceptions to which no physical objects correspond. The pile of money I dreamed of last night was dream money only. The dagger Macbeth saw before him was not "real." The oar which appears bent in water is objective enough, but its "bent-ness" is not. The common-sense realist admits the *subjective* character of dreams and illusions. But this admission does not affect his basic claim that we can and do perceive physical bodies which have objective and independent existence.

The Dualistic Theory of Perception

Common-sense realism tells us that we perceive objects directly. The penny I see and the penny itself are one and the same thing. But is there not some kind of distinction between the penny and our perception of it? Our perception of the penny can and does *vary*, whereas the penny (we assume) does not. If you and I are sitting before a table upon which a penny rests, you perceive the penny as *elliptical* in shape. From my angle of vision, the penny is of a slightly different elliptical shape. Only when we stand up and in turn look directly down upon the penny does it appear *round*. Now despite the many elliptical penny shapes we experience, we believe that the penny, that is, the object itself, is round. We find ourselves, therefore, compelled to admit that the penny and our perception of the penny are *two* different things.

Suppose, however, we insist that our perception of the penny—though it is distinct from the penny—is *caused* by an objective penny. Suppose we say further that our penny perception is like a copy, picture, or representation, which is *like* its cause, the objective penny. By now our analysis of perception is no longer quite that of common-sense realism. The latter view holds to the *directness* of the relationship between perceiver and object perceived. Our present position, however, suggests that the relationship is *indirect;* that the perception of an object is in some way *intermediate* between the object perceived and the perceiver. We now hold that our perception of an object is *something distinct* from the external object, that it is *causally produced* by the object, and that it is *similar* to the object. Such an analysis of perception is called a *dualistic* theory (or "epistemological dualism") since it claims that our perception of an object and the object itself are *two* distinct entities rather than one and the same thing. It may also be referred to as a *representational* theory of perception in contrast to the *presentational* account given by the common-sense realist. Diagrammatically, we may represent the dualist analysis of perception as it appears on the following page.

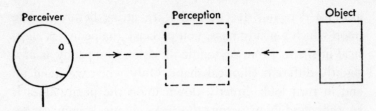

Locke's Analysis of Perception

A classic example of the dualistic analysis of perception is
that offered by the eighteenth-century English philosopher
John Locke. In his book *An Essay Concerning Human
Understanding* Locke tried to determine the scope and limits of human knowledge. He took as his point of departure
the proposition that all knowledge comes from *experience*.
The mind is like a sheet of white paper or a blank tablet
(*tabula rasa*) on which experience makes its marks. Experience furnishes us with *sensations* and the mind *reflects* upon
these. Sensations and the internal operations of the mind
consequent upon sensations Locke calls *ideas*. Ideas are
what we know, and all that we *can* know directly. "We can
have knowledge no further than we have ideas . . . ," says
Locke. "Since the mind, in all its thoughts and reasonings,
hath no other immediate object but its own ideas, which it
alone does or can contemplate, it is evident that our knowledge is only conversant about them."[1]

Locke believed that the *causes* of our sensations are external to us. We do not know the nature of these external
causes immediately, but we infer this from our ideas, which
are representations of the external causes. The *dualistic*
nature of Locke's analysis of perception is evident. The
"understanding" knows (1) the ideas, which are produced

[1] J. Locke, *An Essay Concerning Human Understanding*, A. C. Fraser
(ed.), Oxford University Press, 1894, vol. 2, p. 190 and p. 167.

in us by (2) external causes. Between (1) and (2) there is a likeness or correspondence. The reality of our ideas, says Locke, lies "in that steady correspondence they have with the distinct constitutions of real beings."[2]

Locke's Primary and Secondary Qualities

The correspondence between our ideas and the external objects which cause them is partial only. Following the assumptions of Newtonian physics, Locke divides the qualities of physical objects into *primary* and *secondary* qualities. The primary qualities include extension, figure, rest, motion—those properties which Aristotle had named "common sensibles" since they could be perceived by more than one sense. The secondary qualities ("proper sensibles") are those properties of an object which can be perceived by one sense only—its color, sound, taste, smell, etc. Now, like his scientific contemporaries, Locke states that *only the primary qualities have objective existence;* that is, only those properties like mass and "taking-up-space-ness" exist "out there" independently of the perceiver. The secondary qualities like taste and color have subjective existence only. They are wholly effects produced *in us* by the contact of external objects with our senses. Sugar is not objectively sweet; sweetness is the effect of the sugar upon our sense of taste. The blue is not actually in the flower; it is the effect of the flower upon our visual sense that produces the sensation of blue in us. Locke's doctrine of the subjectivity of secondary qualities, together with his earlier claim that the mind knows not things but ideas, raised difficulties which led to the formation of a new analysis of perception—that known as *subjectivism.*

[2] *Ibid.,* p. 498.

Subjectivism

Locke's analysis of perception tells us (1) that what we know are our sensations or "ideas," (2) that these sensations are produced in us by physical objects external to us, (3) that there is at least a partial correspondence between our perceptions and these external causes. But it is just at this point that a difficulty rises. What assurance have we that there is any correspondence at all between our "ideas" and their external causes? What justifies our belief in this likeness between perceptions and the things which produce them in us, if what we know are perceptions only? There is simply no way of showing that any correspondence whatever exists between our "ideas" and the physical objects which are supposed to cause them. Indeed, there is no way of demonstrating that there *are* any physical objects existing independently of us. Consider the accompanying diagram. In order to show that there is a conformity be-

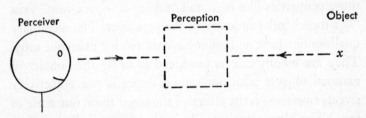

tween our perception *P* and the assumed object *x*, we would have to take a stand at some point *outside* our perceptions in order to compare *P* and *x* to see if there were a similarity between them or to see if there were any object at all. But this is impossible, for no one can stand outside his perceptions. This argument supports a *subjectivist* analysis of perception, since it leads to the conclusion that the character of perceived objects is determined by the character of the perceiving subject.

Berkeley on Things and Ideas

The difficulties implicit in Locke's dualistic analysis of perception were made clear by an eighteenth-century Anglo-Irishman, George Berkeley, who in his later years became Bishop of Cloyne and a Platonist as well. What the youthful Berkeley did was to draw from Locke's analysis certain *subjectivist* conclusions which the older philosopher sought to avoid. Berkeley heartily seconded Locke's announcement that what we know are ideas, and that these ideas are of two kinds—sensations, and reflections of the mind upon these sensations. Now, if what we know consists of ideas and ideas only, if an idea cannot be compared with a "thing," but only with another idea, what evidence is there of the existence of physical objects? None whatever, said Berkeley.

Consider for a moment, says Berkeley, an instance of what we take to be a physical object—a cherry. A cherry is a *collection of sensations*—red color, soft to touch, round shape, tart taste, etc. Can we point to a property of the cherry which is not a sense property? If there is *something more* to the cherry over and above a collection of sensations, we should be able to tell what it is. An underlying substance or substratum perhaps? But there is no contact between us and this *assumed* substratum; there is not one whit of evidence for the existence of anything besides the sensed qualities of the cherry. In Berkeley's words:

I see this *cherry*, I feel it, I taste it: and I am sure *nothing* cannot be seen, or felt, or tasted: it is therefore *real*. Take away the sensations of softness, moisture, redness, tartness, and you take away the cherry. Since it is not a being distinct from sensations; a *cherry*, I say, is nothing but a congeries of sensible impressions, or ideas perceived by various senses; which ideas are united into one thing (or have one name given to them) by the mind; because they are observed to attend each other. . . . Hence, when I see, and feel, and taste, in sundry certain manners, I am sure the *cherry* exists, or is real; its reality being in my opinion nothing abstracted from those sensations. But if by the word *cherry* you mean an unknown nature distinct from all those sensible qualities, and by its existence something distinct from its being perceived; then indeed I own, neither you, nor I, nor anyone else can be sure it exists.[3]

To Berkeley, then, the cherry is a collection of sense qualities and nothing more. The dualist analysis of perception asserts a distinction between a complex of sensations or "ideas" and an external object. Berkeley denies this distinction. The complex of sensations *is* the object. The dualist claims that this complex of sensations is *caused* in us by something outside us. Berkeley replies that he admits that our sensations are caused by a source other than ourselves. He maintains, however, that the nature of this source is *not* physical. We cannot demonstrate the existence of the "material substances" which common opinion wrongly supposes to exist. For we cannot compare our sensations with their alleged physical causes.

Berkeley reinforces his argument by collapsing the distinction between primary and secondary qualities. He agrees with Locke that secondary qualities have subjective status only and do not exist independently of perception. "The red and blue which we see," he says, "are not real

[3] G. Berkeley, "Three Dialogues," in *A New Theory of Vision and Other Writings*, E. P. Dutton and Co., 1934, p. 287.

colours, but certain unknown motions and figures which no man ever did or can see."[4] To prove the subjectivity of secondary qualities Berkeley uses the argument (as old as the Greek Sophists and Skeptics) of the relativity of sense perception. What is sweet to one man may be sour to another. Lukewarm water can be made to seem hot to one hand and cold to another. But the same substance cannot be sweet and not-sweet or hot and not-hot.

The primary qualities, "extension, figure, solidity, gravity, motion, and rest," are just as relative to perception as the secondary qualities. Take extension, for example. A tower, looked at from nearby, appears large and square-cornered. Seen from afar, however, it seems small and round. Moreover, we infer the very existence of the primary qualities from the secondary or sense qualities. How do we know that an object takes up space except by our *seeing* a colored patch, *touching* something hard, etc.? Now if both primary and secondary qualities are relative to perception—if neither has absolute or independent existence in itself—then *all* the qualities of so-called physical objects are relative to the perceiving mind. No idea can exist without the mind, says Berkeley. Things are collections of ideas. Therefore, things do not and cannot exist apart from minds. *Esse est percipi.* For a thing to be, it must be perceived.

When asked by Boswell how he would refute Bishop Berkeley, the illustrious Dr. Johnson fetched a nearby stone a mighty kick and roared, "I refute him *thus!*" Like many who read Berkeley, Dr. Johnson thought that the philosopher was denying that objects in the external world are "real." But if we have followed Berkeley's argument carefully, we can see that it was not his intention to deny the

[4] *Ibid.,* p. 218.

reality of objects. Tables and chairs and stones are real. They are *not* "optical delusions." They are exactly what they appear to be and no more. What Berkeley is denying is that these things are material substances. Experience gives us tables and chairs and stones as collections of sensations and nothing more. They have no existence apart from a perceiving mind. Of course, many would retort that what *they* mean by "real" *is* existence independent of anyone's mind. To which Berkeley would reply that reality in *that* sense is an indemonstrable and unnecessary assumption.

Solipsism

If the subjectivist analysis is correct, what warrant have I to assume that there are any perceiving minds besides my own? I do not perceive another person's mind, but *infer* this via analogy by observing his body. But the body of another is just as much a congeries of my sensations as a cherry or a tower. If all I know are perceptions, and these perceptions are my perceptions, what evidence have I for the existence of other perceivers? Indeed, how do I know that there exists anything but *myself?* Thus, by pushing the subjectivist analysis of perception to its logical conclusion, I find myself in what Ralph Barton Perry calls the *egocentric predicament*. I cannot get beyond my own "ideas." I am walled in by my perceptions. I find myself forced into the strange position of *solipsism*, which is the belief that only I and my thoughts exist.

Further, the proposition "Only I and my perceptions exist" is a halfway weak-kneed form of solipsism. For it assumes the existence of an "I" or "self." But if the subjectivist analysis is strictly applied, the existence of such an entity cannot be demonstrated. If I cannot know anything beyond perceptions, I cannot infer the existence of something which *has* these perceptions, something in which the perceptions of the past, which are not given in present experience, are linked up with the perceptions of the present. Therefore the only tenable form of solipsism seems to be

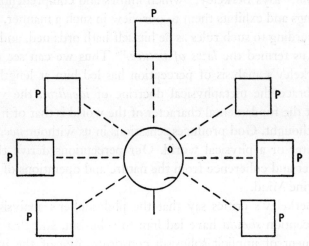

solipsism of the present moment, in which can be stated no more than the proposition "There are sensations now."

Berkeley's Alternative to Solipsism; God

No major philosopher has ever accepted solipsism.[5] On the contrary, philosophers have done everything they could to avoid it. Berkeley himself pulls up short of solipsism, although his arguments seem to lead in that direction. There *are* other minds, he says; there are other perceivers to whom the external world is given as a system of ideas. Above all,

---

[5] Bertrand Russell states that he once received a letter from the eminent logican, the late Mrs. Christine Ladd Franklin, saying that she was a solipsist and was surprised nobody else was. "Coming from a logician," Russell remarks, "this surprise surprised me." *Human Knowledge,* Simon and Schuster, 1948, p. 180.

there is a Supreme Mind or Spirit which is the cause, distinct from myself, of the mighty complex of ideas which is the external world. This Mind is God, who produces in us that system of perceptions which, taken as an ordered whole, we call Nature. "There is an *omnipresent eternal Mind*," says Berkeley, "which knows and comprehends all things and exhibits them to our view in such a manner, and according to such rules as he himself hath ordained, and are by us termed the *laws of nature*."[6] Thus we can see that Berkeley's analysis of perception has led him at length to embrace the metaphysical doctrine of *idealism*, the view that the fundamental character of the world is that of mind or thought. God produces sensations in us without *need* of matter or a physical world. Our perceptions derive their order and coherence from the nature and operations of the Divine Mind.

Berkeley's critics say that the philosopher's analysis of perception *should* have led him to solipsism, and that this element of implicit solipsism constitutes one of the principal objections to the philosopher's doctrine. He saves himself from solipsism only by bringing in God to act as the cause of all perceptions. Such a God, however, is a *deus ex machina*, a metaphysical device arbitrarily introduced to solve an epistemological difficulty.

Can Solipsism Be Refuted?

It is sometimes said that solipsism cannot be refuted. Since the world and everything in it is known to me by sense perception, I cannot get outside my percepts to verify the independent existence of something other than these percepts. Therefore there is no way of disproving that my per-

[6] G. Berkeley, *op. cit.*, p. 266.

ceptions alone exist. Hence solipsism is logically irrefutable. But, because a certain position is "logically irrefutable," it does not on that account follow that there is the slightest reason to suppose it to be true. Moreover, we can ask what is meant by the word "refutable." Even those who state that solipsism is irrefutable admit that it is psychologically impossible to hold this position and that the attitude of a sane person who pretends to hold it may be dismissed as trivial and artificial. But is this not a refutation of solipsism? "If solipsism cannot be a serious conviction," asks A. P. Ushenko, "why not take this fact as a refutation of solipsism?"[7]

Russell's Analysis of Perception

Bertrand Russell once said that a physiologist examining the brain of a patient is actually seeing his own brain.[8] When he made this startling remark, Russell was thinking of the scientific analysis of perception. From a physiological point of view, sense perception is a highly complex and indirect affair. When we see a cat or any other physical object, certain light waves coming from an external source act upon the eye in such a way that nerve currents produce a stimulus within the brain. The effect of this brain stimulus is "seeing a cat." If what science tells us is true, our eyes and ears function as intermediate transmission stations in the chain of events which constitutes sensory perception. Our visual and auditory apparatuses act as delicate selectors of certain light and sound waves. They transform these impulses, which are sent along nerve paths to certain areas of the

[7] A. P. Ushenko, *Power and Events*, Princeton University Press, 1946, p. 87.
[8] B. Russell, *An Outline of Philosophy*, Allen and Unwin, London, 1927, p. 146.

brain. In the brain the impulses are further transformed into sensory experiences which fall into patterns instantaneously interpreted by us as "cat" or "table." Indeed, it is theoretically possible, by means of application of electrical stimulus to the proper brain area, to produce the sight of a cat when there is no cat in the ordinary sense.[9]

Now if scientific analysis of perception is reliable, thinks Russell, we must admit that seeing a cat or a star is in a very important respect an event in the brain. "What occurs when I see a star," he says, "occurs as the result of light-waves impinging on the retina and causing a process in the optic nerve and brain; therefore the occurrence called 'seeing a star' must be in the brain."[10] But if we concede this, then we must also concede that the external world as a whole is a series of brain events. And if the external world is no more than this we seem to be moving rapidly toward solipsism. How does Russell avoid the solipsist's predicament?

Russell's answer takes the form of a dualistic theory of perception. Percepts have independently existing external causes. Between the two exists a relationship of correspondence, although this correspondence is limited. If science is true, our percepts do not greatly resemble their ultimate sources. To common observation, the sun is a rather small yellow disk. To the atsrophysicist, the sun is a body many times larger than the earth, the scene of enormous electrical activity. But there *is* a correlation between our perceptual

[9] One of the practical consequences of current researches by the neuroanatomist W. J. S. Krieg of Northwestern University Medical School may be the possibility of artificially stimulating the brain in blind persons to produce significant flashes so that by means of these "letters" they may be able to read.

[10] B. Russell, *Our Knowledge of the External World* (rev. ed.), Allen and Unwin, London, 1949, p. 129.

world and the world of external objects. This correlation Russell explains in terms of the *continuity of causal lines* between the two.

$$\text{Source} \longrightarrow a \longrightarrow b \longrightarrow c \longrightarrow d \longrightarrow \text{Percept}$$

Each one of the terms in this series, which represents the chain of events leading to a perception, in independent and may be qualitatively quite different from any other. For example, the nerve impulse traveling along a nerve path toward the brain is an event independent of the percept of the sun, and it does not resemble its source, which is the sun itself. But the percept of the sun may be correlated with the sun in that the percept is causally connected with the sun through the chain of intermediate events.

We may say further, Russell tells us, that there is a *similarity* between the "ordinary" world of experience and the system of events which causes these experiences, if we understand by "similarity" a correspondence of *structure*. Consider (A) the score of Beethoven's *C Minor Symphony* as it rests on the stand before the conductor, and (B) the sounds we hear when we listen to a radio broadcast of a recording of the conductor's interpretation of the symphony. Now A and B have a structural similarity despite the many intermediate stages which occur between the score and our hearing of the music. While some of these stages are qualitatively different from and independent of one another—the musicians' translation of notes into sounds, the transcription of sounds into microgrooves on wax, the change of sound waves into radio waves—they all center about a structure which is constant. Analogously, the perceptual world and the system of external causes which produces these perceptions in us have a common structure. The principle of constancy of structure, says Russell, "implies that in circumstances which occur frequently, but not invariably, the structure of a percept is the same as that of each of a series of occurrences, leading backward in time to an original occurrence. . . . This original occurrence is what we are said to 'perceive' when it is held that different people can 'perceive' the same object. . . . The sameness of structure between our sensational experiences and their physical causes explains how it comes about that naive realism, though false, gives rise to so little confusion in practice."[11]

Phenomenalism

Phenomenalism is a doctrine concerning perception which *denies a dualism* between perceptual experiences and their supposed causes. The object as perceived by me and the object which "causes" the perception are one and the same. As perceived, a table is a combination of percepts or *sense data*—rectangular brown surface, hard and smooth, etc. Now consider the "real" table which the dualist thinks of as existing independently of us and causing the appearance of the table in us. But there is no distinction between the two; the "real" and the perceived table are one and the same thing. Appearance is reality. Describing the phenomenalist position, W. P. Montague (himself not a phenomenalist) says: "There are no things in themselves, but only things in relation to our experience. There is no 'reality' hidden behind the veil of sensory appearance; the appearances of

---

[11] Bertrand Russell, *Human Knowledge*, pp. 473–474.

things are their reality. And for the sceptic to bewail the fact that we can know nothing but appearance is as silly as it would be to bewail the fact that we have nothing to wear but clothes and nothing to eat but food."[12]

The phenomenalist analysis of perception is usually associated with certain types of extreme empiricism or positivism, that is, with doctrines which claim that sense observation is the most reliable form of knowledge. Hume defined physical objects as collections of sense data and no more. Ernst Mach imported phenomenalism into nineteenth-century philosophy of science, stating that "Bodies do not produce sensations, but complexes of sensation make up bodies."[13]

The phenomenalist's analysis of perception resembles Berkeley's in that both hold that what is experienced (sense data) is real, and that there is nothing "behind" sense data— no Lockian "substance" or substratum distinct from the sense qualities and "causing" them. But phenomenalism denies Berkeley's doctrine of *esse est percipi*—that for an object to exist it must be perceived. Admitting Berkeley's contention that we cannot prove that anything exists unperceived, the phenomenalist states that the independent existence of objects can easily be verified if only "independent existence" is taken in the proper sense. To say of a physical object that it exists is to say that it is possible to perceive it. Consider the sentence "There is a telephone in that cabinet." If this sentence is taken (and the phenomenalist thinks it should be so taken) as the equivalent in meaning of the

[12] W. P. Montague, *The Ways of Knowing*, Allen and Unwin, London, 1925, p. 185.
[13] E. Mach, *Analysis of Sensations*, Open Court Publishing Co., 1915, p. 29.

sentence "If you were to open that cabinet, you would see a telephone," then there is no problem at all about verifying the independent existence of the telephone.

One of the principal difficulties with phenomenalism is the situation the phenomenalist meets when he tries to reconcile his doctrine of "appearances are reality" with scientific descriptions of objects. To the normal observer, a table is a brown, hard, solid, static object. To the physicist, however, the table is a dynamic society of atoms, continually gaining and losing electrons. If appearances *are* reality, how does the phenomenalist dispose of the scientific description of the table, which is certainly not a description in terms of ordinary appearances or sense data?

One answer to this difficulty is that given by the nineteenth-century philosophers Ernst Mach and Hans Vaihinger, to the effect that scientific descriptions like the atomic theory are *fictions* which do not correspond to anything real. Scientific statements about unobservable entities like atoms are to be taken only "as if" they were true. Such descriptions are instruments for finding our way about more easily in the world. They are not descriptions of what is real. Such fictions, says Vaihinger, are "practically useful and necessary though theoretically false deviations from reality."[14] Variations of this "fictionalism" are present in certain more recent positivistic philosophies of science.

Some contemporary phenomenalists, however, reject the fictionalist account of scientific descriptions because it appears to reduce scientific propositions about the external world to false statements. While atomic events cannot be observed in the same way we observe rocks and trees, yet

[14] See H. Vaihinger, *The Philosophy of "As-If,"* C. K. Ogden (trans.), Harcourt, Brace and Co., 1924, pp. 15, 16.

these micro-events are observable *theoretically*. An electron may be very much smaller than the wave length of light needed to make it visible to a human observer. Yet we may suppose the existence of a hypothetical superhuman observer who could directly see an electron with the help of light of wave lengths smaller than the electron. In other words, while micro-events are unobservable in the ordinary sense, they are observable *in principle*.[15]

Critics of phenomenalism feel that this reply does not dispose of the original difficulty. If what we observe and what is real are one and the same thing, are the atoms which we do *not* observe real or not? The introduction of a superhuman observer, say the anti-phenomenalists, is a strained attempt to "save the appearances." It amounts to no more than saying that all real things, whether ordinary objects or micro-events, are observable; but the latter are observable only in a very peculiar or Pickwickian sense.

Is the External World Real? Moore's Realism

Reading about the odd problems that turn up when philosophers analyze the nature of perception may give one the impression that philosophy is a subject in which one spends a great deal of time wondering whether tables and chairs are real. The English analyst G. E. Moore believes that philosophers themselves are largely to blame for creating this impression. From Locke to Russell, philosophers have begun their analysis of perception with the assumption that *sensations* are real. They have then tried to solve the problem, which is in large part created by this questionable starting point, of whether there is anything real corresponding to sense data. But like the problem of "certainty," the prob-

[15] See A. Pap, *Elements of Analytic Philosophy*, The Macmillan Company, 1949, p. 138.

lem of the reality of physical objects can be solved quite simply if we ask the following question. What do people *mean* by the word "real"?

The ordinary meaning of the word "real" with reference to physical objects is something which has existence independent of the perceiver. Now, that objects have independent existence can be established quite easily by public inspection. Objects in dreams are not real in the ordinary sense of the word because they are parts of subjective and private experiences. Physical objects, however, are real since they are open to public inspection. "Here is my right hand," says Moore. "You see it. I see it. Therefore it exists. Therefore the external world exists." What more do we want by way of proof of the reality of physical objects? What further specifications should the external world fulfill in order to qualify for the "reality" of the philosophers? Those who say that only sense data are real and that the reality of physical objects is not a matter of simple inspection are guilty of a *misuse of language.*[16]

Analysts who do not subscribe to Moore's brand of realism frequently reply with some irritation that when they want a lesson in the correct use of the English language they know where to get it. Of course physical objects are real in the ordinary sense of the word. But there are problems concerning the status of physical objects which careful analysis of perception discloses. Moore's proof does not meet the questions that the analysts are trying to ask. His proof is effective only on the assumption that the problem of perception is no problem at all.

[16] G. E. Moore, "Proof of an External World" (British Academy Annual Philosophic Lecture, 1939), British Academy, *Proceedings,* 1939, vol. 25.

CONCEPTUAL KNOWLEDGE OF THE EXTERNAL WORLD

Percepts and Concepts

Sense percepts may be the simplest elements of human knowledge; but we cannot give an adequate account of our knowledge of the external world solely in terms of sense perceptions. A world consisting of sense data alone would be confused and meaningless, a world like that present to a tiny infant, echoing with the sound of "a thousand twangling instruments" and shot through with random shapes and lights. In a world composed of percepts alone, all knowledge would be immediate and none inferred.

Now human knowledge is largely *inferred* knowledge. This is not to say that animals cannot infer, and that they are restricted to sense data. Animals *build up* knowledge out of sense data as humans do. But human knowledge is distinguished by its power to *explain* and to *interpret* immediate happenings. It has the capacity to perform inferences of a complexity and generality that far outrun those within the powers of the cleverest nonhuman animal.

We may call that all-important area of human knowledge which goes beyond what is immediately given in sense experience *conceptual* knowledge. Percepts are immediate and particular, like a flash of light or the sound of a bell. Concepts are more general and abstract, like the notion of "mammal" or "electron." Whether it concerns the realm of everyday experience or that revealed to us by science, our knowledge of the external world is saturated with concepts. No description of the world is possible without their constant employment.

There is no wide and observable gulf between percepts and concepts. What some call concepts others call percepts. Indeed, it is very difficult to say just where the percepts leave off and the concepts begin. For example, we would naturally be inclined to say that our knowledge of *physical objects*, like tables and trees, is perceptual rather than conceptual. But the notion of a physical object existing independently of me and preserving its identity from moment to moment is to some extent a learned, built up, or inferred notion. Anyone who doubts this should watch the behavior of a very young baby who drops his rattle out of sight. When this happens, the infant behaves as if the rattle had dropped out of existence as well. Small babies are Berkeleyans; to them, *esse est percipi.*

There are *gradations* in concepts, or *constructs*, as they are sometimes called, according to the degree of abstractness they represent. The notion of an independently existing physical object may be regarded as a concept of the lowest grade, a very elementary construct. Above this may be ranked other types of concepts of progressively higher degrees of abstractness. A sample selection from the hierarchy of concepts may be given as follows:

1. The concept of an independently existing physical object.
2. The concept of "minds" or selves other than our own.
3. Concepts of general classes such as "plant" or "metal."
4. Concepts of general properties such as "red" or "heat."
5. Concepts of "laws" of physical nature such as "Gases expand when heated."
6. The concept of "cause."
7. Concepts of a highly abstract nature employed in scien-

tific descriptions of the external world such as that of "gravity" or "relativity."
8. Purely mathematical or logical concepts.

If we concede that only percepts or sense data are immediately given in experience, then all of our knowledge employing notions like those above must be considered to be in lesser or greater degree *conceptual* knowledge. Now the question is: If these concepts are not given to us directly by sense experience, what validity do they have? How can we be sure that there are situations in the external world which correspond to these concepts? Two famous answers to this question are those given respectively by David Hume and Immanuel Kant. Hume says that most of these concepts have no demonstrable validity simply because they are *not* given in experience. Kant says these concepts *have* validity, but that their nature is essentially mental. They are the products of the *mind* operating upon material of unknowable character.

The Skepticism of David Hume

From premises laid down by Locke and Berkeley, Hume proceeded to draw some remarkably skeptical conclusions. Like his predecessors, Hume took the primary data of human knowledge to be perceptions and reflections about perceptions. To the question "What do we know?" Hume answers that we know (1) sense impressions and (2) ideas or "faint images" of these impressions (by the latter we "remember" the impressions). According to Hume, human knowledge is built up by *association* of these impressions according to certain patterns: (a) similarity, (b) contiguity, and (c) invariable sequence. All we are given in experience is impressions, perceptions, sense data.

Now Hume claims that these impressions are always given to us as *separate* and *distinct* from one another. "All our distinct perceptions," he says, "are distinct existences, and the mind never perceives any real connection among distinct existences."[17] Through *habit* we associate these impressions with one another, as, for instance, our association of the visual impression we name "dog" with the auditory impression we call "bark." But as far as *experience* goes, these impressions are all given as distinct and separate elements.

Consider a physical object—for example, a box. Locke admitted that all we know directly of the box is a complex of sense percepts—"red," "hard," "square," etc. On the basis of these distinct impressions, Locke concluded (though not without hesitation) that underlying the impressions was a *thing*, a substance, something enduring through time; something that was the *same*, although its qualities might change. But, Hume points out, if all we know of the box amounts to a collection of separate percepts, we have no right to infer the existence of a supposed enduring substratum which is the "same" from one moment to the next. Hume agreed with Berkeley that since all we know of physical objects is that they are collections of sensible properties, there is no proof that physical objects are anything more than "ideas" in our minds.

But Hume disagreed with Berkeley on the latter's assumption without proof that there were "minds" other than his own. Experience gives us no warrant for the assumption of

[17] D. Hume, *A Treatise on Human Nature*, Clarendon Press, Oxford, 1896, p. 636.

any such thing as a mind or self. Just as experience tells me that this box is a collection of sense data and nothing more, so experience tells me that my "mind" or "self" is just a bundle of perceptions and no more. Says Hume: "What we call a *mind* is nothing but a heap or collection of different perceptions united together by certain relations, and supposed, tho falsely, to be endowed with a perfect simplicity and identity."[18]

Now if we grant, says Hume, that all we know are sense impressions, or ideas built up out of them, and if we grant further that experience gives us no hint of any necessary connection between them, then we must concede that we have no ground (other than that of habit or custom) to justify belief in the existence of enduring *physical objects* which preserve their identity from one moment to the next; we have no basis on which to infer the existence of enduring *selves* or *minds* which underlie the string of sensory impressions or memories of these.

Hume's Analysis of Causality

Having shown to his own satisfaction how infirm are the foundations of our belief in the existence of physical objects and enduring selves, Hume next turns to demolish two other presuppositions of science and practical life—induction and causality. We have already encountered Hume's arguments on induction. Experience presents us with *particulars*, that is, with separate and detached instances of sensory impressions. With no warrant other than habit, we slip in a *connection* between these instances. Upon a set of given particulars we superimpose a *general* principle which experience has failed to provide. Experience gives us sepa-

[18] *Ibid.,* p. 207.

rate occurrences of "This A is B," "This A is B," etc. After a while, we conclude that "All A is B" and use this generalization to predict that future A's will be B's. But, Hume tells us, however much habit may incline us to such general conclusions, we must admit that they are not given to us in our observation of natural bodies.

Hume's analysis of *causality* is similar to his approach to induction. Does experience provide us with any instance of A causing B? If by "cause" is meant some *necessary relation* between A and B, a relation which is more than A *together with* B, the answer is "No." A proper definition of cause, says Hume, amounts to no more than this: "An object precedent and contiguous to another, and so united with it that the idea of the one determines the mind to form the idea of the other, and the impression of the one to form a more lively idea of the other."[19]

Experience may furnish us with numerous separate instances of A *attended by* B. Experience may even go so far as to offer us *invariable sequences* in each of which A is followed by B. But each experience of B following A is always something separate and distinct from the next. Sense observation tells us "A then B," "A then B," and so on. No more. Now through *habit*, says Hume, we insert between A and B a fictitious necessary connection—which we call a "causal relation"—and conclude that "A causes B." But we do not find this necessary connection in experience.

Hume asks us to consider an example. Whenever I go into my garden, he says, I notice that a certain stone is warm to touch. At the same time, I also observe that the sun is shining. I then infer that *the sun warms the stone*. But sense

[19] *Ibid.*, p. 172.

observation does not disclose this causal connection. What I do observe is (A) the sun, and (B) warm stone, and again (A) the sun, and (B) warm stone, and again and again, if you like. Since human inclination tends to supply the necessary connection which experience does *not* supply, I say, "The sun causes the stone to get warm." The moral is that causality is conceived to be a general and necessary relation holding between the particulars which experience presents to us. But the ground of this concept is not to be found in sense experience, but simply in the expectation born of habit.

Thus, by pushing the Locke-Berkeley analysis of knowledge to extreme conclusions, Hume has reached a position of skepticism concerning the validity of concepts. Percepts are given in experience, but concepts are not. There is no reasonable proof of the existence of those universal and necessary connections which men suppose to exist in Nature and to which they appeal to justify inductive and causal inference.

We should note that Hume's skepticism, and the solipsism to which this skepticism appears to lead, is cheerfully admitted by its author to have no relation to practical life. Hume tells us that he does not for a moment doubt that there are independently existing physical objects like the backgammon board before him. Nor does he doubt that he, David Hume, is something more than a bundle of sensations. Nor does he doubt general statements like "Fire burns" or causal inferences like "Water quenches thirst." What I do doubt, says Hume, is the *possibility of any rational justification* of these beliefs. I hold them on no basis other than instinct, inclination, habit, or custom.

Kant's Problem

Hume's skepticism struck the great German philosopher Immanuel Kant as a challenge to the very foundations of philosophy and science. It was the warning voice of David Hume, Kant tells us, "which many years ago first interrupted my dogmatic slumber, and gave my investigations in the field of speculative philosophy a quite new direction."[20] Both philosophy and science, Kant perceived, presuppose the validity of universal or general judgments such as those of inductive generalization and causal inference. If Hume is right, and there is no foundation in *experience* for these indispensable general judgments, what basis can there possibly be for them? If there is no rational justification of our belief in necessary connections between things in Nature, then the foundations of both philosophy and science rest on thin air. Should the situation actually be as Hume represents it, thought Kant, the only defensible philosophic attitude is skepticism.

If skepticism is to be avoided, says Kant, we must show how those universal and necessary connections, which Hume claims experience does not provide, are rationally justifiable. Or, in Kant's formidable terminology, we must show how a priori synthetic judgments are possible.[21] Hume pointed out that in inductive inference sense experience gives us separate and unconnected particulars, "This *A* is

[20] I. Kant, *Prolegomena to Any Future Metaphysics*, P. Carus (ed.), Open Court Publishing Co., 1902, p. 6.

[21] Inductive and causal judgments are *synthetic* and unlike *analytic* judgments, because the definition of their subjects does not disclose their predicates. They are a priori since their general or universal character is never given in experience; that is, we do not directly observe that *all* phosphorus is inflammable. Contrasting with a priori judgments are a posteriori judgments which *are* supported by direct experience. "This box is red" is an example of an a posteriori judgment.

B," "This *A* is *B*," etc. In causal inference sense experience offers us again only separate particulars, "*X* then *Y*," "*X* then *Y*," etc. Whence comes the universal and necessary character of the judgments "All *A* is *B*" and "*X* causes *Y*" which we so swiftly form from these particular and disconnected items of experience?

Kant's Categories

Kant's answer is this: The universal and necessary quality of causal, inductive, and other judgments of a general nature is determined *by the structure of mind itself*. The mind is not like an inert block of wax passively receiving and recording the impressions of sense, as Locke and the other British sensationalists held. The mind is a creative, dynamic, *active* process. It is equipped with certain innate forms which order and interpret sense experience.

The data which sense experience presents to us are first oriented in *space* and *time*. Now space and time have no objective existence independently of us. They are forms of the mind which impress themselves on all human experience. After the data of experience are coördinated in space and time, that part of the mind Kant calls the "understanding" takes over. The "understanding" possesses twelve innate forms or *categories*. It is from the categories that our experience derives its quality of universality and necessary connectedness. Those general and necessary judgments which Hume declared impossible to justify are the products of the operation of the categories of the mind upon the stuff of experience. In a causal inference, for example, experience provides us with the data "*X* then *Y*," "*X* then *Y*," etc. These data are then interpreted by the category of *causality*, and the judgment "*X* causes *Y*" results. Different types of general judgments are produced by the operation of other appropriate categories upon the data of experience. The role of Kant's categories may very roughly be illustrated by the accompanying diagram.

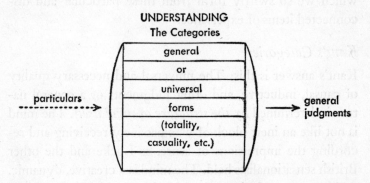

UNDERSTANDING
The Categories

general
or
universal
forms
(totality,
casuality, etc.)

particulars ⤑

general judgments →

"Percepts Without Concepts Are Blind"

Knowledge in which universal and necessary judgments are present is *conceptual*. Both percepts and concepts are elements of human knowledge, the former distinguished by their *particular* and immediate character, the latter by *general* nature. Percepts are provided by experience. Concepts, according to Kant, are formed by the internal structure of the mind itself. Both percepts and concepts are necessary ingredients in any act of knowledge which does not lead to deception. "Concepts without percepts are empty," says Kant. "Percepts without concepts are blind."[22]

Any concept formed without a basis in sense experience will be little better than a fiction, and percepts, without concepts to order and interpret them, cannot advance knowledge one step beyond themselves. For percepts lack the quickening, moving, creative element of conceptual

[22] See I. Kant, *Critique of Pure Reason*, Norman Kemp Smith (trans.), The Humanities Press, 1950, p. 93.

knowledge which distinguishes human thought from the simple immediacy of sensation.

Kant's Subjectivism

According to Kant, then, conceptual knowledge is *subjective* in the sense that concepts come to us as products of the categories of our minds rather than from the external world. Percepts derive from an objective source external to us. But, since percepts are organized by concepts which owe their nature to the structure of the mind, everything that we know is indelibly colored by our knowing faculty. Now the dramatic consequences of Kant's theory of knowledge come into view. We can never know the "real" nature of the external world or of any object within it, if by "external world" is meant the world as it exists independently of human knowledge. *Things-in-themselves,* as Kant calls them, are unknowable and forever hidden from us. What we *do* know are the appearances (*phenomena*) produced by the operation of the forms of the mind upon this unknowable X-world. The mind transforms things-in-themselves in such a way as to make them intelligible. Our world is one of appearances only; behind those appearances the understanding can never penetrate. In Kant's words: ". . . Things which we see are not by themselves what we see. . . . They cannot, as phenomena, exist by themselves, but in us only. It remains completely unknown to us what the objects may be by themselves and apart from the receptivity of our senses. We know nothing but our manner of perceiving them, that manner being peculiar to us and not necessarily shared in by every being, though, no doubt, by every human being."[23]

[23] I. Kant, *Critique of Pure Reason* (rev. ed.), Max Müller (trans.), The Macmillan Company, 1922, p. 34.

Kant's "Copernican Revolution"; Conclusion

Perhaps Kant's meaning can be made clearer by a familiar simile. A man born with undetachable blue spectacles of whose presense he was unaware would see the world blue and think it *was* blue. But we know that the blueness comes, not from the world, but from the glasses. Now, if Kant's theory is correct, we are all born with minds like *ordering glasses*. Through these mental lenses there filters the flux of the external world in such a way that we see this world as an ordered, connecred, rational whole. "Common sense" attributes this order, connectedness, and rationality *to the world*. But Hume's analysis of experience shows that experience does not warrant any such assumption. The only alternative, Kant believes, is to place the origin of the world order in the human mind itself. By finding the source of time, space, and the natural order as a whole within *man* rather than in the external world, Kant believed that he had accomplished a "Copernican revolution" in philosophy.[24]

Kant has offered a theory of knowledge to explain and to justify belief in the existence of orderly, scientific knowledge of the external world. He has claimed for concepts, such as those of general laws and causal relations, the rational justification which Hume declared impossible. But this justification has been achieved only at the cost of a surrender of all claims to knowledge of the properties of the world as it is independent of human perception. In place of such claims, Kant offers an epistemology which holds that

[24] Our exposition of Kant's theory of knowledge is oversimple. For one thing, we make him too much of a "subjectivist." In Kant's view, it is more than just the *human mind* that orders our experience. He seems to hold that in the nature of things, over and above the individual human consciousness, is some sort of rational order with a logical structure in its own right. (We shall see in Chapter 7 how Hegel develops this notion.)

what we know is a world which reflects the structure of the human mind, a world fashioned and shaped by the categories of the understanding out of a raw material whose existence is indubitable but whose nature we can never know. Historically, this Kantian theory of knowledge led to significant developments in the metaphysics of *idealism*, the philosophic doctrine that the world of our experience is essentially of the nature of *thought*.

THE ROLE OF CONCEPTS IN SCIENTIFIC KNOWLEDGE

An Alternative to Hume and Kant

Does conceptual knowledge give us reliable descriptions of the nature of the external world? Hume's analysis of knowledge appears to have shown that conceptual knowledge does not come to us directly from sense experience. Must we then accept as the only alternative Kant's theory that conceptual knowledge is valid but phenomenal only, that the external world we know is no more than *appearance*, an ordered image created by the human mind?

Let us consider some conditions of a third alternative. Such a theory would hold that concepts, while to an important degree the products of the human mind, are nevertheless *correlated with the structure of the external world*. That is, concepts are, to a degree, *constructed* by us; but they are not fictions, nor are they wholly products of innate forms of the mind.[25] Concepts are not given to us *as such* by experience, yet they have a foundation in and some

[25] A persuasive analysis of conceptual knowledge in science in terms of "constructs," which are neither fictions nor products of Kantian categories, may be found in Henry Margenau's *The Nature of Physical Reality*, McGraw-Hill Book Co., 1950.

conformity to the external world which exists independently of human thought. In conceptual knowledge we *interpret* the world rather than describe it literally. Yet this interpretation is neither wholly arbitrary nor subjective, but in some way approaches correspondence to the nature of the external world. Defense of such a position would entail a careful analysis of the nature of the correlation between concepts and percepts, and the role of concepts in scientific descriptions of the external world. This task is difficult, and we shall carry it no further than to show why some such analysis is necessary for a "philosophy of science."

Concepts and Scientific Descriptions; the Atomic Theory

The terms used by physical science to describe events in the external world are highly conceptual. It is true that these concepts are correlated by the scientist with sensory observation, but the lines connecting the two are frequently very long and indirect. Consider a few sample notions in modern atomic theory. Physics tells us that physical objects are composed of "atoms," which are entities that cannot be directly observed. These atoms are not tiny hard pellets of matter but electrical activities of a highly complicated nature. An atom is a complex of electrical events, composed of a center or nucleus plus a number of negatively charged particles called "electrons," which occur at a relatively great distance from the nucleus. Within the atomic nucleus itself activities of various types have been distinguished. There is the "proton," a positively charged particle; the "neutron," which has a relatively heavy mass and no electrical charge; the "meson," which exerts a force which holds the nuclear particles together, etc. The nature of the activities which compose the atom is so very different from the everyday notion of "physical object" or "material thing" that they can only very roughly and inadequately be represented by a diagram or mechanical model. Their behavior can best be described by using mathematical formulas of a complex kind.

Neither atoms nor the subatomic entities that compose them are directly observable. Their existence was established by logical inference. Democritus and his colleagues in ancient Greece, who first put forward the atomic theory, concluded that all things are composed of atoms, *because a physical object must have a smallest part.* Although the crude Greek concept of the atom has today been refined almost beyond description, the method by which the modern scientist establishes the existence and nature of atomic particles is still to some extent the same *sort* of reasoning which led to the Greek theory—despite present opportunities for experimental observation which the Greeks did not have. The Japanese physicist Yukawa postulated the existence of the meson ten years before experimental evidence confirmed his hypothesis. He *inferred* the existence of the meson. Some such concept was needed to explain why the atomic nucleus does not fly apart. Experimental observation may *suggest* highly conceptual theories, and experimental observation may to a great extent *confirm* them. But observation does not *give* the concept; that is, concepts are not direct transcriptions of the observed behavior of physical objects.

Scientific descriptions, such as those found in atomic theory or in relativity or quantum theory are highly conceptual interpretations of the nature of the external world. The concepts involved in such descriptions, however, are neither pure fictions nor constructs of a wholly mental origin. So far as these concepts enable us to understand and to control the behavior of the external world, just so far do they approach adequacy as descriptions of the nature of the external world taken as existing independently of human thought.

Concepts of Wave and Particle in Modern Physics

Consider two concepts used today in describing the nature of the atom. Scientists speak of the atom as a group of *particles* or *corpuscles*. Yet in dealing with certain problems it is often necessary to describe the basic processes of physical nature in terms of *waves* or stresses within an electrodynamic *field*. The ancient concept of the atom was that of a particle, although of an indivisible particle. The notion of the atom as a tiny indivisible bit of matter was held in modern physics until the late nineteenth century, when the behavior of radioactive elements, such as uranium and radium, forced the beginning of a radical revision of the concept of the atom. Now we see the atom no longer as an indivisible particle but as a group or society of particles—protons, electrons, neutrons, etc., held together by powerful forces. Yet even in this highly modified contemporary view of the atom, the notion of ultimate micro-events as *particles* still remains.

In classical physics, *light* was successfully described in terms of *waves* rather than particles. True, Newton had suggested that light was made up of corpuscles, but it was generally felt that there was little evidence for this theory. But in our own century, certain fundamental problems arose which required a reinterpretation of light in terms of corpuscles, and the name "photon" was given to the basic particle of light energy. To this day, the behavior of light seems to require description in terms of *both* wave and particle. These two concepts, however, do not seem compatible or consistent with one another, for the concept of "particle" entails that of "mass," while the notion of "wave" is related to mass only in a much more shadowy way. An analogous problem exists in regard to the nature of the electron. Evidence exists which supports the concept of the electron as a particle; evidence also exists which suggests that the electron is a wave.

Now the lesson of the wave-particle dualism in modern physics may be this: "Wave" and "particle" are *concepts*, and concepts are not literal descriptions or mental photographs of the external world. They are human constructs which *interpret* the nature of the world even though they do not *create* it out of whole cloth. The conflict between the wave and particle concepts seems to indicate a certain lack of adequacy in these valuable notions, a lack which up to the present time it has been impossible to remedy. But reflection on the history of science encourages us to believe that sooner or later a *new* concept will appear in modern physics which will reconcile and unify the wave and particle concepts, and which will at the same time achieve even great success in explaining the nature of events in the external world.

Einstein on Concepts

At a meeting of the British Association for the Advancement of Science in 1951, the president of the Royal Institute of Philosophy, Viscount Samuel, reproached contemporary physicists for their reliance upon what he called concepts analogous to the "smile of the absent cat." Samuel singled out for particular attack Albert Einstein's theory of relativity, charging that certain concepts essential to that theory as well as the "whole mathematical apparatus" involved were nothing more than abstractions invented by the human imagination. Einstein's reply should interest us, for it concerns the role of concepts in scientific knowledge.

According to Einstein, the nature of the external world is not immediately given in experience. What are given are *data*, the data of consciousness. There is only one way to pass from the data of consciousness to knowledge of the external world, and that is the way of *intellectual construction*. The most elementary concept of everyday experience is that of independently existing objects, such as the table in the room. The table, however, is not given to us an an independently existing object, but rather as a complex of sensations to which we attribute the name and concept "table." In Einstein's words: "In my opinion, it is of the greatest importance to be conscious of the fact that such a concept ['table'], like all other concepts, is of a speculative-constructive kind. Otherwise one cannot do justice to those concepts which in physics claim to describe reality, and one is in danger of being misled by the illusion that the 'real' of our daily experience 'exists really' and that certain concepts of physics are 'mere ideas' separated from the 'real' by an unbridgeable gulf."[26]

"Speculative-constructive" though they may be, such concepts as those of independently existing physical objects are not mere fancies, Einstein maintains. These concepts "stand in a relation of correspondence with our sensations." Now in physics, the correspondence or correlation between concepts and sensations becomes more and more indirect.

[26] H. L. Samuel, *Essay in Physics*, Harcourt, Brace and Co., 1952, p. 158.

But because the concepts of physics are highly abstract and only indirectly correlated with ordinary experience, it does not follow that they are fictions. Euclidean geometry contains the concept of a straight line. This concept may be correlated with physics if for a straight line we substitute a rigid rod. But a rigid rod is conceptual also, for we do not find perfectly rigid rods in everyday experience. Yet the notion of a rigid rod may be correlated with the metal rods of everyday experience if we coördinate this concept with others such as that of heat expansion. Scientific concepts are tied to experience in so far as they help us to establish correct and verifiable relations between our experiences.

Although convinced that our knowledge of the physical world is highly conceptual, Einstein believes that we should not feel ourselves confined to a choice of two alternatives between which contemporary physicists seem to him to waver: (1) that there is a physical reality, but its laws do not permit of any other than statistical expressions; (2) that there is nothing at all which "really" corresponds to the description of a physical situation—only "probabilities" exist. In opposition to this attitude, which seems to him undesirably skeptical, Einstein maintains a remarkably optimistic and "realist" position. "We believe," he says, "in the possibility of a theory which is able to give a complete description of reality, the laws of which establish relations between the things themselves and not merely between their probabilities."[27]

FURTHER READINGS

Adrian, E. D., *The Physical Background of Perception*, Oxford University Press, 1947.

[27] *Ibid.*, p. 161.

Berkeley, George, "Three Dialogues Betwewen Hylas and Philonous," in *A New Theory of Vision and Other Writings*, E. P. Dutton and Co., 1934.

Berkeley, George, *A Treatise Concerning the Principles of Human Knowledge*, Open Court Publishing Co., 1903.

Blanshard, Brand, *The Nature of Thought*, The Macmillan Company, 1940.

De Broglie, L., *Matter and Light*, W. W. Norton and Co., 1939.

Eddington, A. S., *The Nature of the Physical World*, The Macmillan Company, 1929.

Einstein, A., and Infeld, L., *The Evolution of Physics*, Simon and Schuster, 1938.

Hume, David, *A Treatise on Human Nature*, Clarendon Press, Oxford, 1896.

Hume, David, *An Enquiry Concerning Human Understanding*, Open Court Publishing Co., 1935.

Kant, Immanuel, *Critique of Pure Reason* (rev. ed.), Max Müller (trans.), The Macmillan Company, 1922.

Kant, Immanuel, *Prolegomena to Any Future Metaphysics*, P. Carus (ed.), Open Court Publishing Co., 1902.

Lewis, C. I., *Mind and the World Order*, Charles Scribner's Sons, 1929.

Locke, John, *An Essay Concerning Human Understanding*, A. C. Fraser (ed.), Oxford University Press, 1894.

Mach, Ernst, *Analysis of Sensations*, Open Court Publishing Co., 1915.

Margenau, Henry, *The Nature of Physical Reality*, McGraw-Hill Book Co., 1950.

Meyerson, Emile, *Identity and Reality*, K. Loewenberg (trans.), The Macmillan Company, 1930.

Montague, Wm. Pepperell, *The Ways of Knowing*, Allen and Unwin, London, 1925, Part II.

Moore, G. E., "Proof of an External World" (British Academy

Annual Philosophic Lecture, 1939), British Academy, *Proceedings*, 1939, vol. 25, pp. 273–300.

Pap, Arthur, *Elements of Analytic Philosophy*, The Macmillan Company, 1949, chap. 7.

Russell, Bertrand, *Human Knowledge*, Simon and Schuster, 1948, Part 3.

Russell, Bertrand, *Our Knowledge of the External World* (rev. ed.), Allen and Unwin, London, 1949.

Samuel, H. L., *Essay in Physics*, Harcourt, Brace and Co., 1952.

Vaihinger, H., *The Philosophy of "As-If,"* C. K. Ogden (trans.), Harcourt, Brace and Co., 1924.

Werkmeister, W. H., *The Basis and Structure of Knowledge*, Harper & Brothers, 1948.

5

METHODS OF KNOWLEDGE

Are data from the world of sense
In that case valid evidence?
— W. H. AUDEN

IN A dialogue called the *Theaetetus*, Plato has Socrates ask the young mathematician for whom the dialogue is named, "What is knowledge?" Theaetetus replies in effect, "Well, Socrates, there is the knowledge of the geometricians; the knowledge of the cobblers; the knowledge of the carpenters . . ." But Socrates interrupts him, saying that he is not interested in having the various kinds of knowledge enumerated. He wants to find out what knowledge *is*. One of the answers suggested by Theaetetus is that "Knowledge is true belief." A similar answer is given by Bertrand Russell, who defines knowledge as a subclass of true beliefs.

If knowledge is "true belief," from what general sources do we derive our beliefs? Are these sources reliable? We have already raised these questions in a *particular* form in connection with the problem of our knowledge of the external world. There we say that our knowledge of physical nature derives from sense observation (percepts) and from the intellectual interpretations of sense observation (concepts). Now we wish to put the question in a more general way. We all carry about with us a very large number of beliefs about many different things, and these beliefs we hold to be true. Now what are the various ways by which we derive our beliefs? What is the comparative reliability of these methods of obtaining belief? These questions are quite common in modern philosophy, and the term *methodology* or *theory of inquiry* is used to name that part of philosophy which considers them.

In 1877 C. S. Peirce published an article called "The Fixation of Belief." *Belief*, said Peirce, is the opposite of *doubt*, and the two attitudes of mind may be contrasted as follows: "Doubt is an uneasy and dissatisfied state from which we struggle to free ourselves and pass into the state of belief; while the latter is a calm and satisfactory state which we do not wish to avoid, or to change to a belief in anything else. On the contrary, we cling tenaciously, not merely to believing, but to believing just what we do believe."[1] The irritation of doubt, Peirce said, causes a struggle to obtain belief. This struggle is *inquiry*. The object of inquiry is to find out, on the basis of what we already know, something else which we do not know. Now there are four ways of removing doubt and fixing our beliefs firmly. One is the method of *tenacity*, in which we hold fast to our beliefs simply because we want to continue believing them. Another is the a priori method, in which we support our beliefs by appealing to their alleged *reasonableness*. A third way is the method of *authority*, in which propositions are held to be true on the word of a powerful social agency such as church or state. (For the mass of mankind, says Peirce, there is perhaps no better method than this.) A fourth way of fixating belief is *scientific method*. This method begins with the study of observable occurrences.

[1] C. S. Peirce, "The Fixation of Belief," in *Chance, Love, and Logic*, Morris Cohen (ed.), Harcourt, Brace and Co., 1923, p. 15.

Hypotheses are formed to explain these occurrences. The conclusions derived from these hypotheses are then subjected to experimental verification. Of the four methods of fixating belief, Peirce held scientific method by far the most reliable, since it involves test by sensory observation and is open to public inspection.

Since Peirce's time American philosophers have shown much interest in classifying the various means of obtaining knowledge and in estimating their comparative value as methods of inquiry. The following division of the sources of knowledge may be considered typical:[2]

Authority
Intuition
Reason
Experience

AUTHORITY

A moment's reflection on the number of our beliefs that we have acquired through authority should convince us that this number is very great. Nearly all of what we know through "book learning" comes to us on the testimony of others. The proportion of our beliefs that we have taken on the say-so of parents, teachers, friends, neighbors, government officials, clergymen, physicians, newspaper writers, and radio speakers is impressively large. That we are thus able by means of authority to increase our knowledge so greatly without going to the trouble of investigating the situation personally is a very wonderful thing. Indeed, the capacity to accumulate and to pass along large bodies of knowledge to others is a human talent which gives man an immense advantage over the other animals.

[2] See, for example, W. P. Montague, *The Ways of Knowing*, Allen and Unwin, London, 1925, Part I.

Of course, there are dangers implicit in the way of knowledge of authority. Man is a credulous animal and tends to believe what he is told. Historically, philosophers (like Bacon and Descartes) have taken great pains to point out that authority is at least as important a source of error as it is of knowledge. But there are certain precautions which can be employed to reduce the perils implicit in the way of knowledge of authority. Some of these safeguards will become apparent as we examine the following distinctions.

In the first place, authority is not, strictly speaking, a "true" way of knowledge at all; it is a way of knowing in a derivative sense only. That is, authority always reduces to some other way of knowing which is not authority. For example, I may believe the statement "Copper is a better conductor of heat than iron" because I have read it in my physics textbook. But this proposition is originally derived *from somebody's experience*. Back of the propositions "Lhasa is the largest city in Tibet" and "Caesar crossed the Rubicon" stands somebody's presence in Lhasa and somebody's sight of Caesar. These propositions have been communicated to us by the testimony of others. But the persons who first believed in their truth did not derive their beliefs from someone's say-so but from personal experience.

In the second place, we must distinguish between authority as a means by which we *come to know* a proposition to be true and authority as the reason *why* a proposition is true. A reliable authority communicates truth; it does not make it. Any agency which claims that its authority *constitutes* the truth of the propositions it utters should be regarded with the most profound distrust. Suppose a child, told by its father that "Spinach is good for you," asks why, and is informed, "Because I say so. That's why." In making his authority constitute the goodness of spinach, the father allows his temper to cloud his good sense. It is authority conceived in this second way—that of constituting rather than communicating truth—that is today widely repudiated under the label of "authoritarianism." Rulers of twentieth-century totalitarian states have not hesitated to manufacture their own truth. The techniques employed in this efficient method of preserving power over ignorant men have been wittily satirized by George Orwell in his novel *1984* and by Ignazio Silone in *Bread and Wine*.

"An authority is only as good as his argument" is a sound saying. It tells us that the reliability of an authority is inseparable from the *possibility of that authority's being checked by some other way of knowing*. It would be foolish of us not to accept a proposition stated by a competent authority unless we had personally checked it. The technical and specialized character of much of modern knowledge requires our reliance on the opinions of experts within their respective fields of competence. The fact that the statements made by the authority in question are open to independent investigation is usually a sufficient warrant of reliability. If a reputable physicist who has been investigating the properties of the metal niobium tells us that it has a very low lattice heat capacity, we would not think of subjecting ourselves to rigorous training in laboratory technique simply in order to verify his statement. The possibility that we *could* do so, if we so desired, is assurance enough.

If, however, my history book tells me that Napoleon

was defeated at Waterloo, and I am disposed to doubt the truth of that statement, it is not even theoretically possible for me to check it by personal observation. What I can do is to check it against the statements of other authorities trained in the field of history. If I find that all competent historians agree that Napoleon was defeated at Waterloo, I am faced with the following alternatives: (1) The statement "Napoleon was defeated at Waterloo" is true, or (2) expert historians, who have made independent investigation of the documents concerned, have one and all been made victims of an incredible deception or they themselves have engaged in an inexplicable conspiracy to deceive the students of the present day. Now I can ask: Of these alternatives, which is the more *reasonable?* That is, which alternative is more nearly consistent with a large number of propositions which we have independent grounds to believe to be true? Thus we have introduced as a check on authority a method of inquiry independent of authority, a method to which the classical name *reason* may be applied.

When authorities *disagree*, the question of determining which is in the right may be very complicated. Suppose two experts of roughly equal competence have examined a painting and have subjected it to exhaustive tests. Expert X says that it is a genuine Titian. Expert Y says that it is not. A third expert brought in to settle the dispute is unable to decide. In situations like this, evidence may exist which can be interpreted to support both contentions. But the total evidence may not be complete enough to be conclusive. Sometimes in such unsettled cases the only thing one can do is to suspend judgment in the hope that some further evidence can be turned up.

INTUITION

A Feeling in the Bones?

Intuition is commonly taken to mean a direct, immediate, and certain way of knowledge which dispenses with both the element of logical inference present in *reason* and the element of sensory observation associated with *experience*. When the writer of this book was a small boy, he secretly decided one Sunday to go to a baseball game instead of attending Sunday School. Now he had never before absented himself from Sunday School for a reason of this kind. On the day in question, he left the house at the usual time and walked part of the way through the usual streets. After enjoying as much of the ball game as coincided with the Sunday School period, he returned home to find his mother waiting for him at the door with lightnings playing about her head. Long after the storm had blown over, the mother confided that, as she was working in the kitchen that afternoon, a sudden conviction came to her that her boy was not in Sunday School. "It was a feeling that came over me all at once," she said, "I didn't know why, but I just *knew* you weren't there." From that day onward, the writer has entertained a wholesome respect for the way of knowledge called intuition.

Intuition and Mysticism

"Intuition" has been applied to many different kinds of knowledge situations. Its common meaning (as in the incident related above) refers to a person's sudden feeling of certain knowledge for which there is no *apparent* evidence other than the power of the conviction itself. A related meaning concerns knowledge which has come to many remarkable characters in history by way of visions, interior illuminations, *aperçus*, inner voices, and the like. Such intuitions commonly have the effect of suddenly resolving metaphysical, moral, or religious conflicts within the person concerned. In many cases they effect a complete reorientation of life and action. Ancient Indian sages taught that a holy man, who subjected himself to long periods of self-discipline, would suddenly know the reality that lay behind the veil of Maya which is this world. In a famous passage of the *Symposium*, Plato says that a philosopher, after laboriously mounting upward by way of the disciplines of earthly love and mathematics, may achieve a vision of eternal beauty. Socrates and Joan of Arc differed widely in beliefs and culture, but both listened to inner voices at critical moments of their lives. St. Paul had a shattering vision on the road to Damascus and went forth to spread Christianity throughout the Roman world.

Such intuitions are characteristic of the way of knowledge of *mysticism*. The mystic is a saintly person who, after long exercise in prayer and ascetic self-denial, suddenly "sees" beyond the world's illusion that one Divine Reality with which he feels himself united. Mystics of the religions of the West—St. Theresa, Ruysbroeck, Meister Eckhart, and others—all speak of an exhausting spiritual struggle (St. John of the Cross calls its most depressing moment "The Dark Night of the Soul") which is brought to an end by climactic experience of incandescence in which the mystic no longer "knows" but "sees."

Other Meanings of "Intuition"

"Intuition" is frequently used to refer to the direct and immediate way in which we apprehend an artistic object.

Philosophers of art often refer to a certain instantaneous insight into "form" as essential to the creation or appreciation of a work of art. The sudden clarity with which important hypotheses sometimes present themselves to great scientists is commonly labeled "intuition." The history of science, from Archimedes to Darwin, furnishes dramatic examples of revolutionary scientific ideas which have come to their authors "all at once." "Every one of these great discoveries," says Schopenhauer, "is an immediate intuition, and as such the work on an instant, an *aperçu*, a flash of insight. They are not the result of a process of abstract reasoning."

Propositions of which we can have immediate certainty without proof ("self-evident" propositions) are often said to be intuitively known. However, as we have seen, there may be disagreement as to just what kinds of propositions may properly be described as self-evident. Some philosophers restrict the class of propositions intuitively known to statements about simple perceptions, such as "This is blue." Others hold that the axioms of logic are intuitively known. Descartes used "intuition" as a synonym for his "clear and distinct" basic knowledge. "Each individual," he says, "can mentally have intuition of the fact that he exists, and that he thinks; that the triangle is bounded by three lines only, the sphere by a single superficies, and so on."[3] Some moral philosophers hold that the fundamental principles of ethics are intuitively known. Since basic moral axioms can be neither rationally demonstrated nor experimentally confirmed, they say, the truth of such ethical principles is "self-evident" and can be grasped only by direct and immediate knowledge.

[3] R. Descartes, "Rules for the Direction of the Mind," in *The Philosophical Works of Descartes*, E. S. Haldane and G. R. T. Ross (trans.), Cambridge University Press, 1931, p. 7.

Limitations of Intuition

Intuition is usually taken to mean a way of knowledge which is immediate, direct, and certain. It is the opinion of most analysts that, while such knowledge may exist, it does not come to us by way of a mysterious faculty set apart from other channels of knowledge. Many psychologists agree that the larger number of instances of "intuition" can be explained in terms of reflection upon sense experience. The mother of the truant boy, they would say, probably observed a certain unusual tenseness or caution in his behavior that day. Subsequent reflection on these observations, below the level of her conscious attention, produced a build-up of latent responses which finally "broke through" in the form of a sudden conviction of her son's absence from Sunday School.

While psychologists generally agree that the solution of problems frequently comes to us "in a flash," they tend to deny that such insight affords sufficient evidence of the existence of a special intuitive faculty.[4] The sudden illumination which discloses to a Newton or a Lavoisier the hypothesis for which he has been searching can be taken simply as the product of a long period of mental incubation in which concepts built up from sensory observation and logical inference have been mentally matched against

[4] In recent years certain psychologists have investigated the possibility of the existence of a quasi-intuitive way of knowledge known as "extrasensory perception." During the thirties and forties the American psychologist J. B. Rhine conducted a long series of experiments at Duke University designed to discover whether or not certain persons have the power to "know" if something is so without observing the situation. In these experiments, the subject tried to identify concealed cards upon which special designs were printed. According to Rhine, the results of these experiments indicate that some people actually do possess a special way of knowing by means of which unobserved states of affairs are directly disclosed to them in consciousness. A considerable number of psychologists and other scientists disagree with Rhine on the value of these experiments.

one another in an imaginative process of trial and error. Psychologists interested in the phenomena of religious experience, yet skeptical of revelations and visions, have analyzed the illumination of religious mysticism in terms of complex forms of latent sensory and emotional build-ups. An example of such an analysis may be found in J. H. Leuba's *The Psychology of Religious Mysticism*, in which the author claims that any information obtained by mystics in their moments of illumination has "really" come to them through their senses.

Perhaps the most important limitation of intuition as a way of knowledge is its *lack of public character*. Critics of intuitionism point out that what is disclosed in intuition is not publicly verifiable; it is an essentially private affair. We are quite properly suspicious of those people who say they "see" things which others do not see, and who claim that they have interior illuminations in which important truths are revealed to them alone. Indeed, the claim of private revelation is all too often the first mark of a psychotic state. Lunatic asylums are full of persons who claim such particular visions. Now most contemporary methodologists are inclined to believe that truth is not a private but a social affair. If a proposition is true, they say, what it designates should in some way or other be open to public inspection. An important reason why the methodology of the sciences is so productive is that scientific statements are amenable to public test and confirmation.

At this juncture, however, a distinction should be made. Suppose, for the sake of argument, that on occasion it is possible for one to arrive at the knowledge of important propositions via the direct and private route of intuition. Now if the truth of these propositions, disclosed in intuition, can be confirmed by some way of knowing which *does* have a public character, then the objection to intuition on the ground of its essentially private character will lose something of its force.

Intuition and Intellect; Bergson's Theory of Knowledge

The modern French philosopher Henri Bergson offers an interesting theory of knowledge in which *intuition* and *intellect* are suggested as the two basic ways of knowing. This dual analysis of knowledge leads the philosopher to a remarkable metaphysical theory in which something analogous to, but more generic than, organic life is taken to be the ultimate source of all things. Of the two ways of knowing, Bergson says: "The first implies that we move round the object; the second that we enter into it. The first depends on the point of view at which we are placed and on the symbols by which we express ourselves. The second neither depends on a point of view nor relies on any symbol. The first kind of knowledge may be said to stop at the *relative;* the second, in those cases where it is possible, to attain the *absolute.*"[5] The first kind of knowledge is the indirect, conceptual, rational, abstract way of intellect. The second is the direct, immediate, concrete, life-penetrating way of *intuition.* The way of intellect is best observed in *science,* whose function is to understand and to control material objects. The way of intuition may be found in artistic creation, human love, and in the experiences of the saint and the mystic. By means of the conceptual, symbolic way of intellect we *know about* the object—that is, we move all around it and see it from every side. By means of

[5] H. Bergson, *Introduction to Metaphysics* (rev. ed.), T. E. Hulme (trans.), G. P. Putnam's Sons, 1936, p. 1.

the direct, immediate way of intuition we *know* the object —that is, we enter into the object and become at one with it. The task of philosophy, says Bergson, is to integrate *both* these fundamental ways of knowing.[6]

Bergson's view of intellect is pragmatic and instrumental. Intellect, he tells us, has a *functional* character. It is an instrument which man has acquired and developed in the course of evolution, a natural tool by means of which the human organism is able to cope with its environment. Intellectual knowledge enables us to handle, to manipulate, and to control the material world. Because the function of intellect is the handling of matter, the intellect cannot help but see the world as if it were made up entirely of material bodies. Thus, when faced with an object it seeks to understand, intellect by its very nature tends to conceive of it in terms of an assemblage of material particles. Intellect *analyzes* the object which confronts it, splits it up into parts, then moves round the parts, examining them from every side, ever striving to establish the relation of these parts to each other as well as the relation of the object as a whole to other objects. This is the way of knowledge of science, which is intellectual knowledge *par excellence*— indirect, analytic, conceptual, rational, abstract.

But intellect, says Bergson, is not all there is to human consciousness; it is a contraction, a focusing, a special use

[6] William James distinguishes between (1) knowledge by acquaintance and (2) knowledge "about." A similar distinction is made by Bertrand Russell between (1) knowledge by acquaintance and (2) knowledge by description. I know New York City by acquaintance, but I only know *about* Hankow. I know Schubert's *D Minor Quartet* by acquaintance, but I only know *about* atoms.

In medieval philosophy, the meaning of the term "connatural knowledge" is somewhat similar to Bergson's "intuition." Thomas Aquinas says that while it is possible to acquire considerable knowledge *about* virtue by studying moral philosophy, only a *good* man has *connatural* knowledge of virtue.

of that consciousness. Surrounding intellect, as a vague but luminous fringe, is *intuition*. In man, this way of knowledge is a higher development of what appears in the animal world as *instinct*. Intuition is not analytic; it does not break up the object which confronts it into a collection of movable parts. It does not seek to understand its object, as does intellect, by indirect reference to concepts and ideas. In intuition, we grasp the object as a whole. We no longer move around it; we are at one with it.

Now if the object of intellect is matter, what then is the object of intuition? Bergson answers: *Life*. When science (which is to say the intellectual or rational way of knowledge) is faced with the phenomenon of life and seeks to understand the nature of the organic, it breaks up the unified living thing into parts, into atoms, into material bits, and seeks to "explain" life in terms of physical particles combined in some complex way. But, Bergson is convinced, life will never thus be understood. For intellect, striving to grasp the nature of life, handles it as if it were *not* living. It turns life into a collection of tiny material blocks and, in so doing, presents us with a conception of life which is one-sided and misleading, if not actually false. Intuition, on the other hand, is at home with life. Directly, immediately, without need of conceptual reference, we know life as it flows and wells up within ourselves. We know, without intellectual demonstration, that our *mode of being* is fundamentally different from the mode of being exhibited by physical objects:

Intelligence, by means of science, which is its work, will deliver up to us more and more completely the secret of physical operations; of life it brings us, and moreover only claims to bring us, a translation in terms of inertia. It goes all round life, taking from outside the greatest number of views of it, drawing it into itself instead of entering into it. But it is to the very inwardness of life that *intuition* leads us—by intuition I mean instinct that has become disinterested, self-conscious, capable of reflecting upon its object and of enlarging it indefinitely.[7]

Bergson tells us that if we extend beyond ourselves this intuition of life—given to us in our awareness of the inward flow of our own consciousness—we can at significant moments touch the pulse of life as it surges in the world behind the crust of matter. For, Bergson believes, something analogous to organic life, but far more fundamental, strives to unite itself with everything that is. This *élan vital*, conceived as a primordial cosmic impulse, is the ultimate source of organic life. In such a way does Bergson's concept of intuition lead him to a particular *metaphysical* theory, that is, to a general doctrine of the nature of things. It should not surprise us to learn that in his later years Bergson became absorbed with the problem of *mysticism* and underwent himself the experience of religious conversion.

REASON

The Rational Animal

Long ago, Aristotle said that the definition of "man" is "*rational animal.*" According to the Greek philosopher, the function of definition is to set forth the essence, the nature, the "what-ness" of that which is defined. We do this by first giving the *genus* or *kind* to which the thing we are defining belongs. In the case of man, the genus is "animal,"

---

[7] H. Bergson, *Creative Evolution*, A. Mitchell (trans.), Henry Holt and Co., 1911, p. 176.

for he shares with animals capacities which are characteristic of them. The second element in definition is *difference*, the characteristic which marks off what is being defined from all other members of its genus. In man, said Aristotle, the "difference" is *reason*. Like animality, rationality is part of man's essence or nature, but it is that element which man does *not* share with other members of his genus. Reason is that property which sets man *apart* from other animals. Man's rational capacity, said Aristotle, is the source of all properly human activities—our ability to talk, to laugh, to engage in scientific inquiry, etc.

Contemporary philosophers, as a rule, do not accept the implication in Aristotle's definition that "reason" is a unified inborn faculty with which man is "by nature" endowed. Such a conception of reason, thinks John Dewey, draws attention away from the fact that "reason" is a set of learned habits, achieved with difficulty through long runs of trial and error in experience. Dewey prefers the word "intelligence" to "reason." Nevertheless, most philosophers have agreed with the *spirit* of Aristotle's definition. Human knowledge can certainly be distinguished from animal knowledge by virtue of its *results*. At the very least, it is a legitimate linguistic convenience to include under one name —whether this be "reason" or "intelligence"—those capacities by means of which men produce mathematical theorems, Diesel locomotives, systems of both cost accounting and philosophy.

The classical word "reason" has many senses, all of them more or less closely related, which are determined by the particular context of subject matter in which the word is used. Two or three of these related meanings of "reason" are rather important to an understanding of frequently heard discussions in which the word "reason" occurs, and we shall try to distinguish between them.

Reason and Impulse

One of the many shades of meaning which have gathered about "reason" is that taken on by the word when it is used in opposition to "impulse." Impulse plays a tremendous part in human life. The *power* of the instinctive, dynamic, infrarational side of human nature has been a matter of serious concern to Western thinkers from Plato to Freud. The way of impulse is to act without reflection, to "shoot first and ask questions afterward." Impulse is powerful and, if undirected, blind. Poets and moralists alike have mourned the havoc wrought in human affairs by uncontrolled sexual love and the compulsion to strike down one's fellow man. Human beings have the capacity to achieve, at the cost of pain and frequent defeat, control of impulse and the ability to channel it in productive directions. To that specifically human capacity to foresee the results of impulse, and to govern and direct compulsive drives accordingly, we give the name of "reason" or "intelligence."

Some moralists have been content to stress the *negative* role of reason in relation to impulse. Like the Stoics and Spinoza, they have focused one-sidedly on the power of reason to control or even to eliminate the emotions. Other analysts of human nature—aware of the thin and ineffective quality of thought without the driving force of passion— have insisted that the function of reason is not to conquer impulse but to guide it. The function of reason, *positively* conceived, is to direct impulse and vital energy toward the achievement of fruitful ends. Impulse urges us to act—to act at once without thought of consequences. The part of reason is to make us look before we leap; to foresee the consequences of the act to which impulse drives us; to reflect upon these consequences; and to adjust our plan of action accordingly. Such a conception of reason in relation to impulse is presented by John Dewey in his analysis of "intelligence."

Impulse is primary and intelligence is secondary and in some sense derivative. There should be no blinking of this fact. But recognition of it as fact exalts intelligence. For thought is not the slave of impulse to do its bidding. Impulse does not know what it is after; it cannot give orders, not even if it wants to. . . . What intelligence has to do in the service of impulse is to act not as its obedient servant but as its clarifier and liberator. . . . Rationality . . . is not a force to evoke against impulse and habit. It is the attainment of a working harmony among diverse desires. "Reason" as a noun signifies the happy cooperation of a multitude of dispositions, such as sympathy, curiosity, exploration, experimentation, frankness, pursuit—to follow things through—circumspection, to look about at the context. . . . The clew of impulse is, as we say, to start something. It is in a hurry. It rushes us off our feet. It leaves no time for examination, memory and foresight. But the clew of reason is, as the phrase also goes, to stop and think.[8]

Reason and Sense Perception

A somewhat different sense of "reason" is used when we contrast reason with sense perception. Here "reason" refers to our capacity for *conceptual knowledge*, the power of the human mind to go beyond the particular and separate items of sense experience to form abstract concepts or "laws" of a general nature. To describe and to interpret the world it is

[8] J. Dewey, *The Philosophy of John Dewey*, J. Ratner (ed.), Henry Holt and Co., 1928, pp. 292–293.

necessary to go beyond what is immediately given in sense perception, to fix upon general patterns of experience rather than on particular and isolated bits of it. Since Plato, who believed that "the mind, by a power of her own, contemplates the universal in all things," it has been traditional to associate reason with conceptual knowledge.

A very broad division of types of philosophic thinking is suggested by the contrast between reason and sense experience. Those philosophers who stress the importance of sense observation in reliable knowledge are called *empiricists.* Those who emphasize the power of reason or conceptual knowledge are labeled *rationalists.* Historically, no philosophers have said of sense perception and conceptual knowledge that one was utterly valueless and the other completely trustworthy. But there have been major differences of emphasis on the relative importance of these two ways of knowing.

Philosophic Rationalism

Generally speaking, philosophic rationalism can be identified with confidence in the capacity of human reason or conceptual knowledge to attain to truth. With this confidence is associated a tendency to relegate sense experience, as a way of knowledge, to a role of secondary importance.

It is only natural to be impressed by the power of the human mind to carry on complex processes of inference without the need of constant stopping and turning to the observable world to verify conclusions established at each link of the chain of thought. The mathematical disciplines most clearly reveal the successful working of this human talent. Philosopher-mathematician that he was, Plato exulted over the ability of the human mind to reach knowledge without apparent aid of sense observation. Knowledge is not sense perception, he says; it is not even reasoning about sense perceptions. The objects to which reason leads us are not observable at all. They are the universal patterns of being to which mind alone can penetrate. Those who place their trust in sense perception Plato calls "the earth-born," and scornfully refers to them as "the people who believe in nothing but what they can hold in their hands." This is rationalism of an extreme sort.[9]

Philosophers of the seventeenth century were similarly struck by the power of mathematics, which was brilliantly developed in their age. Continental rationalists like Descartes, Leibniz, and Spinoza were convinced that the human mind possessed certain innate capacities or a priori truths upon which complex inferences could be built up without important aid from sense perception. Kant was a rationalist in that he believed our knowledge of the external world is primarily conceptual; the material which these concepts order is unknown. Thinkers as different as Thomas Aquinas and Hegel are frequently described as rationalists

[9] Perhaps the most radical philosophic rationalist of all time was Plato's predecessor Parmenides, who convinced himself and his disciples by apparently sound reasoning that neither multiplicity nor motion exists. There is only one thing that is, says Parmenides, and that is Being. Since Nothing is not, it does not exist. Now space is nothing. In order for there to be *many* things, there must be space between them. But space does not exist; therefore there is only *one* Being. Similarly, in order for there to be motion, there must be space to move in. But there is no space; therefore motion is impossible. The one eternal Being does not move or change in any way. If the senses tell us that there are many different things, and that there is motion, so much the worse for the senses.

Parmenides' pupil Zeno used paradoxes or puzzles to prove the impossibility of motion, the best known of which is that of Achilles and the tortoise. See J. Burnett, *Early Greek Philosophy*, A. & C. Black, Ltd., London, 1920, chaps. 4, 8.

because of their reliance on the powers of conceptual inference in their construction of grand-scale philosophic systems.

Another Meaning of Rationalism; Reason and Faith

A large number of educated persons of the seventeenth and eighteenth centuries shared with Descartes and Leibniz the general confidence of the period in the competence of human reason to reach true knowledge. Not everyone, however, (particularly in England) agreed with the Continental rationalists in believing that sense observation plays a minor role in reliable knowledge. Many showed their confidence in human reason by crying down, not sense experience, but another type of knowledge—hitherto considered as basic. This was knowledge derived from *religion* —from faith and the authority of sacred revelation.

In medieval culture it was generally held that there were two primary ways of knowledge, which we may distinguish as *faith* and *reason*. To the philosopher of the Middle Ages the information contained in Scriptures (which he considered as divinely revealed knowledge) together with the teaching of his religion constituted a broad path of knowledge which reached farther and higher than reason. But the medieval philosopher did not think that religious faith supported by the authority of Scriptures and tradition was the only way of knowing or even the only important way. He believed that reliable knowledge could also be attained through the exercise of the natural power of human reason unaided by revelation. Men like Aquinas and Maimonides set themselves the task of organizing systems of human knowledge in which the findings of faith and reason would be integrated within a synthesis which did justice to both.

Religious faith was never considered by medieval thinkers to be an *obstacle* to human thought; they took it as a *stimulus* to intellectual activity. *"Credo ut intellegam,"* said Anselm. "I believe in order that I may understand."

Modern times, beginning with the Renaissance, saw the gradual breakup of the medieval synthesis. Little by little, educated men pushed the presuppositions of faith further and further into the background. By the eighteenth century, the rise of confidence in the power of human reason was paralleled by a decline of trust in religious beliefs. Faith became associated with clericalism, superstition, fanaticism, and "enthusiasm." All necessary knowledge of God and his relation to the world could be obtained by natural reason. No need of revelation, Scriptures, or a teaching church. In this climate of eighteenth-century rationalism there developed the "rational" or "natural" religion known as deism.

Nineteenth-century scholars turned to the scriptural writings themselves, and, treating them as they would any other set of historical documents, subjected them to critical analysis. They challenged the authenticity of some parts of the Scriptures, called into question the authorship of others, pointed out interpolated and corrupt passages, and so forth. In this way the term "rationalism" became associated with the so-called "higher criticism" of the Bible.

Thus we can distinguish two basic meanings of the difficult word "rationalism," each of which has an element in common with the other. *Philosophic rationalism* entails (1) confidence in the power of human reason to reach true knowledge (2) without important aid from sense perception. What we may call *secularist* or *naturalistic* rationalism implies (1) confidence in the power of human reason to at-

178   *The Meaning of Philosophy*

tain to true knowledge (2) without the aid of faith, revelation, or a teaching church. In the definition of philosophic rationalism, "reason" is taken as synonymous with conceptual knowledge in contrast to sense perception. In secularist rationalism, reason is interpreted in a broader sense which does not necessarily exclude the element of sense observation.

EXPERIENCE

Some Meanings of "Experience"

"We learn by experience," we say. "Experience is a great teacher." But what is experience? The word is even more difficult to define than "reason." Its varied usages form concentric rings of meaning that blur into one another in such a way that it is impossible to separate them clearly.[10]

The narrowest meaning of "experience" is *sensation*. In this sense, the perception of a colored shape, a flash of light, or a feeling of warmth is said to be an experience. A less restricted meaning is *observation*. We know via experience that it is raining, that the stove is hot, that the subway is crowded, etc. Another meaning refers to an event or happening in which we are involved and which makes a *strong impression* on us. Thus a man who has just been robbed may say, "I had a terrible experience last night."

If we translate Descartes's famous "*Je pense, donc je suis*" as "I am experiencing, therefore I am," we are using "experience" as a synonym for *consciousness*. A person whose capacity to do a job has been built up by *past practice* in the skills required is referred to as "experienced." A still broader

[10] For various meanings of "experience," see J. H. Randall and J. Buchler, *Philosophy: An Introduction*, Barnes and Noble, Inc., 1942, p. 85.

usage of "experience" suggests *knowledge by acquaintance* in contrast to *knowledge about*.[11] I know from experience that my father was a gentle and kind man while my children know this only by my testimony. When I ask, "In your experience, did you ever encounter a case like this?" I refer to a series of past events in which you were concerned and your response to these. This last usage gives us a clue to a working definition of "experience" in a fairly comprehensive sense. *Experience is what happens to us and what we do about it.*

Philosophical Empiricism

An empiricist is one who believes that experience is the most reliable method of knowledge. Such a person is the legendary man from Missouri who said, "Show me." Philosophical empiricism is associated with confidence in the reliability of experience as a way of knowing together with a tendency to distrust conceptual knowledge. The philosophical empiricist is critical of the rationalist's claim that the mind has powers of its own to disclose the nature of things. He also tends to suspect intuition and many forms of authority as ways of knowing.

Credit for the most eloquent and influential defense of *experience* as the most important source of human knowledge goes to John Locke. In his *Essay Concerning Human Understanding* Locke rejects the teaching of the rationalist Descartes that the human mind is by nature endowed with certain innate ideas: "Let us suppose the mind to be, as we say, white paper, void of all characters, without any ideas. How comes it to be furnished? Whence comes it by that vast store which the busy and boundless fancy of man has

[11] See footnote 6, p. 168.

painted on it with an almost endless variety? Whence has it all the *materials* of reason and knowledge? To this I answer in one word: EXPERIENCE. All our knowledge is founded in experience, and from experience it ultimately derives itself."[12]

Locke never tells us just what he means by "experience," but he tends much of the time to take it in the narrow sense of *sensations*. British empiricists who succeeded Locke applied his doctrine "All knowledge from experience" strictly as "All knowledge from sense data." A rigorous application of this sensationalistic interpretation of "experience" led to Hume's doctrine of objects and minds as clusters of sensations. Thus empiricism turned into skepticism. The greatest twentieth-century representative of British empiricism is Bertrand Russell. Russell himself inclines toward an analysis of "experience" in terms of sensations or "brain states." But he admits that a theory of knowledge based on "experience" alone is inadequate. Our knowledge of the general principles which guide human behavior, he says, "cannot be based on experience, though all their verifiable consequences are such as experience will confirm."

The contemporary doctrine known as *logical empiricism* is descended in part from the British empiricist tradition. This fact may throw some light on the tendency of many of its adherents toward a sensationalistic analysis of experience. We have seen earlier that logical empiricists hold (with Hume) that informative statements must be either formal or factual if they are to be significant. It follows that for the logical empiricist there are two basic methods of re-

[12] J. Locke, *An Essay Concerning Human Understanding*, A. C. Fraser (ed.), Oxford University Press, 1894, vol. 1, pp. 121-122.

liable knowledge: (1) logical and linguistic analysis and (2) inferences from observed "facts." Propositions which are analytic are true in virtue of the rules of logic and language. "Factual" propositions are meaningful only if verifiable; their truth can be determined only by a testing process in which some element of sensory observation is present. In our discussion of "Language," we have noted some opinions concerning the limitations of this form of empiricism.

A great part of contemporary American philosophy may be described as "empiricist," if we interpret the word in a broad sense to refer to a general underlying assumption that the most reliable knowledge is that which is subject to confirmation by scientific experiment or social practice. American philosophy was given its empiricist orientation by the philosophers of the pragmatist tradition, Peirce, James, and Dewey. The current popularity of "philosophy of science" and "philosophy of language" and the influence of logical empiricism have introduced more specialized and technical strains of empiricism into philosophic tendencies in the United States.

A Broader Concept of Experience; Dewey's Empiricism

John Dewey's interpretation of "experience" is probably the broadest of any philosophy this side of rationalism. He forcefully rejects the notion that experience is *sensation*, and that what we know are *sense data*. He has no patience with those self-styled empiricists who tell us that when we look at a chair we "really" experience only a colored patch. A man experiences the chair most fully, says Dewey, not when looking at it, but when he is intending to sit down in it. And he can intend to sit down in the chair precisely because his experience of the chair is *not* limited to a colored shape. Far from experiencing only a colored patch which is *less* than a chair, that man experiences a good deal *more* than a chair. He "lays hold of a wide spatial context, such as the room where the chair is, and a spread of its history, including the chair's period, price paid for it, consequences, public as well as personal which follow from its use as household furniture, and so on." In Dewey's opinion, the contemporary "colored-patch" empiricist is not talking about experience or knowledge at all:

> Sensations are not parts of *any* knowledge, good or bad, superior or inferior, imperfect or complete. They are rather provocations, incitements, challenges to an act of inquiry which is to *terminate* in knowledge. . . . When the isolated and simple existences of Locke and Hume are seen not to be truly empirical but to answer certain demands of their theory of mind, the necessity ceases for the elaborate Kantian and post-Kantian machinery of *a priori* concepts and categories to synthesize the alleged stuff of experience. The true "stuff" of experience is recognized to be adaptive courses of action, habit, active functions, connections of doing and undergoing; sensori-motor co-ordinations. Experience carries principles of connection and organization within itself.[13]

What then is experience? Of all the varied definitions of the term we have outlined in a previous section, the one closest to Dewey's conception is "Experience is what happens to us and what we do about it." But Dewey would insist that the primary stress be put on the *doing* rather than the *undergoing*. As we have said earlier, Dewey sees man

[13] J. Dewey, *Experience and Nature*, Open Court Publishing Co., 1925, p. 5.

as an organism acting upon and being acted upon by the dual environment of Nature and society. The human organism does not stand passive and inert, like Locke's blank tablet, waiting for something to impress itself upon it from outside. Man *acts* upon his environment, changing its character, and the environment, so modified, reacts upon him. Experience is the *product* of this interaction between the human organism and its natural and social environment. Experience is the outcome of transactions between man, Nature, and society. This Dewey takes to be the business of human knowledge, whether common-sense, scientific, or philosophical.

Like Bergson, Dewey holds a *genetic* theory of knowledge—although, unlike the French philosopher, he does not separate intuition from intellect. To Dewey, intelligence has arisen in the course of evolution as a means of successful adaptation of the human organism to its environment. Ideas, says Dewey, are tools of practical action, not objects of contemplation. It is not the business of human thought to uncover a "reality" which has always been "there." The primary function of intelligence is to grapple with the succession of problems, obstacles, difficulties, and doubtful situations which man's natural and social environment presses constantly upon him.

Dewey's Analysis of Thinking

With Peirce, Dewey holds that knowledge begins with a doubtful situation and moves toward a settled one. Knowledge does not spring up out of nothing. A problem, an obstacle, a sense of trouble and unease must exist to stimulate productive thought. Dewey distinguishes five stages in the process of reflective thinking which practical everyday thought and scientific investigation have in common.[14] We may illustrate these phases by an example of our own:

Suppose a man who wants to listen to a ball game turns on his radio and finds that it will not work. Here is the typical start of a thinking process—the situation is uncertain; action is blocked. (1) The first phase, *suggestion:* Action blocked leads to hasty notions as to how action may quickly be resumed. The man twists the dials of his radio at random, then taps the instrument with his hand. (2) The second phase, *intellectualization:* A problem clearly formulated is a problem half-solved. The man observes that no current is flowing through his radio. This is the central difficulty. What has cut off the current? Why no power? (3) The third phase, *hypothesis:* Ideas now occur as to the possible causes of the situation. Perhaps a tube has blown. Maybe the ground connection is cut. Or perhaps there is a break in the circuit within the set itself. (4) The fourth phase, *reasoning:* Here the hypotheses are tested mentally by comparing them with what we already know. The man considers the suggestion that a tube has blown, but rejects it on the ground that the tubes are new, and that it is unlikely that one would fail so soon. He also rejects the idea that the ground wire is broken, since this would not cut off his power but only weaken it. Finally he considers the possibility of a circuit break in the radio itself. (5) The fifth phase, *testing the hypothesis:* A hypothesis which has survived the test of consistency with what we already know is ready for test in action. The man examines the circuit wires within the set, finds one which is badly frayed. Rubbing the separated strands together, he hears a crackle followed

[14] See J. Dewey, *How We Think* (rev. ed.), D. C. Heath and Co., 1933, chap. 7.

by the sound of the announcer's voice. A little solder does the rest, and the man settles back at last to listen to the ball game. The troubled situation is over. Equilibrium has been restored.

Is All Knowledge Problem Solving?

Dewey has been reproved for reducing all knowledge to problem solving, for representing every worth-while situation of human thought in terms of fixing an automobile engine. He has also been criticized on the ground that his analysis of knowledge leaves no room for theoretical research which does not have practical application in mind. It is true that Dewey's view of man in the universe struggling with the problems imposed on him by his environment orients his theory of knowledge toward practical action. But Dewey would insist that practical action need not be problem solving in the narrow sense of the world. It may mean the resolution of doubtful situations on purely theoretical levels. "Ideas may be of intellectual use to a penetrating mind," says Dewey, "even when they do not find any immediate reference to actuality, provided they stay in the mind for use when new facts come to light."[15] It is not to speculative knowledge that Dewey objects, but to knowledge which is *merely* speculative. Ideas, concepts, theories, and speculations are utterly necessary to productive knowledge. But unless they make some difference one way or another, they are just ideas and no more. Ideas which are not used as *instruments,* as operational plans to guide future action, are no better than daydreams. Dewey would be the first to admit that the ideas which contribute to great poetry and art are very valuable. But he does not

[15] *Ibid.,* p. 106.

(at least in his earlier writings) consider them the material of knowledge.

Rationalism and Empiricism as Methods of Science; Conclusion

In the sciences we can observe a happy union of the two great methods of knowledge we have labeled rationalism and empiricism. The truth of a proposition may be determined by testing it. But there are two general methods of testing propositions. We may show that the proposition may be deduced by logical inference from other propositions already established. Or we may try it out in an experiment in which some element of sense perception is involved. The first is the way of deduction or *rationalism*, the second the way of observation and experiment or *empiricism*. In the realm of logic and mathematics only does the method of rationalism operate successfully *solo*. To be sure, it is prominent and successful also in those physical sciences in which mathematics plays an essential role. But even theoretical physics—which carries on so much of its work by mathematical reasoning—requires an occasional crucial check by experiment. *All* the natural sciences are more or less rationalistic. There is no science which confines itself to sense observations without reasoning about them. But the propositions of the empirical sciences (in contrast to those of logic and mathematics) must somewhere along the line be subject to confirmation by experiment. And experiments are procedures in which some kind of sense observation is concerned.

From propositions contained in his revolutionary theory of relativity Einstein deduced by a complex process of inference that light rays are bent as they pass near the sun.

Some years later, astronomers at Greenwich took photographs of an eclipse of the sun which showed the bending of the light waves. The astronomical photographs which correlated Einstein's theory with sense observations showed, as Whitehead expresses it, that a great adventure in thought had come safe to shore.[16] In the form of observation and experiment, the empiricist element plays an indispensable role in the methodology of the physical sciences. But observation and experiment of themselves do not produce great scientific theories. These are the products of the creative, speculative, *rational* aspects of human thought stimulated by the problems and uncertainties of the world of sense.

FURTHER READINGS

Bergson, Henri, *Creative Evolution*, A. Mitchell (trans.), Henry Holt and Co., 1911, chap. 2.

Cohen, Morris, *Reason and Nature*, Harcourt, Brace and Co., 1931.

Cohen, Morris, and Nagel, Ernest, *An Introduction to Logic and Scientific Method*, Harcourt, Brace and Co., 1934, chaps. 10, 11, 20.

The Columbia Associates, *An Introduction to Reflective Thinking*, Houghton Mifflin Co., 1923.

Descartes, René, "Discourse on Method," in *The Philosophical Works of Descartes*, E. S. Haldane and G. R. T. Ross (trans.), Cambridge University Press, 1931.

Dewey, John, "Changed Conceptions of Reason and Experience," in *Reconstruction in Philosophy*, Henry Holt and Co., 1920.

Dewey, John, "The Instrumental Theory of Knowledge," in

---

[16] A. N. Whitehead, *Science and the Modern World*, The Macmillan Company, 1925, p. 15.

188   *The Meaning of Philosophy*

The Philosophy of John Dewey, J. Ratner (ed.), Henry Holt and Co., 1928.

Dewey, John, *How We Think* (rev. ed.), D. C. Heath and Co., 1933.

Feigl, Herbert, "Logical Empiricism," in *Readings in Philosophical Analysis*, Appleton-Century-Crofts, Inc., 1949.

James, William, *Pragmatism*, Longmans, Green and Co., 1928, chaps. 1 and 2.

Leuba, J. H., *The Psychology of Religious Mysticism*, Harcourt, Brace and Co., 1925.

Maritain, J., "On Knowledge through Connaturality" in *The Range of Reason*, Charles Scribner's Sons, 1952.

Montague, Wm. Pepperell, *The Ways of Knowing*, Allen and Unwin, London, 1925, Part 1.

Peirce, Charles Sanders, "The Fixation of Belief," in *Chance, Love, and Logic*, Morris Cohen (ed.), Harcourt, Brace and Co., 1923.

Plato, Socrates' Speech in "The Symposium," *The Dialogues of Plato*, B. Jowett (trans.) Random House, 1937, vol. 1.

Plato, "Theaetetus," *The Dialogues of Plato*, B. Jowett (trans.), Random House, 1937, vol. 2.

Reichenbach, Hans, "The Empiricist Approach," in *The Rise of Scientific Philosophy*, University of California Press, 1951.

Russell, Bertrand, "Knowledge by Acquaintance and Knowledge by Description" in *Mysticism and Logic*, Longmans, Green and Co., 1918.

Russell, Bertrand, *Scientific Method in Philosophy*, Open Court Publishing Co., 1914.

Walsh, W. H., *Reason and Experience*, Oxford University Press, 1947.

PART III

METAPHYSICS OR SPECULATIVE PHILOSOPHY

6

WHAT IS METAPHYSICS?

> *"Those Platonists are a curse," he said.*
> —W. B. YEATS

METAPHYSICS or speculative philosophy may be tentatively described as that division of philosophy which raises some very general questions about the nature of the world and man's place in it. Many philosophers today hold that metaphysics is an altogether useless study, in fact quite nonsensical, and should be discarded permanently from philosophy. Our approach to the subject will be more tolerant for the following reasons. The term "metaphysics" can be taken in several different ways. It is possible that, defined in one way, metaphysics will not appear to be anything but a fruitless enterprise, while defined in another way, it may seem quite legitimate. The reader should be acquainted with two or three different opinions as to what the object of metaphysical inquiry is. He may also prefer to examine for himself some of the topics associated with metaphysical discussion rather than having his mind made up for him in advance.

METAPHYSICS AND SCIENCE

Metaphysics as Prescientific Speculation

The ancient Greeks made little distinction between philosophy and what we would call physical science. In fact, the study of the nature of the physical world was considered the business of the philosopher until quite modern times. As a synonym for "physics" the term "natural philosophy" has not been extinct very long. The very first philosophers in the West, the Ionian Greek cosmologists of the sixth century B.C., were absorbed by the question "What kind of stuff is the world made of?" Thales, the first philosopher of whom we have any record, said that all things ultimately derived from water. Anaximenes stated that the elemental principle of things was a primordial vapor. Heraclitus held that fire was the cause of all things. Democritus' theory that the simplest units of world stuff were tiny, indivisible, material particles or *atoms* is the most remarkable product of the same ancient line of inquiry. Such prescientific speculations as to the ultimate principle of things are frequently called "metaphysical."

Today we believe that the constitution of matter and the structure of the physical universe are no longer questions for philosophy to answer, but rather for the empirical sciences, physics, astronomy, and the rest. These sciences are special disciplines which do not rely wholly upon speculation and logical reasoning but employ experimental means of confirming the hypotheses they put forward. These methods include the use of sensitive instruments of measurement which the Greeks did not have. To be sure, most scientists today will quickly decline to answer the question which the prescientific Ionian cosmologists had in mind: What is the ultimate origin or "first cause" of the universe? They usually explain their reluctance by stating that such a question is "metaphysical"; that it cannot be answered by science, since there are no methods by which it can be settled.[1]

[1] Two recent scientists have committed themselves on the question of the origin of the physical universe. In his *The Nature of the Universe*, Harper & Brothers, 1951, Fred Hoyle says that the universe had no be-

Metaphysics as the Synthesis of Conclusions of Sciences

One modern view of the task of metaphysics is this: While metaphysics should not occupy itself with questions which the special sciences have experimental means of treating, yet it is possible to construct a metaphysical doctrine on the basis of the findings of these sciences. According to this opinion, the business of metaphysics is to fashion a synthesis of the general conclusions of the special sciences and in this way to arrive at a world perspective more comprehensive than any one of the particular sciences can offer. The aim of metaphysical philosophy, says the Danish philosopher Höffding, "is to attain points of view from which the fundamental phenomena and the principles of the special sciences can be seen in their relative importance and connection." Comte arranged the sciences according to the order of their abstractness, beginning with mathematics and ending with sociology. Referring with approval to this classification, the American philosopher W. P. Montague says:

We now have the six fundamental branches of science: Mathematics, Physics, Chemistry, Biology, Psychology, and Sociology, each of them (except, of course, the first) logically dependent on its predecessor. And all of them are to be represented as the successive spokes of a wheel . . . but so far there is nothing to bind the spokes together. It is this binding or unifying function which *metaphysics* aspires to perform. . . . Accepting humbly and gratefully from the sciences their verified discoveries of this and this and that and that, we must still ask, *what is it all about?*[2]

ginning, while George Gamow, in his *The Creation of the Universe*, The Viking Press, 1952, maintains that it had a definite beginning. This is an interesting case of the disagreement of two authorities.

[2] W. P. Montague, *The Ways of Things*, Prentice-Hall, Inc., 1940, pp. 10–11.

Even the anti-metaphysical Carnap, whose view of philosophy is very different from Montague's, has no quarrel with "those theories—sometimes called metaphysical—whose object is to arrange the most general propositions of the various regions of scientific knowledge in a well ordered system."[3]

Some metaphysicians object to this conception of the task of their subject as one of integrating the broad conclusions of the special sciences. Among their number are those who believe that speculative philosophy should be constructed from material drawn from every major phase of human experience—poetic, moral, and religious, as well as scientific. To these philosophers the "scientific synthesis" view of metaphysics is too narrow. Such a view seems to take for granted that scientific propositions are the most important if not the only true propositions. Such a conception of metaphysics, says Bergson, is altogether too modest; it reduces metaphysics to the role of a "registration court, charged at most with wording more precisely the sentences that are brought to it, pronounced and irrevocable."[4] Such a view leaves to the metaphysician only the passive role of awaiting delivery of various sets of propositions which he must assume in advance to be true as well as adequate representations of the character of things. But, say the critics of this conception of metaphysics, scientific descriptions, though true, may be somewhat abstract and one-sided. Metaphysicians, restricted to the task of integrating the general statements of science, may be content to offer a world picture which is no more than a pastiche of

[3] R. Carnap, *Philosophy and Logical Syntax*, Kegan Paul, Trench, Trubner and Co., London, 1935, p. 15.
[4] H. Bergson, *Creative Evolution*, A. Mitchell (trans.), Henry Holt and Co., 1911, p. 195.

scientific conclusions. Such an outlook will be limited in its perspective; it will fail to do justice to many basic aspects of human experience.

METAPHYSICS AS THE STUDY OF BEING

Aristotle's "First Philosophy"

We do not know just how the word "metaphysics" came into use. According to a plausible explanation, a Greek editor, collating the writings of Aristotle, inserted the published lectures in which the philosopher deals with what he calls "first philosophy" or "theology" *after* (μετά meta) the treatise titled *Physics*. In any event, this particular work of Aristotle is now known as the *Metaphysics*.

According to Aristotle, "first philosophy" investigates *being*. The special sciences treat of particular *parts* of being; zoölogy, for example, deals with animals and political science with constitutions. But "first philosophy" deals with being *qua* being, that is, with being in general, without primary reference to some particular variety of being: "There is a science which investigates Being as Being and the attributes which belong to this in virtue of its own nature. Now this is not the same as any of the so-called special sciences; for none of these treats universally of Being as Being. They cut off a part of Being and investigate the attribute of this part."[5]

Ontology

Taken in the special sense of an inquiry into being, metaphysics is frequently called *ontology* (literally, the study of being). Since there is no category more comprehensive

[5] Aristotle, *Metaphysics*, W. D. Ross (trans.), Book 4, 1003a21.

than being, ontology is the most generic and abstract of all intellectual inquiries. Some analytic philosophers, such as Carnap, hold that ontology consists wholly of pseudo problems; that metaphysicians who ask questions about being and its kinds are under the impression that they are discussing actual objects, while in fact they are merely talking about special grammatical forms. Others, like Tarski, maintain that ontology is not objectionable, if we understand by it "a general theory of objects . . . a discipline which is to be developed in a purely empirical way, and which differs from other empirical sciences only by its generality."[6] Without further ado about the various senses in which "ontology" may be taken, we shall proceed to mention a few well-known classic and contemporary distinctions between various *modes of being*.

Modes of Being; Permanence and Change

Aristotle divides being into two basic kinds: (1) *immutable* or changeless being and (2) *mutable* or changing being. The study of the second kind, mutable being—which, according to Aristotle, is the only kind we see in the world about us—belongs to the subject of physics or (as we would say) philosophy of Nature.[7] The study whose subject matter is the first kind of being, immutable being, is theology; for there is only one being "eternal and immovable" and this is God.

The belief that there is a mode of being which is *changeless* is characteristic of a large part of Greek metaphysics.

---

[6] A. Tarski, "The Semantic Conception of Truth," in *Readings in Analytic Philosophy*, H. Feigl and W. Sellars (eds.), Appleton-Century-Crofts, Inc., 1949, p. 72.

[7] Aristotle, *op. cit.*, Book 6, 1026a10.

Aristotle derived his dual classification of being from Plato, his teacher, who held that "true being" was something not subject to change and decay. According to Plato, our world exhibits only *becoming;* in the world of sense everything coming into being and going out of being, but nothing really *is*. Only that which is changeless is real, thought Plato; reality is permanent and immutable. The world of sense experience in which everything is subject to generation and corruption is only a reflection of reality. Of the two primary modes of being, permanence and change, permanence is primary, more important, "realer," while change is derivative, secondary, less real.

The conviction that permanence is the primary mode of being has an interesting relationship to the classical doctrine of *substance*. One of Aristotle's classifications of being divides being into the two modes of "substance" and "accident." A substance or "thing" manifests a relatively *independent* "way" of being. Examples of substances are objects like books or men. An accident or quality has no independent being, but exists *in* a substance. Blue and soft do not have the relatively self-contained being of trees and men. Qualities must "inhere" in substances such as coats or fruit. Now substances, in some fundamental way, remain the same, although their qualities may change; that is, substances retain their identity through change. A man may display the property of running or talking. But these modifications of the "basic" man pass away and are replaced by different ones. Yet the "basic" man remains; his identity is preserved through change. Substances, then, represent the relatively permanent side of Nature. The substantial aspect of things enables us to identify them on separate occasions. Thus the old and bald Socrates is in some important way the *same* Socrates as he was when he was young and had curly hair.

The Greek notion that permanence is the "realer" or "better" mode of being and that change is derivative and, by comparison, less "real" is not at all characteristic of recent systems of metaphysics. In many of the outstanding metaphysical theories of the nineteenth and twentieth centuries the situation is quite the reverse. In the world perspectives of men like Whitehead (as we shall see), Bergson, and the German idealists, change, process, passage is taken as primary, while the permanent and stable side of things is considered derivative, secondary, less fundamental. Along with the general concept of the primacy of permanence, modern metaphysicians have also tended to abandon the particular notion of substance. To them, the concept of substance is inseparable from a view of the universe in terms of basic units which are fixed, static, and enduring.

The discovery of modern science that basic physical entities are electrical agitations, dynamic processes rather than static pellets of enduring matter, reinforces the "process philosopher's" conviction that ultimate units are happenings rather than substances.

Several reasons have been offered to account for the shift from permanence to change as a basic ontological category in the transition from classical to modern metaphysics. Some cite the influence of the philosophy of Hegel, who viewed the world primarily as a process of *becoming*. Others refer to the impact of the concept of evolution, which inclined many thinkers to see the cosmos in terms of *development*. Still others claim that the nineteenth-century socioeconomic ideal of progress (a notion unknown to the classical world) is an important cause of the turn in modern speculative philosophy from permanence to change as the primary mode of being or reality.

Essence and Existence

When Aristotle remarked " 'What man is' and 'That man exists' are two different questions,"[8] he formulated the distinction between essence and existence and sent it off to a distinguished metaphysical career which has lasted to the present day. "Essence" refers to *what a thing is*, to its definition or its description, if you like, while "existence" refers to *whether it is*. An example may clarify this distinction. A fictitious being is an essence. We can answer the question "What is it?" Thus, Shakespeare's Miranda is the daughter of Prince Prospero; she lives with her father on a remote and magic island where she meets a young man cast up by the sea, etc. Miranda is an essence. But she does not exist, in the sense of "actual existence." The reader of this book, on the other hand, is both an essence and an existence. He can not only define himself by answering the question "Who are you?"; he is also an actual as opposed to a merely possible being. New York City combines essence and existence; it is both possible and actual. But the land of Hy Brasil, where the Celtic heroes rest, is an essence or possible only. In classical metaphysics, the distinction between essence and existence raised questions which concern the so-called ontological argument for the existence of God. We shall see something of this in our discussion of theism.

The Realm of Essence; Santayana

When the existence of something comes to an end, we can no longer say that the thing exists. But we can still talk of

[8] Aristotle, *Posterior Analytics*, II, 7, 92b, 10–11.

its "what-ness" or character. The lost continent of Atlantis may once have been an existing thing; now it is an essence only. As George Santayana says: "After things lose their existence, as before they attain it, although it is true of them that they have existed or will exist, they have no internal being except their essences, quite as if they had never broached Existence at all: yet the identity of each essence with itself and difference from every other essence suffices to distinguish and define them all in eternity, where they form the Realm of Essence."[9]

In Santayana's philosophy there are two worlds. Over against the world of natural facts and events, there is an immense realm of possibilities or essences. Through sense observation and practical action we know the world of natural fact; but we reach the realm of essences through the clear intuitive insight of the imagination. The realm of essences is a world of ideal eternal objects, incredibly rich in variety, infinite in number. God and the devil are essences, as well as sky blue and B flat. The human mind has laid hold of a small part only of this inexhaustible store of timeless forms. The domain of essences is full of things no one has yet imagined, "tortures undreamed of in hell and delights unthought of in heaven." From this non-actual region come the things that matter most—all the values that enrich our lives and make our natural existence bearable. The metaphysical speculations of Plato, the theology of the Catholic church, the great visions of the poets, moralists, and saints—all are products of fertile contact between the creative imagination of man and the limitless world of essences.

[9] G. Santayana, *The Realm of Essence*, Charles Scribner's Sons, 1927, p. 24.

The natural world has only one advantage (if it can be called an advantage) over the realm of essence—that of actual existence. Essences have "aesthetic immediacy and logical definition," says Santayana, but they have no natural being. Men have cherished the illusion that essences particularly precious to them have somewhere, somehow a footing in the world of natural fact. Frequently such men try to force their belief on others. But the wisely doubting spirit knows that essences do not exist, yet loves them all the more:

Thus a mind enlightened by scepticism and cured of noisy dogma, a mind discounting all reports, and free from all tormenting anxiety about its own fortunes or existence, finds in the wilderness of essence a very sweet and marvellous solitude. The ultimate reaches of doubt and renunciation open out for it, by an easy transition, into fields of endless variety and peace, as if through the gorges of death it had passed into a paradise where all things are crystallised into the image of themselves, and have lost their urgency and their venom.[10]

"Our" Kind of Being; Bergson; Pascal; Heidegger

Many philosophers have been struck by the peculiar and immediate "feel" of our personal existence, as it is given to us directly in consciousness. Bergson, as we have seen, believed that there were two kinds of knowledge: the inward, direct knowledge he calls "intuition"; and the external, indirect, and conceptual knowledge he terms "intellect." Each of these ways of knowing deals with one of two basic modes of being. By intuition, "our" kind of being, *life*, is disclosed to us directly in the immediate data

[10] G. Santayana, *Scepticism and Animal Faith*, Charles Scribner's Sons, 1923, p. 76.

of consciousness. By intellect or conceptual knowledge, we reach and control *matter*, the kind of being physical objects represent. We have seen also that, long before Bergson, the great Descartes was so impressed by the immediacy of his knowledge of his own existence that he drew from it a primary principle upon which to base all human knowledge. Descartes's contemporary Pascal pondered not only on the immediacy with which we know our individual existence but also on the *unique quality* of this existence. That he, Blaise Pascal, should exist at this time, in this place, with this utterly personal and inimitable *individuality* seemed to him a subject worthy of much meditation. In Pascal's words: "When I consider the short duration of my life, swallowed up in the eternity before and after, the little space which I fill, and even can see, engulfed in the infinite immensity of spaces of which I am ignorant, and which know me not, I am frightened, and am astonished at being here rather than there; for there is no reason why here rather than there, why now rather than then. Who has put me here? By whose order and direction have this place and time been allotted to me? . . . The eternal silence of these infinite spaces frightens me."[11]

The contemporary German metaphysician, Martin Heidegger, takes as the starting point of philosophy what he terms *Dasein*. *Dasein* or "being there" is the kind of being exhibited by human life as it is disclosed to us, with all its uniqueness and immediacy, in our consciousness. The type of being represented by things which are not *Dasein*, such as physical objects, Heidegger terms *vorhanden*—that is, things which are present or at hand. "Our" kind of be-

---

[11] B. Pascal, *Pensées*, 205, 206, Everyman's Library ed., W. F. Trotter (trans.), E. P. Dutton and Co., 1948, p. 61.

ing or *Dasein* is attended by a deep-rooted feeling of in-security. We are aware that our foothold in being is fundamentally shaky. As Heidegger puts it, we sense that we are *"thrown"* into being. At rare moments, we are pervaded by a feeling Heidegger calls dread (*Angst*). Dread is to be distinguished from fear. The object of fear is always *something*—a storm, an enemy, the loss of a job, etc. But the object of dread is *Nothing*. To Heidegger (as to Plato long ago), Nothing is not a metaphysical zero. Nothing is related to being. It is Other-than-being. On those infrequent occasions when we apprehend Nothing, what oppresses us is the feeling that everything has slipped away and ourselves with it.[12]

Existentialism

Heidegger's conception of being was taken up by the French philosopher and literary man, Jean-Paul Sartre, who popularized the doctrine known as *existentialism* which attracted world-wide attention after the close of the second great war. It is not easy to explain just what existentialism is, for men who are labeled "existentialists" frequently differ in basic beliefs. Sartre, for example, is an atheist, while Karl Jaspers is a Christian.

The term "existentialism" has several layers of meaning. Very generally, it refers to that type of philosophy in which the starting point is the personal experience of the philosopher himself. In their writings, men like St. Augustine, Pascal, Nietzsche, and Kierkegaard develop their thought autobiographically. Their deepest insights are drawn from their own personal histories. More particularly,

[12] M. Heidegger, "What Is Metaphysics?" R. F. C. Hull and Alan Crick (trans.), in *Existence and Being*, Henry Regnery Co., 1949, p. 366.

existentialism designates a certain quality common to the thought of such men as those named above—their sense of the *predicament of man*. It is not man in the abstract, not man as an "essence" that they write about; they care neither for Aristotle's "rational animal" nor for John Dewey's "intelligent agent." The man who interests the thinkers of the existentialist tradition is, as the Spanish philosopher Unamuno puts it, "The man of flesh and bone," *this* man in his individual and unique *existence* which is inseparable from his passion and his suffering.

Sartre's existentialism draws from two sources. The general source is the tradition of such philosophers as we have mentioned above who have what Unamuno calls "the tragic sense of life"; men who have emphasized the uniqueness of the individual man and the importance of his passion and his hopes. The more specific source of Sartre's existentialism is the teaching of Heidegger that philosophy must start from *Dasein*, the kind of being we know better than any other because it is our own. The conclusions Sartre draws from his doctrine of existence are not cheerful. For him, to exist is to be trapped. Each man is enmeshed in his own existence; that is his predicament. Sartre does not deny human freedom. Man cannot *not* be free. It is my awareness that I, and no other, am the source of my own acts which is at the root of that anguish which is the human condition. Most people try to hide from their own freedom by pretending that they are not free, that they are bound by moral rules which transcend them, or by some other being upon whom they are dependent, etc. But each man is alone with his own freedom. No one can take this burden from him. The only alternative to despair is to *act*, knowing existence for what it is, without deluding oneself with the hope of ultimate success or happiness. In this "engagement" lies the only meaning of human life. Commenting on Sartre's book *L'Être et le néant* (*Being and Nothing*), J. A. Bede says:

> Reality has no meaning save *for* the mind. It does not follow that all reality is *in* the mind. The outer world exists. "Human reality" [Heidegger's *Dasein*] is a centrifugal force incessantly directed toward physical objects or other persons treated as physical objects. It yearns to achieve the wholeness and self-identity which is the attribute of things without losing self-consciousness which is the attribute of man. This is a logical contradiction. Human existence then will be characterized by a lack, void, frustration. But by this very incompleteness we are capable of freedom; liberty—born in anguish—is a function of "le néant."[13]

CRITICAL CONCEPTIONS OF METAPHYSICS

Since the eighteenth century there have been a number of conceptions of metaphysics which agree on this: that *metaphysics is concerned with things which cannot be shown to have actual existence*. While these critical conceptions of metaphysics are generally in accord concerning the indemonstrability of the actual existence of those entities talked about by metaphysicians, they differ as to the value or importance of metaphysics as an intellectual discipline.

Kant's Metaphysical Agnosticism

According to Kant, metaphysics is a study peculiar to that department of the knowing mind he calls reason. *Intuition* or sensibility furnishes us with the concepts of mathematics.

[13] J. A. Bede, "Sartre," in *The Columbia Dictionary of Modern European Literature*, Columbia University Press, 1947.

Understanding is divided into categories which supply the general concepts necessary for physical science. *Reason* provides the concepts of metaphysics. Now the "ideas" of mathematics and physical science order or pull together some kind of material which comes to us in *experience*, even though we can never know the nature of that material as it exists independently of our minds. But, says Kant, the "ideas" of metaphysics have *no* foundation in experience.

What are these metaphysical "ideas" for which experience fails to provide any basis? There are three of them: (1) the *psychological idea* deals with the question of the permanence of the "self" and the immortality of the soul; (2) the *cosmological idea* treats of the question whether the world is eternal or had a beginning in time and whether *freedom* exists anywhere in the series of causes and effects which constitutes the world; (3) the *theological idea* concerns the existence of God, the first cause or "ground" of the world. In sum, the three primary metaphysical "ideas" are God, freedom, and immortality.

Kant uses the word "idea" in a special sense in this connection. "By idea," he says, "I understand the necessary concept of reason to which the senses can supply no corresponding object."[14] In other words, sensory experience gives us no ground to support convictions such as the existence of God, freedom, and the immortality of the soul. Metaphysics can never tell us more than this: it is *possible* that objects exist which correspond to these concepts. It may be that there is an enduring self and a God upon whom the world depends. But human reason can never show that these things have actual existence. Metaphysics, says Kant,

[14] I. Kant, *Critique of Pure Reason* (rev. ed.), Max Müller (trans.), The Macmillan Company, 1922, p. 266.

is a study for which we have a natural inclination; but it is deceptive and *dialectical* in its nature. For reason will provide us with arguments of equal force for *either side* of the disputed issues. For example, the weight of the arguments supporting free will are exactly balanced by the weight of the arguments which prove that all our acts are determined.

But Kant has a word of comfort for metaphysicians. Even though reason cannot establish the actual existence of metaphysical objects, such as God, neither can reason demonstrate that they do *not* exist. Therefore, metaphysics can at least teach us not to adopt uncritical dogmatic views such as atheism and materialism. If nothing else, the ideas of reason are valuable as *ideals*. Moreover, the concern of metaphysics for subjects like God, freedom, and immortality can prepare us for sympathetic consideration of these topics in *moral philosophy*. There we learn that, while we cannot *prove* the existence of God, freedom, and immortality through our knowing minds, nevertheless as moral agents we must *postulate* their existence.

Metaphysics as the Study of Nonnatural Objects; G. E. Moore

The British philosopher G. E. Moore takes the position that metaphysics deals with things which are *possible* rather than things which are *actual*. Moore calls anything which has actual existence a "natural object." Now metaphysical statements, he believes, are never about natural objects. Such propositions are always statements about something *supersensible*. That is, they concern things which are not objects of perception and which cannot be inferred from things which *are* objects of perception. According to

Moore, inquiry into the realm of things which have not actual but only possible existence is by no means an illegitimate enterprise. Metaphysics has the edifying effect of teaching us that not all objects of knowledge are natural objects. In other words, metaphysics can inform us that there are many interesting forms of *being* which do not have actual *existence*. According to Moore, the trouble with most metaphysicians to date is that they do not realize that they are talking about objects which have no actual existence. When, like Plato, they refer to a supersensible reality—a world of eternal Forms, for example—they mistakenly suppose that this nonobservable realm has actual existence. In Moore's words:

I admit that "metaphysics" should investigate what reasons there may be for belief in such a supersensible reality; since I hold that its peculiar province is the truth about all objects which are not natural objects. And I think that the most prominent characteristic of metaphysics in history has been its profession to *prove* the truth about non-natural existents. I define "metaphysical," therefore, by a reference to supersensible *reality;* although I think that the only non-natural objects about which it has succeeded in obtaining truth, are objects which do not exist at all.[15]

To put what Moore is saying in another way: Metaphysics would be a thoroughly admirable enterprise if only metaphysicians would realize that they are talking about those objects which Santayana calls "essences"—things which are quite wonderful in their way, but which have no status in the world of natural fact.

[15] G. E. Moore, *Principia Ethica* (1902), Cambridge University Press, 1951, p. 112.

The Empiricist Critique of Metaphysics

The conceptions of metaphysics examined in the preceding sections are *critical* in that they set limits to the subject. Yet they are essentially friendly criticisms, since they concede to metaphysics a legitimate, if restricted, status. There are, however, many contemporary philosophers whose attitude toward metaphysics is not only critical but skeptical. The most that metaphysics can offer, they say, is poetry; the rest is nonsense.

Most of these anti-metaphysical philosophers belong to that tradition of extreme empiricism which derives from Continental positivism and from Hume. Comte, the father of positivitism, considered metaphysics as a prescientific stage of the development of human knowledge.[16] With science available, Comte believed, philosophers should abandon metaphysical speculation and devote their energies to constructing a unified encyclopedia of the sciences. Hume, as we have seen, believed that there were only two kinds of significant statements: those which treat of formal relations such as we find in mathematics and those which refer to observable facts. Metaphysics consists of statements which fall into neither one of these categories. Therefore, the study should be abandoned as a vain pursuit. In Hume's words: "If we take in our hand any volume; of divinity, or school metaphysics, for instance; let us ask, *Does it contain any abstract reasoning concerning quantity or number?*

---

[16] Comte distinguished three stages in the development of the intellectual life of man: (1) the *theological* stage, during which men explained everything by gods and spirits, (2) the *metaphysical* stage, in which men accounted for things by invoking essences and hidden causes, (3) the *positive* stage, under which men would not go beyond the observable facts in constructing explanations.

No. *Does it contain any experimental reasoning concerning matter of fact and existence?* Commit it to the flames. For it can contain nothing but sophistry and illusion."[17]

Contemporary anti-metaphysical empiricists and "philosophers of language" attack metaphysics, as we have noted before, on the ground that metaphysical propositions are unverifiable by procedures involving sense experience. From such propositions we are not able to deduce any statement asserting any experience whatever which may be expected for the future. Metaphysical propositions, says Carnap, assert nothing at all.[18] Carnap's disciple A. J. Ayer opens his assault on metaphysics with Hume's gambit: "We may . . . define a metaphysical sentence as a sentence which purports to express a genuine proposition, but does in fact express neither a tautology nor an empirical hypothesis. And as tautologies and empirical hypotheses form the entire class of significant propositions, we are justified in concluding that all metaphysical assertions are nonsensical."[19]

Consider, says Ayer, a statement chosen at random from the pages of a metaphysical book *Appearance and Reality* by F. H. Bradley: "The Absolute enters into, but is itself incapable of, evolution and progress."[20] No means whatever can be specified which would determine whether this statement is true or false. It is therefore not a genuine proposition but a pseudo proposition. The quantity of metaphysical statements about such topics as "being" or "tran-

[17] D. Hume, *An Enquiry Concerning Human Understanding*, Open Court Publishing Co., 1935, Section 12, part 3.
[18] R. Carnap, *op. cit.*, p. 17.
[19] A. J. Ayer, *Language, Truth and Logic* (rev. ed.), Victor Gollancz Ltd., London, 1948, p. 41.
[20] F. H. Bradley, *Appearance and Reality* (rev. ed.), Oxford University Press, 1946, p. 442.

scendental reality" arises from defective linguistic analysis. Because philosophers have found that they can talk about all sorts of names which do not designate actual existents, they have supposed that there must be a special mode of being, differing from actual existence, which is inhabited by these nonexistents. What remains in metaphysics, Ayer concludes, over and above statements about some transcendent reality or other entities generated in linguistic confusion, are a number of passages which manifest genuine mystical feeling and which may have some moral or aesthetic value.

Can Metaphysics Be Defended?

F. H. Bradley, the author of the now notorious proposition about the Absolute and evolution quoted above, once jocosely defined metaphysics as "the finding of bad reasons for what one believes on instinct." In a more serious vein, Bradley remarks that a man who is ready to prove that metaphysics is impossible is a brother metaphysician with a rival theory of his own. With reference to Bradley's second statement, his critics point out that this type of *tu quoque* argument ("You yourself do it!") can easily be overworked. For example, it is not a very powerful argument against atheism to claim that a man who says "There is no God" is himself making a theological statement. Nevertheless, there is some strength in Bradley's implicit charge of dogmatism against the anti-metaphysical empiricists. It is probably never wise to include in one's philosophic doctrine a rule that people are forever barred by that rule from pursuing certain lines of inquiry, however unprofitable they may appear to be. For such an attitude tends to suggest that the critic is thoroughly familiar with what lies beyond the boundary he has marked "Closed."

But now to the point. The question of the legitimacy of metaphysics depends in large part on how one interprets the term "metaphysics." It is doubtless true that philosophic minds of certain types are inclined to construct systems of explanation which have little to do in any important way with human experience. In so far as critiques of metaphysics serve to recognize this inclination and to expose the absurdities to which it frequently leads, such critiques are valuable *correctives*. But the usual empiricist criticism assumes that metaphysics *must* by its very nature lack contact with experience. Metaphysics is identified as a subject which *by definition* deals with that which lies beyond experience. The subject is alleged to be the study of a "transcendent reality" or some other inaccessible domain. "I will call *metaphysical*," says Carnap, "all those propositions which claim to represent knowledge about something which is over and beyond all experience."[21] It would be pretty difficult to find any philosopher today who would defend a subject defined in those terms.

There is no compulsion to believe that metaphysics can be defined only as an inquiry into things which are beyond experience. A metaphysician is not necessarily committed to belief in the existence of some mysterious realm which has no contact at all with the world of sense. "Metaphysics" may be understood in some other way—for example, as *an attempt to provide some unified and systematic explanation of the numerous and widely different kinds of experience we have.* To those (like Carnap) who believe that science can provide such explanation, and that this explanation is adequate, metaphysics will have the task of arranging the broad conclusions of the special sciences in systematic form. To those (like Whitehead), on the other hand, who do *not*

[21] R. Carnap, *op. cit.*, p. 15.

believe that scientific statements can adequately describe all phases of human experience, metaphysics will have the work of integrating scientific conclusions with accounts of those phases of human experience for which scientific explanations are deemed insufficient. In either case, metaphysics would appear to be quite unobjectionable, and its study a legitimate and important intellectual pursuit.

METAPHYSICS AND EXPERIENCE; WHITEHEAD

Whitehead's Conception of Metaphysics

Metaphysics or speculative philosophy is defined by Whitehead as the endeavor to frame a system of general ideas in terms of which every element of our experience can be interpreted.[22] In contrast to conceptions of metaphysics as a subject which inquires into things no one can experience, Whitehead's definition emphasizes that speculative philosophy can have meaning only in so far as it is based on and continuous with experience. "Experience," in Whitehead's view, is not just one especially selected set of experiences like science. The data of science are important and must be taken up into any system of speculative philosophy which pretends to be adequate. But science takes a special and abstract view of things. There are important facts, Whitehead believes, which elude scientific method. An example of an experience which cannot adequately be described in scientific concepts would be that arising from a poet's contact with Nature, the sort of experience Wordsworth had when he wrote:

---

[22] Whitehead's exact wording is: "Speculative Philosophy is the endeavor to frame a coherent, logical, necessary system of general ideas in terms of which every element of our experience can be interpreted." *Process and Reality*, The Macmillan Company, 1929, p. 4.

> Ye Presences of Nature in the sky
> And on the earth! Ye visions of the hills!
> And Souls of lonely places! . . .

Speculative philosophy, Whitehead believes, must be constructed on the basis of *all* phases of experience; this includes poetic, moral, social, and religious experiences, as well as scientific. The task of metaphysics is the endeavor to bring together under a general system of explanation the abstractions of science and the concrete experiences for which scientific explanations are inadequate.

The Character of Whitehead's Metaphysics

It is possible to agree with Whitehead's conception of *what metaphysics is* without accepting his own highly individual metaphysical doctrine. Nevertheless, it is only natural that this philosopher's definition of metaphysics should tie in with his particular view of the universe. Basic to Whitehead's world view is his teaching of the *interconnectedness of things.* For purposes of a particular interest—such as scientific experiment or religious meditation—we may fix our attention on certain aspects of experience as if they were separate from the total context of experience. But within that total context all things are interrelated.

The word "things" may be misleading. In Whitehead's lexicon there are no things; there are *events.* The basic units of experience are not *substances*—fixed, permanent, static entities which can be separated and isolated from changing qualities. Change is at the very heart of "things." "One all-pervasive fact," says Whitehead, "inherent in the very character of what is real is the transition of things, the passage one to another."[23] We are involved in a great *process* which includes myriads of interrelated events. Within

[23] A. N. Whitehead, *Science and the Modern World*, The Macmillan Company, 1925, p. 135.

this shifting flux we can point to unities or patterns, such as a mountain, the American nation, or a rose. These unities or patterns have varying degrees of stability and definiteness. But even the most permanent of these unities are ever shifting and blurring their lines with those of other unities with which they are fused. The most stable of patterns fade and finally disappear as fresh forces of creative novelty emerge in the world process. For practical purposes, we speak of the world as if it were made up of "facts." But facts are not ultimate. Process is ultimate.

The universe, then, consists not of passive enduring matter but of centers of activity. Now these active unities which constitute the world are *interrelated*. They are entwined with one another as organisms merge with their environments. And, just as organism and environment reciprocally influence one another, so it is with all the events we discern in the world process: each contributes to the other's character and qualities. "There is no possibility of a detached, self-contained local existence," says Whitehead. "The environment enters into the nature of each thing."[24]

To Whitehead, Nature is a seamless web. Throughout the world process run feelings of mutual awareness. Each individual activity takes account of all the activities with which it is connected. We participate in natural processes, and these, in some way, take account of us and of each other. There are no gaps, no sharp-cut divisions, no "bifurcations" in the nature of things. Feeling and consciousness, life and mind, are no monopolies of man. They are qualities of the world process with which we are integrated. *Value*—the quality we sense in aesthetic, moral, social, or religious experience—is not a purely subjective reaction

[24] A. N. Whitehead, *Modes of Thought*, The Macmillan Company, 1938, p. 188.

confined to the human sphere. Value is an ingredient in the cosmos, an element of the total metaphysical situation, not just of that part of it man occupies. Nature, of which all these factors are components, cannot be described in terms of one isolated set of categories—moral, poetic, or scientific. Description of Nature in terms of sense perception approaches adequacy least of all: "Sense-perception, for all its practical importance, is very superficial in its disclosure of the nature of things. . . . My quarrel with modern epistemology concerns its exclusive stress upon sense-perception for the provision of data respecting Nature. Sense-perception does not provide the data in terms of which we interpret it."[25] These are the words of a philosopher in the great rationalist tradition.

Through the many-sidedness of human experience, Whitehead tells us, we become aware of the multiple aspects of the great cosmic adventure in which we are involved. The mathematician, the poet, the religious teacher, the physicist, the social reformer, the political leader—each has experiences which yield partial insights into the character of the world process. The task of speculative philosophy is to show this character in its totality. The metaphysician's view must be synoptic.

FURTHER READINGS

Aquinas, Thomas, *Concerning Being and Essence (De Ente et Essentia)*, G. G. Leckie (trans.), D. Appleton-Century Co., 1937.

Aristotle, *Metaphysics*, Books 3–9.

Ayer, A. J., *Language, Truth and Logic* (rev. ed.), Victor Gollancz Ltd., London, 1948.

[25] *Ibid.*, p. 182.

Bergson, Henri, *An Introduction to Metaphysics,* T. E. Hulme (trans.), G. P. Putnam's Sons, 1912.

Carnap, R., *Philosophy and Logical Syntax,* Kegan Paul, Trench, Trubner and Co., London, 1935.

Collingwood, R. G., *Metaphysics,* Clarendon Press, Oxford, 1940.

Feibleman, James K., *Ontology,* John Hopkins Press, 1951.

Kant, Immanuel, "Transcendental Dialectic," in *Critique of Pure Reason* (rev. ed.), Max Müller (trans.), The Macmillan Company, 1922.

Kant, Immanuel, *Prolegomena to Any Future Metaphysics,* L. E. Beck (ed.), Liberal Arts Press, 1950.

Plato, *Sophist.*

Santayana, George, *The Realm of Essence,* Charles Scribner's Sons, 1927.

Whitehead, A. N., "Nature and Life," in *Modes of Thought,* The Macmillan Company, 1938.

Whitehead, A. N., "The Romantic Reaction," in *Science and the Modern World,* The Macmillan Company, 1925, p. 135.

In Connection with Existentialism

Collins, James, *The Existentialists,* Henry Regnery Co., 1952.

Grene, M., *Dreadful Freedom: A Critique of Existentialism,* University of Chicago Press, 1948.

Harper, R., *Existentialism: A Theory of Man,* Harvard University Press, 1948.

Heidegger, Martin, "What Is Metaphysics?" R. F. C. Hull and Alan Crick (trans.), in *Existence and Being,* Henry Regnery Co., 1949.

Kierkegaard, Soren, *A Kierkegaard Anthology,* Robert Bretall (ed.), Princeton University Press, 1946.

Pascal, B., *Pensées,* Everyman's Library, E. P. Dutton and Co., 1948.

Wahl, J., *A Short History of Existentialism,* F. Williams and S. Maron (trans.), Philosophical Library, 1949.

7

MIND, MATTER, AND NATURE

*Almost all philosophers have confused
ideas of things. They speak of material
things in spiritual terms, and of spiritual
things in material terms.*

—PASCAL

THERE seem to be two very different kinds or states of
"being" in the world. On the one hand, there are physical
objects and events. On the other, there are our thoughts
and feelings. We often refer to this distinction as that between *mind* and *matter*. The distinction is complicated by
the fact that we who have these thoughts and feelings are
also physical objects. However significant a man's thoughts,
however noble his loves, when you trip him with a stick,
he falls downstairs just like any other physical object.
Granting (as it seems we must) that both types of being,
mental and physical, have some kind of status in the world,
the question may be raised: Which kind of being is primary
and basic, and which is secondary or derivative?

Metaphysicians frequently tell us that the subject of their
study is the nature of reality. What is reality? It is that to
which we refer when we are pushed to ultimate explanations of the character of things. In terms of which kind of
being, mental or physical, is reality most adequately described? To this question the philosophical *idealist* will reply: the basic character of reality is analogous to mind,

thought, consciousness. Physical being cannot be understood without reference to the activity of a knowing mind. The order of physical things and events is secondary to and dependent upon the order of mind and knowledge. On the other hand, the philosophical *materialist* will tell us that the basic character of reality should be interpreted in physical terms. All things and events, including life, consciousness, and mind, are most adequately explained as particular states of matter or energy. The philosophical *naturalist* will answer that both the idealist and the materialist focus onesidedly on two genuine aspects of what is essentially *one* real situation, that is, Nature. To the naturalist, Nature is the real. From Nature arise both mind and matter, and to Nature both must be referred as their ultimate source. Nature is all that there is; no supernatural order exists. Our present task is to gain some further understanding of these three world perspectives, which we may label respectively idealism, materialism, and naturalism.

IDEALISM

The Meaning of "Idealism"

In ordinary conversation we use the word "idealist" to refer to a person who envisions and strives to reach goals so high that their complete achievement is unlikely. Thus, we say that Woodrow Wilson was an idealist or that the supporters of the United Nations are idealistic men and women. Philosophical idealism must be taken in a different sense. Very generally, the philosophical idealist takes the position that what is real, what is fundamental in the nature of things, resembles or has some important affinity to human thought, mind, consciousness, or spirit. "Outside of spirit," says idealist F. H. Bradley, "there is not, and there cannot be, any reality, and the more that anything is spiritual, so much the more it is veritably real."[1]

We may distinguish three main types of idealism: (1) ancient Greek idealism, particularly that of Plato, (2) the "empirical" idealism developed by Berkeley in the eighteenth century, (3) modern German idealism and its related forms. German idealism comprehends the doctrines of a whole line of philosophers including Leibniz, Kant, Fichte, Schelling, Hegel, and Schopenhauer. What is called "absolute idealism" is related to the Hegelian type and includes among its proponents the late nineteenth-century English philosophers Bernard Bosanquet and F. H. Bradley, the Italian Benedetto Croce, and the American Josiah Royce, who was a colleague of William James at Harvard. The metaphysics of the "transcendentalist" movement in America, of which Emerson is the best-known representative, derives in part from German idealism.

Platonic Idealism

Plato's "Ideas" are not psychological states; they are not simply ideas "in somebody's head." They are neither the subjective sensations of Berkeley nor the innate categories of Kant. Platonic Ideas are timeless and heavenly models of which things in the world are imperfect copies and of which thoughts in our minds are dim reflections. Plato, following a line of thought suggested by his master Socrates, arrived at this position in the following way.

Experience conveys to us this truth, says Plato, that there is nothing that can be observed by the senses which endures. All objects perceived by the senses are perpetually

[1] F. H. Bradley, *Appearance and Reality* (rev. ed.), Oxford University Press, 1946, p. 489.

changing, becoming, perishing; they never really *are*. Now, in contrast to the shifting quality of the multiple and ephemeral objects which make up the world of sense, there is the quality of general notions or concepts like "man," "triangle," or "justice" which are constantly employed in human discourse. To these general notions sense experience gives us no corresponding objects. For no one of us ever did see triangle; we see only this triangle. Nor did we ever observe good; we see only this good man. Now any particular triangle is subject to erasure; any individual good man changes with age and finally dies. But the concepts of triangle, man, good, justice, and the rest survive the passing away of any one of their particular embodiments. Long after the death of Socrates, we continue to speak of "good" and "man" in connection with other individuals.

How can we explain the existence in our minds of these universal concepts whose originals are never disclosed by sense experience, yet which outlast the objects we perceive by our senses? These notions, says Plato, are the products of reason or intelligence. To these notions correspond real objects. Unlike the objects of sense perception which are multiple and subject to change and decay, the objects with which reason puts us in touch are single and changeless. But where are these changeless unities? Plato tells us that they inhabit another world, a world that is stable and eternal in contrast to the shifting world of sense: "But of the heaven which is above the heavens, what earthly poet ever did or will sing worthily? It is such as I will describe. . . . There abides the very being with which true knowledge is concerned; the colourless, formless, intangible essence, visible only to the mind, the pilot of the soul."[2]

The hierarchy of eternal Ideas is the original source of

[2] Plato, *Phaedrus*, B. Jowett (trans.), 247.

what poor measure of reality our world possesses. Whatever imperfect suggestion of order and unity we may find in the world of sense must be traced back to these deathless models which are the prototypes of all order and unity. Not only are the Ideas the cause of all *being;* they are the cause of all *knowledge* as well. For the universal concepts of general notions we have in our minds are but reflections within us of the light from this realm of real being. Sense percepts report only the unstable, flickering character of the physical world. "There are two patterns eternally set before us," says Plato, "the one blessed and divine, the other godless and wretched."[3] Or again, "There are two ruling powers, and one of them is set over the intellectual world, the other over the visible."[4] In sum, the world disclosed by sense perception is appearance or semi-real only, in contrast to "true being," the supremely rational order of things upon which the world depends and to which "mind" alone can penetrate.

Berkeley's Idealism

Berkeley's idealism, unlike that of Plato, whose theory of knowledge is strongly *rationalistic*, arises out of an *empiricist* analysis of knowledge he shares with Locke and Hume. This consists, as we have seen, in taking sense data as the material of knowledge. The line of argument Berkeley uses to establish the proposition that the real world is a mental world is familiar to us. What we know are our sensations and ideas compounded from these. These sensations are popularly (and wrongly) believed to be caused by material things to which they correspond. Berkeley tells

[3] Plato, *Theaetetus*, 176.
[4] Plato, *Republic*, 509.

us that there is no way of demonstrating that physical objects exist independently of us with the properties they
appear to have, for every object of which we can have
knowledge is a "sensed" or "experienced" object. Since
we cannot know objects apart from our experience of them,
the properties of objects, and indeed their very existence,
depend upon a perceiving mind or experiencing consciousness.

On the basis of these arguments Berkeley concludes that
the external world is the sum total of a series of effects
produced in our consciousness by a cause which is not a
physical thing at all. This ultimate cause of our ideas is God,
a Supreme Mind or Spirit who presides over a society of
finite minds or spirits. Berkeley's God is the benevolent
counterpart of Descartes's malignant demon; a good genius
rather than an evil one, and real rather than possible. What
we call "Nature" is the result of God's stimulating in our
several minds a coherent and rational system of sensations
or ideas. By his constant production of ideas in human consciousness, God sustains the existence of the world. In
Berkeley's words:

Some truths there are so near and obvious to the mind that
a man need only open his eyes to them. Such I take this important one to be, to wit, that all the choir of heaven and
furniture of the earth, in a word all those bodies which compose the mighty frame of the world, have not any subsistence
without a mind, that their *being* is to be perceived or known;
that consequently so long as they are not actually perceived
by me, or do not exist in my mind or that of any other created
spirit, they must either have no existence at all, or else subsist
in the mind of some Eternal Spirit. . . .[5]

[5] G. Berkeley, *Principles of Human Knowledge*, Open Court Publishing Co., 1903, p. 32.

Hegel's Idealism

Kant's theory of knowledge implies idealism. According to Kant what we know is appearance only. Things as they exist independently of ourselves (things-in-themselves) are unknowable to us. The world of appearance, however, is not a deceptive phantasm. It is an orderly and rational world. And it is orderly and rational because its structure is the product of the knowing *mind*. Now is the rational character of our world entirely the effect of the *human* mind ordering and arranging the data of experience by means of its innate categories? Or does the nature of things possess of itself a rational or intelligible character which transcends the human mind? Kant never made his answer to these questions wholly clear. But Kant's great successor, G. W. F. Hegel, leaves us in no doubt. Hegel denies that the rational structure of the world is simply the creation of the human mind. In Hegel's view, the human mind is but one particular aspect of a cosmic process, a world-embracing system which has a logical and rational structure in its own right. That is why Hegel's brand of idealism is sometimes called "Objective Idealism."

According to Hegel, there is at work in the heart of things something we may call "self-consciousness." Now self-consciousness is a property of human thought. Not only do we know; we know that we know. Self-consciousness, however, transcends or goes beyond the thought of the individual human. The universe is an all-encompassing organic whole which is in a constant state of development toward greater consciousness of itself. This cosmic process is something like a mighty system of logical thought which contains both mind and Nature. The world is a series of progressive stages of development toward a state of supreme self-consciousness, free of limitation, which Hegel calls Absolute Spirit. If we view things and events—history, art, religion, science, Nature itself—against the background of their widest set of relations, we see that they are stages of development thrown off, as it were, by Spirit as it moves through the world via progressively higher levels of growth toward complete self-realization. Now the meaning of this rational, spiritual First Principal cannot be grasped until we have studied its development from the partial and limited forms in which it reveals itself to its final all-embracing unity. The task of philosophy is to chart the development of Spirit. In order to accomplish this, we must understand the laws through which the stages of Spirit's growth are disclosed.

First we must construct a logic, says Hegel. Not a formal logic composed of tautologies, but a "real" logic which has *content*. Since human thought and Nature are but interrelated parts of a rational cosmic process, the laws of thought are inseparable from the laws of reality. The rational is the real. We shall discover that thought moves *dialectically*, and we shall find that Nature moves in the same way. What is dialectic? It is an advance through opposites. An ordinary town-meeting argument provides a homely illustration, if the opposed points of view genuinely advance the discussion and lead to a solution of the problem under consideration. Such a solution will contain propositions advanced by each of the opposed parties but will be more comprehensive than any one of their one-sided views. To Hegel, thought is a dialectical process manifesting an interplay of opposing tendencies and forces. But the existence of these polar opposites in thought does not block the progressive realization of what Hegel calls the Absolute Idea. On the contrary, the Idea must move *through* opposites in order to manifest itself on higher levels.

Take any element in the thought process, be it concept or judgment, and call it *A*. Now *A* has its own self-identity and is what it is. This is *thesis*, the first stage of the dialectical process. But it is not the whole story, for perfect self-identity presupposes that *A* is immune to change, which it is not. What happens is that *A* from within itself generates its own opposite—let us call it *not-A*. This is *antithesis*, the second stage of the dialectic. The third stage is marked by a reconciliation of these opposites, but on a higher or more advanced level, which we may call *B*. This is the stage of *synthesis*. But *B* itself is also subject to dialectical development and generates its own opposite within itself, following which these opposites are reconciled in a higher synthesis *C*, and so on.

Hegel invites us to consider the concept of *Being*. Analysis of Being discloses that this concept is so empty and abstract that it may be identified with its opposite, *Nothing*. In the dialectical process, Being and its opposite Nothing are "taken up" into the "higher" concept of *Becoming*, which includes them both and yet transcends them: "Being, as Being, is nothing fixed or ultimate: it yields to dialectic and sinks into its opposite, which also taken immediately, is Nothing. . . . Nothing, if it be thus immediate and equal to itself, is also conversely the same as being is. The truth of Being and of Nothing is accordingly the unity of the two: and this unity is BECOMING."[6] Thus the process of thought is carried to successively higher stages in which that

---

[6] *The Logic of Hegel* (rev. ed.), Wm. Wallace (trans.), Clarendon Press, Oxford, 1892, pp. 161, 163.

final rational synthesis Hegel calls "Idea" becomes progressively more manifest. The highest unity of thought, within which all opposition is finally reconciled and integrated, is the Absolute Idea.

Now we move from the order of logic to the order of reality. The Absolute Idea which is the goal of the dialectical process of thought is but the first stage in the ultimate dialectic of the real. In that final process of the whole, we see *Idea* as thesis, *Nature* as antithesis, and *Spirit* as synthesis. Here we see the "objective" character of Hegelian idealism on grand dimensions. The *subjective* side of things—mind, thought, Idea—forms but one pole of reality. The opposite pole is the sphere of the *objective*, which is Nature. But subject (Idea) and object (Nature) do not exhaust reality, for these two polar realms are "taken up" within one final all-containing synthesis. This ultimate reconciliation of all opposites is Absolute Spirit, the history of whose progress toward self-realization is the ground of all histories, political as well as cultural. Thus philosophy, which begins with the particular self-consciousness of the individual human mind, at length discovers itself on the universal scale in the self-knowledge of Absolute Spirit.

Hegel was convinced that the various stages of historical development of science, art, religion, politics, and human culture generally could only be understood as phases of the process of self-realization by Absolute Spirit. He fleshes out the theoretical and abstract side of his doctrine by reference to striking examples of human experience which lend themselves to dialectical interpretation. It is a matter of regret that we cannot examine the evidence Hegel draws from various levels of cultural activity to support his formidable rationalism. Hegelian metaphysics is regarded by many critics as an outrageous farrago of nonsense. Nonsense or no, Hegel's philosophy made a deep impression on a modern century's thought. His dialectical method was adapted by Marx and Engels (as we shall see) in such a way as to provide a theoretical basis for communism. His metaphysical doctrine became a powerful factor in the development of absolute idealism, considered by many as the most important stage in the development of philosophical idealism.

Absolute Idealism

In Hegelian idealism we find that the world is described as a process akin to a system of thought, this thought system being a partial aspect of a comprehensive principle or absolute which is the ground of everything. What is called absolute idealism—the doctrine associated with thinkers like Bradley, Croce, Royce, and the rest—may be regarded as a development of this thesis. Absolute idealism prefers not to describe the real as a system of *thought*, but rather (more broadly) as a system of *experience*. The absolute idealist holds that there is no reality apart from some experience, and that reality is a vast unified system of experiences internally coherent and mutually interdependent. Whose experiences? Who or what is *having* the experiences? Human experience is partial and limited; one would not expect human experience to be identical with the ultimate nature of reality. True, says the absolute idealist, but human experience is always developing; our knowledge is constantly growing. As human experience progressively widens, it approximates more and more closely to a total system of interrelated experiences in which no single experience can be completely understood apart from the perspective of the whole. As human knowledge increases, it moves nearer and nearer to identifying itself with an all-embracing system of experiences which contains, and indeed makes possible, any particular experience. This all-containing system of experiences is reality, the absolute. Since human knowledge represents only an approximation of this final system of experiences, we do not know reality, but appearances only. But human experience is constantly widening out. It is at the same time becoming the subject of increasingly more systematic interpretation, with one realm of experience after another seen to be interdependent within the whole. Therefore, appearances may become progressively less unreal. Says F. H. Bradley: "Reality is one . . . it is essentially experience. There is nothing in the Whole beside appearance, and every fragment of appearance qualifies the Whole; while on the other hand, so taken together, appearances, as such, cease. Nothing in the universe can be lost, nothing fails to contribute to the single Reality. . . . And hence, because nothing in the end can be *merely* itself, in the end no appearance, as such, can be real. But appearances fail of reality in varying degrees; and to assert that one on the whole is worth no more than another, is fundamentally vicious."[7]

Perhaps we can see now a little more clearly why a coherence theory of truth is essential to absolute idealism. A judgment is made on the basis of experience. Its truth depends on whether that experience ties in with other experiences. If my judgments, based on my present experience, cohere with other judgments based on a wider set of experiences, my judgments acquire a higher degree of truth. But this wider set of experiences is itself tied in with still

[7] F. H. Bradley, *op. cit.*, p. 453.

wider sets of experience. These in turn derive what reality they possess from the all-embracing system of experiences which is reality itself. Therefore, the truth of any judgment derived from experience is ultimately constituted by its coherence with that complete system of judgments which would be formed if human knowledge could identify itself with the widest possible set of experiences, which is reality or the absolute.

Postscript; Other Varieties of Idealism

We must bring to a close our brief description of idealism without adequate reference to other varieties of this prolific metaphysical doctrine. There is a type of idealism known as *pluralistic* idealism, which sees what is real not as mind, but as *minds*. Reality is not a single absolute but a collection of centers of mental activity or consciousness, each of which has a certain independence. The seventeenth-century German philosopher Leibniz taught that the universe consisted of spiritual atoms called *monads*. All monads are conscious, but they may be graded according to the different degrees of consciousness they possess. The perception of the monads which make up physical bodies is duller than the perception of monads which compose the higher faculties of human beings.[8] This notion that everything which exists is to some degree conscious is called *panpsychism*. There is an element of panpsychism in Whitehead's metaphysics, for he holds that something analogous to *feeling* or mutual awareness pervades the cosmos and is

[8] Bertrand Russell once wondered whether it ever struck Leibniz as odd that the end of his nose should be a colony of spiritual beings. To which a critic of Russell's analysis of knowledge replied that it is just as odd to consider the end of one's nose a collection of brain states.

not restricted to organic life. A form of pluralistic idealism, well known in the United States, is called *personalism*. Personalists maintain that what is real is either a person or "self," or some part or aspect of a person. A person is defined as a "self" capable of rational thought and of forming ideal values.

MATERIALISM

Meaning of "Materialism"

We often hear moralists who deplore the present state of the world blame its shortcomings on "materialism." In this context of meaning, the word has a derogatory flavor; a materialist is one who attaches undue importance to money, property, power, and the like. In philosophy, the word is used rather differently. *Philosophical materialism* is that metaphysical view which holds that physical matter determines the basic character of things and events. The kind of being physical objects have is the only "real" kind; what we call mental or conscious experience derives from matter and can be explained in terms of the behavior of matter. Let us put the basic tenets of materialism in the form of three propositions:

1. All things and events, including life, consciousness, and mind, represent different levels of the organization and behavior of physical matter or energy.

2. Whatever happens is the effect of the operation of a uniform system of physical laws to which all things, conscious or not, are subject.

3. No God or any other spiritual agency is required to explain the existence and nature of the world.

The Monistic Character of Materialism

Both materialism and idealism are *monistic* systems of explanation. Any monism accounts for the world in terms of *one* fundamental category. The idealist's one all-inclusive principle is *mind;* the materialist's is *matter.* In this context, we may take the opposite of monism to be *dualism.* A dualistic position explains things in terms of two basic categories. The traditional account of the nature of man in terms of body and soul is dualistic. So is the traditional distinction between God and the world. Perhaps the most extreme form of dualism in Western philosophy is found in the metaphysics of Descartes, who held that there are two kinds of substances, material things and spiritual things, which are utterly *unlike.*

Now the first proposition of materialism denies any dualism between matter and life or matter and mind. Physical matter or energy, says the materialist, is the *one* fundamental reality; everything which seems to be different from matter or energy may be explained in terms of matter or energy. The second proposition implies that there is but *one* system of laws governing the totality of things and events. These are the patterns of behavior of matter and energy which the investigations of physical science have partly disclosed. The materialist denies any dualism which would set a particular kind of events apart from the uniform control of physical laws—those human actions, for example, which many suppose to be "free." The third proposition of materialism asserts that there is but *one* all-inclusive cosmological category—physical nature. This proposition denies the dualism implied by belief in the existence of any world transcending the physical universe—such as the Platonic ideas or the realm of supernature assumed in traditional theology or religion. Materialism denies the existence of God as a being distinct from the world.

Mechanism

The second proposition of materialism maintains that all things without exception are governed by a uniform system of physical laws. Implicit in this assertion is a doctrine known as *mechanism*, which together with its corollary *determinism* has been defended by most "classical" materialists. Mechanism asserts the primacy of a familiar type of causal sequence called *mechanical causality* in contrast to "free" or "purposive" causality. When one billiard ball knocks another into a certain position, we do not assume that the rolling ball "chooses" to act that way. Rather we assume that the ball "must" act that way if it is impelled by a certain force in a certain direction. Further, we would say that if, before the event occurred, we had all the relevant data—the weight of the ball, the point on its surface where it was hit, the force and direction of the stroke, etc. —we could by prior calculation *predict* the behavior of the ball in advance.

The investigations of the first three hundred years of modern science proceeded on the assumption that some kind of uniform mechanical causality operated throughout Nature. The enormous success of these investigations naturally enough led scientists and philosophers to affirm that *any* event is predictable in principle.[9] The astronomer La-

[9] The reader doubtless knows that contemporary physicists are not quite so sure of the universal predictability of physical events as were their nineteenth-century predecessors. Heisenberg's principle of indeterminacy was formed on the basis of experiments which indicate that certain aspects of the behavior of subatomic particles, taken individually, are not predictable.

place maintained that an intellect which knew the situations of all the bodies in Nature and the forces operating upon them could then calculate with certainty, not only all the past states of the universe, but every future state as well. A similar confidence radiates from Thomas Huxley:

If the fundamental proposition of evolution is true, that the entire world, living and not living, is the result of the mutual interaction, according to definite laws, of the forces possessed by the molecules of which the primitive nebulosity of the universe was composed, it is no less certain that the existing world lay, potentially, in the cosmic vapor, and that a sufficient intellect could, from a knowledge of the properties of the molecules of that vapor, have predicted, say the state of the Fauna of Great Britain in 1869, with as much certainty as one can say what will happen to the vapor of the breath in a cold winter's day.[10]

What does the materialist do with his concept of mechanical causality? He extends it in such a way that he sees it governing *all* things and events, including those we do not ordinarily think of in terms of mechanism. Human behavior can hardly be subject to the same laws that hold for the motion of billiard balls. Now the materialist will concede a far greater *complexity* in the human situation. Human beings are not simple objects like billiard balls. But, he will maintain, if we knew (and through science we are gradually coming to know) as much about the physical structure of the human organism as we do about billiard balls, we would realize that the difference between them is one of *degree* of complexity of structure rather than a radical distinction of *kind*. If we had sufficient data and could

[10] T. Huxley, cited by H. Bergson in *Creative Evolution*, A. Mitchell (trans.), Henry Holt and Co., 1911, p. 38.

control the variables, we would see that whatever a human organism does can be explained in terms of the antecedent physical states of that organism together with those of its environment—just as the motion of the ball may be adequately accounted for by a consideration of all the relevant physical circumstances.

Freedom and Purpose

If a uniform system of mechanical causality holds throughout Nature, then should not purposive or "teleological" causality be abandoned as a category of adequate explanation? The fact that a sunflower orients itself toward the sun is not to be accounted for on the ground that the sunflower *intends* to do so or because it unconsciously fulfills a purpose thereby. The behavior of the sunflower is *determined* by the physical factors present in the situation. The interpretation of physical, chemical, and biological events in terms of nonpurposive causality is basic to scientific method. Struck by the wonderful success of that method, the materialist would like to extend nonpurposive explanation to include everything, including human behavior of the type usually considered purposeful. Some materialists admit the existence of purposive cause in Nature but insist on the primacy of nonpurposive causality. Does it follow that human freedom is an illusion? Many materialists have drawn this conclusion without hesitation. If by "freedom" is meant exemption of any part of our behavior from basic or derivative physical laws, human actions are not "free."

According to John Watson, famous American behavioristic psychologist, human behavior is simply the result of conditioned reflexes. Pavlov's dog drooled at the sight of a steak accompanied by the sound of a bell; at length, the bell's ring alone produced the salivary response. Human behavior, says Watson, can be explained in terms of conditioned reflexes, allowing, of course, for the greater complexity of many human behavior situations. Could society only make up its mind what it wants, says Watson, psychologists with data and technical equipment sufficient to permit application of the necessary conditioning could turn out any kind of human being desired: "Give me a dozen healthy infants, well-formed, and my own specified world to bring them up in and I'll guarantee to take any one at random and train him to become any type of specialist I might select—doctor, lawyer, artist, merchant-chief and, yes, even beggar-man and thief, regardless of his talents, penchants, tendencies, abilities, vocations, and race of his ancestors."[11]

Mind, Life, and Value

But what is *mind?* Surely, human thought cannot be explained in terms of matter in motion! The materialist replies that, while we do not as yet understand fully the nature of mental activity, there is no reason why mind cannot be satisfactorily explained in physical terms. The mind's dependence on matter is evident. A minute fragment of bone driven from the skull into the brain can transform a noble, intelligent man into an obscene and driveling idiot. Nineteenth-century materialists said that mind is an *epiphenomenon*, a by-product of the processes of the physical organism, like the electrical glow that may sometimes be

[11] J. B. Watson, *Behaviorism* (rev. ed.), W. W. Norton and Co., 1930, p. 104.

seen hovering over a machine at work. Later, behaviorist psychologists said that mind can be described adequately in terms of observable behavior. Mental life is a fiction, said Watson, for thinking is but subvocal talking; that is, thinking is essentially motor contractions. Contemporary materialists are confident that recently developed calculating machines will dispel much of the mystery associated with human thought. These marvelous devices, they say, are like human brains; an important difference between the two is that the computers have a comparatively small number of electrical circuits, while the brain has millions.

The materialist reminds us that we inhabit a little planet which revolves about a rather unimportant star which is a member of a galaxy of stupendous dimensions, this galaxy itself only one of thirty million or so composing the physical universe. *Life* has arisen on our small planet as the result of a chance collocation of atoms. Temperature and other conditions happened to be suitable for life's development. The evolution of life is accounted for by the adaptation of living forms to the less highly organized physical environment. The complex character that life forms have assumed in the course of evolutionary history is no more to be put down to purposes inherent within these living forms than the shape of the human nose is to be explained on the ground that such a shape is most suitable for the wearing of spectacles. The universe itself has no inherent purposive direction. The man who said that there is "one far-off divine event toward which all creation moves" was no scientist, but a poet influenced by theology.

The materialist does not deny that human beings have values and ideals. These, however, he generally views as subjective in nature and related to external material factors as effect to cause. Ethical values develop from the desire of the organism to preserve its life and well-being. Aesthetic values arise from the need on the part of the organism to release emotional tensions brought about by physiological or environmental conditions. Religious values have their origin in the fears and insecurities of a highly sensitive animal organism, frightened by physical phenomena and overborne by the immensity of the universe.

Historical Background of Materialism

The doctrine that the ultimate cause of the world is physical stuff is found in the earliest Western philosophy. The Greek atomists (Leucippus, Democritus, and Epicurus) held that this physical material occurs in the form of tiny indivisible particles called *atoms* which move through space or *void* according to a principle of *necessity* inherent in things. All objects are combinations of atoms. The human mind is composed of particularly light and delicate particles. There are gods, but they too are physical beings composed of atoms. They have no control over the laws of Nature, nor do they interfere in human affairs. In his great philosophical poem *On the Nature of Things*, the Roman poet Lucretius sets this metaphysical doctrine to Latin verse. No need to fear death, Lucretius tells us, for death is but the dissolution of the society of atoms of which we are composed. There is no afterlife in which we shall be judged and punished for our misdeeds.

Materialism disappeared during the religious Middle Ages for obvious reasons. The rise of materialism in modern times is directly related to the development of the physical sciences. The conception of a world composed of physical bodies operating upon one another in regular predictable patterns went hand in hand with enormous advances in the understanding and control of natural processes. Newton's wonderful picture of a cosmic mechanism was quickly detached by his materialist admirers from his belief in God. Earlier Thomas Hobbes had already explained everything in terms of bodies in motion. His French contemporary Descartes was no materialist, but the Cartesian dictum that all living substances other than man were machines inevitably led to the question "Why not man also?" The eighteenth-century French materialist La Mettrie wrote a book titled *Man a Machine*. La Mettrie belonged to a group of free-thinking, anticlerical writers of the French Enlightenment—men like Diderot, d'Holbach, and D'Alembert—who helped popularize a rather naive mechanical materialism.

The triumph of Darwin's evolutionary theory in the nineteenth century was followed by a wave of popular materialist essays couched in the idiom of biology rather than physics. Huxley in England and Haeckel in Germany contributed to the growing popularity of the belief that living forms, including man, were but chance products of molecular combinations in a vast process of cosmic evolution. The disciples of the great Hegel in Germany included not only a religious and theologically inclined group (the "right-wing" Hegelians) but also a left wing, sympathetic to materialism and absorbed by problems of social and political reform. The disputations of these men provided an intellectual setting from which Karl Marx and Friedrich Engels developed the most powerful form of modern materialism. This is *dialectical materialism*, today the official metaphysics of the Soviet Union and, as such, well deserving of our separate attention.

Dialectical Materialism

This theory combines the fundamental materialist thesis that matter alone is real with the following propositions whose Hegelian origin is apparent: (1) all things are interconnected; (2) all things are in the process of development; (3) this development proceeds according to dialectical laws. This theoretical framework supports an explanation of human social and economic development in terms of the material needs of men, and of the social classes which have control of the production of necessities which satisfy those needs.

As we should expect, dialectical materialism asserts the primacy of matter. Says Engels: "The material, sensuously perceptible world to which we ourselves belong is the only reality. . . . Our consciousness and thinking are the product of a material, bodily organ, the brain. Matter is not a product of mind, but mind itself is merely the highest product of matter."[12] And Lenin says: "Matter is that which, acting upon our sense-organs, produces sensation; matter is the objective reality given to us in sensation. . . . Matter, nature, being, the physical—is primary, and spirit, consciousness, sensation, the psychical—is secondary. . . . The world picture is a picture of how matter moves and of how *'matter thinks.'* "[13]

To the dialectical materialist the world of matter does

[12] F. Engels, *Ludwig Feuerbach*, International Publishers (n.d.), pp. 39, 43.
[13] V. I. Lenin, *Materialism and Empirio-Criticism*, in *Selected Works*, International Publishers, 1943, vol. 11, pp. 207–208, 402.

not consist in a simple mechanical assemblage of physical
bodies isolated from and independent of each other. This,
they say, is eighteenth-century "mechanical" materialism
which must be corrected. The material world is "a connected and integral whole, in which things, phenomena,
are organically connected with, dependent on, and determined by, each other."[14] Not only is every part of this
material system interrelated with every other part; the entire system is constantly undergoing change and development. The older mechanical materialism, says Marx, fails
to account for change. It treats of change simply as the
relocation of static bits of matter in new positions—which
is no change at all. Dialectical materialism holds that change
is at the heart of Nature. Matter is not static, but dynamic.
It is constantly in development, which continually manifests itself in the formation of new forces and phenomena
and in the breakdown of the old.

How does matter change? The answer given by Marx
and Engels is that matter develops *dialectically*. Hegel was
wrong in claiming primacy for Idea and Spirit. His idealism
must be rejected. But Hegel was right in his belief that the
world process moves dialectically, that is, by means of
opposites inherent in the development of things. "In its
proper meaning," says Lenin, "dialectics is the study of the
contradiction within the very essence of things." The history of every object and event can be understood only in
terms of the development within that object or event of
its own opposite or contradiction, and the emergence of
that opposite upon the dissolution of that which gave it
birth.

[14] J. Stalin, *Dialectical and Historical Materialism,* International Publishers, 1940, p. 7.

To describe the dialectical development of the material world Marx and Engels adapted three Hegelian principles: (1) the law of transformation of quantity into quality; (2) the law of unity of opposites; (3) the law of the negation of the negation.

1. The law of transformation of quantity into quality is invoked to do justice to the genuine qualitative difference of things and to avoid the oversimplification of the older materialism in which qualitative differences are conceived merely as rearrangements of quantities of matter. Dialectical materialists say that in the development of matter new qualities arise at certain critical points or "nodes." The qualitative transformation is not gradual, for when the nodal point is reached, there is a comparatively quick change or "leap" into the new state. This may be illustrated by changing states of natural substances, as in the case of the freezing of a liquid. When the temperature of water is lowered, there comes a critical point at which the liquid changes quickly into a qualitatively new state—ice. Dialectical materialists see this law at work in the realm of social action as well as in physics. Industrial capitalism, a qualitatively new social order, sprang comparatively quickly into being, although the conditions favorable to its development had been in existence for a long time. So also with the Soviet Socialist order.

2. The law of the unity of opposites states the familiar dialectical principal of the essentially contradictory character of things. The unity of all objects and events covers an internal polarity of opposites. This doctrine was taught in early Greek philosophy by Heraclitus, who held that the apparent stability of things was the result of tension between opposite forces, as in the case of a bow or lyre string. Hegel maintained in his *Logic* that opposites, like positive and negative, never represent an absolute difference but are in some way identified. What is negative to the debtor is positive to the creditor. A way to the

East is also a way to the West. We cannot have the north pole of a magnet without a south pole. Applying this law to social theory, Marx asserted that at the basis of social conflict or "class struggle" was a contradiction between the methods of production available to a particular society and the social relationships characteristic of that society. Under capitalism, the proletariat or working class seeks to expand and to change the system of social relations to an extent comparable to the massive changes in the means of production brought about under capitalism. The proletariat, however, is opposed by the "bourgeoisie," who control the means of production; they strive to prevent or to limit the social changes demanded by the working class. When the conflict between the two opposing forces reaches its nodal or "breaking" point, there will occur, in accordance with the first of the three dialectical laws, a sudden and violent leap, via revolution, from bourgeois capitalism to a new social order, *scientific socialism*.

3. The law of the negation of the negation may be clarified if we consider any state of affairs to be developing its opposite or negation within itself in good Hegelian fashion. This negation in time breaks away to stand over against and in opposition to the state which gave it birth. But this second state (the first negation) generates its own opposite, which then stands forth as the negation of the first negation. According to Marx, capitalism cannot exist without its own negations. But these negations will ultimately negate capitalism. An example of the internal contradictions of capitalism is its tendency to overproduction, which brings about unemployment. This in turn prevents the workers from buying the goods produced. Thus arise economic crises or depressions in which the very existence of capitalist economy trembles in the balance. With the final collapse of capitalism will emerge the world socialism envisioned by Marx. This new social order is thus the negation of the negation. Here is Marx's illustration of this law: "The

capitalist mode of appropriation, the result of the capitalist mode of production, produces capitalist private property. This is the first negation of individual private property, as founded on the labor of the proprietor. But capitalist production begets, with the inexorability of a law of Nature its own negation. It is the negation of the negation."[15]

Comment on Dialectical Materialism

We shall see some criticisms of idealism and materialism in our exposition of naturalism which follows. But dialectical materialism deserves separate comment. It is difficult to appraise dialectical materialism impartially. In the first place, its soundness is contingent upon the worth of its Hegelian conceptual framework. Further, dialectical materialism depends heavily upon key concepts drawn from Marx's social philosophy, such as the "materialist conception of history." The adequacy of these concepts has been widely challenged by historians and economists. Moreover, the writings of dialectical materialists are usually so full of violent attacks on other positions that it is not easy to disengage exposition and support of the theory from the mass of polemic in which it is embedded.[16]

Yet many of its critics feel that dialectical materialism represents an important landmark in the development of materialism. It brings into materialism the causal role of social factors which the older materialism neglected. Its

[15] K. Marx, *Capital*, International Publishers (n.d.), vol. 1, p. 789.

[16] An example of the intemperate language typical of recent Soviet philosophy may be seen in the following extract from an outline of a projected Soviet history of philosophy:

"The tasks of this chapter are to subject to partisan Bolshevik criticism the reactionary, bourgeois ideology of the imperialist period; to show its connection with the general crisis of capitalism and with the corruption of all contemporary bourgeois culture; to pull to pieces with particular severity the reactionary philosophical and sociological doctrines used nowadays by the enemies of Marxism; to show that V. I.

Hegelian "rational kernel" enables it to correct many of the inadequacies of "mechanical" materialism. It recognizes the limitations of any materialism founded on a conception of the world as an essentially static system of isolated bodies moving about one another. The Marxian metaphysics replaces this "mechanical" materialism with a world perspective in which change and development are treated as internal and basic, rather than as external and accidental relocations of permanent particles in space.

Nevertheless, critics believe that the dialectical materialist's claim that "matter moves dialectically" is itself open to serious question. While striking instances of "dialectic" can be pointed out in Nature (for example, the polar character of electricity), there are many natural objects and events which do not seem to behave in a particularly dialectical manner. Such phenomena can be accounted for dialectically only by forcing the facts to fit the theory.

NATURALISM

The Meaning of Naturalism

Naturalism may be defined very generally as the belief that things and events have natural rather than supernatural causes; that the cosmos has a natural rather than a supernatural origin; that man has a natural rather than a supernatural end. Naturalism is a "this-worldly" rather than an "other-worldly" view of things. That is why, for example,

---

Lenin and J. V. Stalin tirelessly attacked the rotten anti-Marxist idealistic doctrines and reactionary social ideas of the imperialistic bourgeoisie and mercilessly exposed every kind of tendency toward idealism and priestcraft; and to emphasize that the contemporary bourgeois ideology is an arsenal of reactionary and odious ideas for the right-wing socialists —the lackeys of the imperialistic bourgeoisie." *A Soviet History of Philosophy*, William Edgerton (trans.), Public Affairs Press, 1950.

we speak of the "naturalism" of Chinese classical philosophy. Confucius was averse to any form of supernatural explanation and found all problems of interest to him in Nature and in human relations. For the same reason, we describe Aristotle's general approach to problems as "naturalistic," even though this philosopher believed in a God who was distinct from the world. For, despite his theology, Aristotle tends to explain things pretty generally without reference to another world. In this respect, we contrast Aristotle with the "other-worldly" Plato, who held that the ultimate explanation of things must be sought in the heavenly world of Ideas. Aristotle criticized his master's doctrine of the ideal world on the ground that it is superfluous to erect another world in order to explain this one. Such criticism is typical of the naturalist attitude.

Taken less broadly, "naturalism" refers to an approach to philosophy that has been steadily developing in the United States for the past fifty years. Toward the close of the last century the philosophy taught in American colleges was generally some form of idealism. The reaction against idealist metaphysics, led by Peirce, James, Dewey, and their followers, helped develop interests less concerned with systematic metaphysics than with inquiry into scientific method and an empirical approach to moral and social problems. Nevertheless, the new American empiricism required a metaphysical stand on the question of Nature versus Supernature. The empiricists, generally, declared themselves on the side of Nature, and this is the position of the majority of American philosophers in secular schools today. Thus "naturalism" is defined by S. P. Lamprecht as "a philosophical position, empirical in method, that regards everything that exists or occurs to be conditioned in its existence or occurrence by causal factors within one all-encompassing system of nature."[17]

Critical Naturalism

Contemporary or *critical* naturalism, as it is sometimes called, does not represent any special philosophic movement, such as German idealism, or a specific philosophical doctrine, like dialectical materialism. While critical naturalists would subscribe to our broad definition of naturalism, they do not adhere to any detailed metaphysical platform. For this reason, the philosophic problems which interest one naturalist may be quite different from those which concern another.

In one way critical naturalism stands as a "third force" between the two opposed doctrines of idealism and materialism. Naturalists do not agree with the idealist's view of the world as wholly mind, but they give credit to idealism for calling attention to the powerful role played in our experience by reason and intelligence. Naturalists criticize materialism for reducing everything to matter in motion, yet they support its rejection of supernaturalism. Thus it may seem to us that contemporary naturalism represents an endeavor to take up into philosophy contributions from both idealist and materialist camps. To a certain extent this assumption is correct. But present-day naturalism is not a simple compromise between idealism and materialism. The naturalist's empiricism, his admiration for scientific method, his rejection of a God who transcends the universe, reveal a

[17] S. P. Lamprecht, "Naturalism and Religion," in *Naturalism and the Human Spirit*, Y. Krikorian (ed.), Columbia University Press, 1944, p. 18.

cousinship with the materialist. But it would be a mistake to think of naturalism as a kind of materialism. Rather the reverse. Of the two world perspectives, naturalism is much the broader. Materialism is a narrow, and in some cases a naïve, kind of naturalism.

The Naturalist's Criticism of Idealism

Idealism, says the naturalist, has helped us to realize how important a part is played by mind in our knowledge of the world. But, while he concedes the value of the idealist's contribution to philosophy, the naturalist rejects idealism as a general system of explanation. Idealism explains *everything* in terms of mind and thereby reduces our experience, taken as a whole, to *one category* of experience. The idealist's theory rests upon the questionable assumption that, because we cannot know things apart from our thought of them, therefore thought is the "realest" kind of being. The naturalist's empiricism leads him to distrust what seems to him the excessive rationalism of the idealist. The impressive metaphysical *systems* of idealism in which concepts swing from concepts, too seldom touching down to the observable world, suggest that their authors have forgotten Kant's sober warning that concepts without percepts are empty. Hegel's Spirit, Bradley's Absolute, Leibniz' monads seem to the critical naturalist to lie too far beyond ordinary experience to have anything important to tell us about ordinary experience. The naturalist objects to the idealist's dualism in which appearance is opposed to reality. Finally, many, though not all, idealist systems require the concept of God or something like a God. This element of supernaturalism the naturalist cannot accept, since he believes Nature to be the ultimate category of explanation.

The Naturalist's Criticism of Materialism

Historically, contemporary naturalism may be regarded as an outgrowth and development of materialism. But apart from their common empiricism and rejection of super-naturalism (admittedly important points of agreement), there are marked differences between the two doctrines. Critical naturalism is the broader view and includes corrections of the inadequacies of the older theory.

What most naturalists of our day object to in materialism is its *reductionism*. The reductive or "nothing-but" fallacy is committed when one explains *A* by saying "*A* is nothing but *B*." We are in danger of falling into reductionism whenever we try to account for something by saying it is not what it is, but something else. Extreme examples of the reductive fallacy are assertions like "Romantic love is nothing but glands" or "Religion is nothing but magic." The critical naturalist says that the materialist, in his anxiety to prove that "All is matter in motion," reduces genuinely *different* levels of experience to *one* only. To say that life is simply highly organized matter is to say that life is nothing but matter. But this explanation ignores real differences between living and nonliving things. Instead of explaining life, the materialist explains it away. To say mind is nothing but electrical activity is to refuse to treat mind as an important type of experience. The materialist's treatment of mental events brushes aside problems which arise from the genuine contrast between thoughts and physical objects. Naturalists see no reason to deny the important differences between life and inorganic matter. They hold that mind and physical events show really different levels of natural processes. Moreover, naturalists will defend the autonomy of moral, aesthetic, and (with such qualification as we shall see) religious values:

> Critical naturalism cannot accept the materialist tendency to fit all things into the categories of physics and chemistry. For this . . . is equivalent to the denial that certain kinds of facts are "really" facts. To say that the phenomenon of a living organism is "nothing but" an arrangement of chemical compounds is to disregard relationships of which experience gives clear testimony. To say that values are no more than names given to purely physical situations is to dismiss one portion of experience *in favor* of another. Naturalism thus holds that values, meanings, purposes, ideals, life, mind, and society are not less "real" than the physically measurable world.[18]

The materialist speaks of "the primacy of matter." Now many naturalists readily concede the primacy of matter in the sense that in the history of the universe matter chronologically "came first." They will further concede to the materialist that these qualitatively different levels like life, consciousness, mind, and the rest, have *developed from* a material base. But, granting this, the naturalist sees no reason why we must treat these genuinely different levels as if they were the same. Further, the naturalist finds that the materialist cosmology is often erected on the basis of an outmoded scientific concept of matter. The old materialist slogan "Matter in motion. That is all!" was based on a picture of physical nature which has been radically changed on the basis of new concepts introduced by physicists like Einstein, Planck, Heisenberg, Dirac, and others. Matter, once the solid and irreducible basis to which materialists

[18] J. H. Randall, Jr., and J. Buchler, "The Broader Conception of Nature," in *Philosophy: An Introduction*, Barnes and Noble, Inc., 1942, p. 231.

referred everything for explanation, is today disclosed as a twilit quagmirish affair in which one simply cannot get the solid metaphysical footing the materialist requires. The materialist's "matter" is no longer ultimate, since it seems to be just one particular state that events happen to be in. Things have come to such a pass in modern physics that it is sometimes difficult to distinguish matter from space itself, since space has a way of getting itself mixed up with very small particles of matter. While this state of affairs should not be interpreted as evidence to support theology, says the naturalist, it shows that the old materialism is inadequate even as an explanation of the physical world.

The Naturalist's Concept of Mind

The critical naturalist is both a monist and a pluralist. He is a pluralist in his endeavor to grant full reality to each level of experience, whether it be matter, life, mind, or value. He is a monist in that he tries to bring these things together for explanation within Nature as the ultimate category of reference. He opposes any sharp-cut dualism which seems to him to split experience too widely apart. Consider his interpretation of mind. The naturalist disagrees with Descartes that body and mind are two utterly different kinds of things. He rejects the traditional view that the soul is radically "other" than the body. At the same time, he insists on the crucial importance of mind and the human capacity of intelligence and denies the materialist's thesis that mind is nothing but matter behaving in a complicated way.

In Western thought there developed two great concepts of mind which we may call the Platonic and the Aristotelian views—after the philosophers who started them on their way through history. To Plato the mind is a faculty of the soul, and the soul is an incorruptible spiritual entity radically different from and opposed to the body. The body is composed of matter, the principle of heaviness, sluggishness, and inertia; it weighs down the soul and prevents its clear vision through its highest power—mind. But the soul is not fated to die with the body. Its destiny is immortality in heaven. Says Socrates in the *Phaedo:*

> The body is a source of endless trouble to us by reason of the mere requirement of food; and is liable also to diseases which overtake us and impede us in the search after true being: it fills us full of loves, and lusts, and fears, and fancies of all kinds, and endless foolery, and in fact, as men say, takes away from us the power of thinking at all. . . . In this present life, I think that we make the nearest approach to knowledge when we have the least possible intercourse or communion with the body and are not surfeited with the bodily nature, but keep ourselves pure until the hour when God himself is pleased to release us.[19]

Aristotle has a different notion of soul. Like Plato, he believes that mind is a faculty of the soul. But to Aristotle the soul is not a spiritual principle imprisoned in a body as a bird in a cage. The soul, he says, is *the form of the body*. That is, the soul is the principle of organization of any living thing. A man's soul is his life, and mind or "reason" is the highest activity of that life. Thus conceived, body and soul are as inseparable as the structure of anything is inseparable from the material of which it is composed. "That is why," says Aristotle, "we can wholly dismiss as unnecessary the question whether the body and soul are one: it is as meaningless as to ask whether the wax and shape given to it

[19] Plato, *Phaedo*, B. Jowett (trans.), 66, 67.

by the stamp are one. . . ."[20] Traditional Christian religion, which regards belief in a separable and immortal soul as basic, inclines toward the Platonic concept of the soul— although the soul-body dualism it teaches is not as extreme as Plato's.[21]

Now the naturalist takes his stand with Aristotle rather than Plato. Prescientific as it may be, Aristotle's conception of the relation of mind and body as one of integral unity is naturalistic, and this is one reason why the Greek philosopher is regarded by contemporary naturalists as one of the great precursors of modern naturalism. Present-day naturalistic theories of mind, taken individually, differ in many respects from one another. But they all seem to agree that mind is a way of acting integrated with the human organism, rather than a spiritual substance residing in a body. Mind is not a simple process, for we may distinguish various elements within it—sensations, willing, feeling emotions, thinking, imagining, remembering. But these elements are not cut off from one another; they form a unity within that highly organized natural type of life we call human. The contributions of psychology, psychiatry, physiology, and related disciplines have thrown much light on the problem of mind. So has philosophic analysis of the nature of

---

[20] Aristotle, *De Anima*, 412b6. The neat opposition of the Platonic and Aristotelian concepts of the soul is marred by the fact that Aristotle hesitates over the question whether the "active intellect" might not, after all, be immortal; while Plato in his later years reorients his concept of the soul in a somewhat more "naturalistic" direction. Nevertheless, the contrast between these two classic interpretations of soul remains.

[21] The doctrine of the resurrection of the body made a radical Platonic body-soul dualism unacceptable to traditional Christian philosophers. Thomas Aquinas denied that the soul was in the body "like a sailor in a ship" and tried to reconcile the Aristotelian concept of the soul as the form of the body with the notion of the separable soul. Nevertheless, the language of popular Christian teaching concerning the soul is nearly always Platonic.

thought. There is every reason to believe that our understanding of mental activity will increase. The naturalist is
confident that further investigations of the nature of mind
will continue to confirm the proposition that mind is inextricably rooted in Nature, and that man—body and mind
—is an integral, natural whole.

Naturalism and Human Freedom

The issue of free will versus determinism is raised by the
materialist's assertion that every event is the necessary effect
of antecedent physical circumstances. If physical causes
determine every event, does it not follow that human actions are so determined—since man is a physical being?
That the individual is to some degree responsible for his
acts is a social and legal presupposition. But if all human
actions are determined by physical causes, we are not free
agents. In that case, how can we be held responsible for
our acts?

Materialists have adjusted their doctrines in different
ways in order to meet this difficulty. Epicurus held that the
atoms falling through space have a slight tendency to
swerve, an *exiguum clinamen*, a minute deviation from a
perfectly straight trajectory. In this way, an incalculable
element is introduced into Nature, so that in the human
soul there is present a "nameless element" which accounts
for freedom of choice. French materialists of the eighteenth century met the difficulty head on. They admitted
that their doctrine precluded moral responsibility, claimed
that crime was nothing but a disease, and recommended
hospitals for the wicked. They conceded, however, that
legal punishment was a necessary though regrettable social
expedient; but they recommended that correction should be

as mild as possible. In his fascinating little book *What Is Life?* the contemporary physicist Schrödinger offers an analysis of living organisms in terms of an enlightened but relentless materialism. But when he comes to account for his own unshakeable conviction that it is he, Erwin Schrödinger, who controls the aggregate of molecules that is himself, he confesses that the only plausible answer to the problem seems to be that of the ancient Indian philosophers— "I am God."

Critical naturalists do not favor explanations of human behavior in terms of either a thoroughgoing mechanistic determinism or a unity with the Divine. The "billiard ball" theory of human behavior, they point out, is now generally discredited. Materialistic theories of determinism have too often relied on misleading analogies between men and machines. There can be no question that in ordinary life we draw a distinction between free and compelled action, and any attempt to deny the reality of this distinction is to contradict experience. To give money to a poor man is one thing; to give money to a robber with a gun is another. There is an important difference between a confession given out of a genuine desire to admit a wrong and one wrung from a man by torture. The naturalist points out that determination need not be external—a compulsion upon the organism "from the outside." Human beings are organisms capable of a certain measure of *self*-determination. As John Dewey points out, we are able, as intelligent agents, to foresee the results of different courses of action we contemplate; we are able to weigh the benefits of these results against one another and to make a choice accordingly. While conceding the relative autonomy of human agents, the naturalist reminds us, however, that a large part of

human behavior is directly related to physical circumstances. Modern social analysis has done much to disclose
the importance of material causality in relation to human
action. We realize that poverty is a fertile seedbed of crime,
and we make important allowances for a delinquent youth
who comes from a broken home. Even the most genuine
free act cannot be entirely disassociated from the natural
circumstances that surround it. Beyond these rather broad
considerations it is difficult to suggest any further statements concerning the problem of freedom which represent
the common opinion of contemporary naturalists.

Naturalism and Religion

The old philosophers liked to compare man to a "little
world" or *microcosm* within a "great world" or *macrocosm*
which is the universe. On the scale of the microcosm—that
is, the human being—we have seen that the naturalist rejects any body-mind or body-soul dualism in which mind
or soul is conceived as a spiritual principle separable from
the body. Now if we move from the microcosmic to the
macrocosmic level, we find that here the naturalist rejects
as well any dualism between Nature and Supernature. To
put it bluntly, the naturalist denies the existence of God, if
God is conceived as an actual being distinct from and
transcending Nature. It would seem to follow that naturalists do not believe in the importance of religious values;
that naturalism and a religious world view cannot be reconciled. It is true that, historically, materialistic naturalism has
been identified with militant atheism, aggressive secularism,
and antireligious and anticlerical movements. In present-day
naturalism, however, we may see efforts on the part of some
philosophers to grant religious experience a genuine status,

to recognize religious values, and to integrate religion within a naturalistic world outlook. Contemporary naturalists may be divided into "right-wing" and "left-wing" groups, or, to borrow William James' terminology, into those who are "tender-minded" and those who are "tough-minded." "Tough-minded" naturalists are closer in spirit to the older materialists. They are indifferent to the problem of religious values, or actively opposed to attempts to bring religion in any sense into a naturalistic world outlook. "Tender-minded" naturalists are sympathetic to religion. While they generally reject the forms of orthodox or traditional religions, they feel that religious values are important and can be incorporated within a naturalistic philosophy.

Santayana's attitude toward religion has had considerable effect upon American naturalism. This philosopher, as we know, holds that, in addition to the world of natural fact, there is a world of essences which can be reached through man's creative imagination. These essences are *not* natural facts, but, taken as *ideals*, they can give meaning to life; they can and do lend color, richness, and value to experience. Among these ideals are those of poetry and religion: "Religion and poetry are identical in essence and differ merely in the way in which they are attached to practical affairs. Poetry is called religion when it intervenes in life, and religion, when it merely supervenes upon life, is seen to be nothing but poetry."[22] To Santayana, God is an ideal, not a fact. Theology deals with essences rather than existences. Yet ideals and essences communicate with life by providing centers about which our lives can be organized and made significant. Without them life could hardly be

[22] G. Santayana, cited by J. Dewey in *A Common Faith*, Yale University Press, 1934, p. 17.

human. But, Santayana reminds us, while everything natural has an ideal fulfillment, every ideal has a natural basis. Taken as descriptions of natural fact, the traditional religions can only lead to disillusion. Taken as symbolic interpretations of life, they can help us to accommodate ourselves to destiny in a tranquil spirit.

John Dewey is a naturalist whom it would be misleading to classify as "right-wing" or "tender-minded." Yet he admires Santayana's conception of religion as concerning ideal values. Santayana distinguishes two elements in religion—a moral consciousness and a poetic or mythological conception of things. It is religion's connection with the moral life that interests Dewey. He is concerned with religion's relation to the ideals by which men set their goals and with the effect that these ideals have on practical action. To Dewey the religious life consists of commitment to ideals and continuing efforts to realize them. Since ideals have the power to guide action, religious values occupy a high place among those norms which govern human conduct. God is a name for our ideals conceived as a unity: "Suppose . . . that the word 'God' means the ideal ends that at a given time and place one acknowledges as having authority over his volition and emotion, the values to which one is supremely devoted, as far as these ends, through imagination, take on unity. If we make this supposition, the issue will stand out clearly in contrast with the doctrine of religions that 'God' designates some kind of Being having prior and therefore non-ideal existence."[23]

The general direction taken by Santayana and Dewey is followed by those contemporary naturalists who are anxious to find a place for religious values within a naturalistic

[23] J. Dewey, *op. cit.*, p. 42.

scheme. Their approach is humanistic, since religious values are seen as grounded, not in any supernatural source, but in human nature itself. "Right-wing" naturalists feel that there is a place for religion in a naturalist philosophy, since religion is a fact of human experience. What the naturalist usually means by "religion," however, is not some historical form of religion, not an "organized" religion. Santayana is an exception here, for he believes that the naturalist can enjoy a traditional religion. One cannot speak in language in general, he says, but only in a particular language. But most American naturalists shy away from "orthodox" religions, preferring to take religion as Dewey's "common faith," a devotion to those unified patterns of ideals by which one guides one's life. Says S. P. Lamprecht: "The religious life is . . . a life in which multiple interests and diverse values are brought into effective and organic unity through central allegiance to some integrating ideal. . . . Religion ought to be the ornament of a rich life, not the driving passion of a fixed commitment."[24] It is obvious that such a concept of religion is very different from religion in the sense in which it has been traditionally conceived.

However sympathetic he may be toward religion, the "right-wing" naturalist gently, occasionally almost reluctantly, declines to concede the existence of God as an actual being distinct from the universe. The naturalist position in regard to this question is generally that, while the notion of a transcendent God is not inherently self-contradictory, there is no empirical evidence to warrant belief in the actuality of such a being. In the following chapter we shall examine some elements of traditional theology, as well as certain modern concepts of God as a "real" being. The

[24] S. P. Lamprecht, *op. cit.*, pp. 20, 38.

reader may decide for himself whether these theological considerations have place only within an older religious culture from which our secular age has long since broken away, or whether they have some weight in their own right.

FURTHER READINGS

Idealism

Beck, L. W., *Philosophic Inquiry*, Prentice-Hall, Inc., 1952, chaps. 10, 11.

Berkeley, G., *Principles of Human Knowledge*, Open Court Publishing Co., 1903.

Blanshard, Brand, *The Nature of Thought*, The Macmillan Company, 1941.

Bradley, F. H., *Appearance and Reality* (rev. ed.), Clarendon Press, Oxford, 1946.

Ewing, A. C., *Idealism: A Critical Survey*, The Humanities Press, 1950.

Hegel, G. W. F., *Selections*, Charles Scribner's Sons, 1929.

Leibniz, G. W. F., *Monadology*.

Plato, *Phaedo*.

Plato, *Phaedrus*.

Royce, J., *The Spirit of Modern Philosophy*, Houghton Mifflin C., 1892.

Materialism

Beck, L. W., *Philosophic Inquiry*, Prentice-Hall, Inc., 1952, chap. 12.

Elliot, Hugh, *Modern Science and Materialism*, Longmans, Green and Co., 1919.

La Mettrie, J. de, *Man a Machine* (1748), Open Court Publishing Co., 1927.

Lange, F. A., *The History of Materialism*, Harcourt, Brace and Co., 1925.

Lucretius, *On the Nature of Things*.

Schrödinger, Erwin, *What Is Life?* The Macmillan Company, 1945.

Sellars, R. W., Farber M., and McGill, V. J. (eds.), *Philosophy for the Future: The Quest of Modern Materialism*, The Macmillan Company, 1949.

Smith, Homer, "Kamongo," in *The Woollcott Reader*, Alexander Woollcott (ed.), The Viking Press, 1935.

Watson, J. B., *Behaviorism* (rev. ed.), W. W. Norton and Co., 1930.

Materialism (Dialectical)

Guest, David, *A Textbook of Dialectical Materialism*, International Publishers, 1939.

Haldane, J. B. S., *The Marxist Philosophy and the Sciences*, Random House, 1939.

Lenin, V. I., *Materialism and Empirio-Criticism*, in *Selected Works*, International Publishers, 1943, vol. 11.

Lewis, John (ed.), *A Textbook of Marxist Philosophy*, Victor Golancz Ltd., London (n.d.).

Somerville, John, *Soviet Philosophy*, Philosophical Library, Inc., 1946.

Stalin, J., *Dialectical and Historical Materialism*, International Publishers, 1940.

Naturalism

Beck, L. W., *Philosophic Inquiry*, Prentice-Hall, Inc., 1952, chap. 13.

Dewey, John, *Experience and Nature*, W. W. Norton and Co., 1929.

Dewey, John, *A Common Faith*, Yale University Press, 1934.

Krikorian, Y. (ed.), *Naturalism and the Human Spirit*, Columbia University Press, 1944.

Lamont, Corliss, *Humanism as a Philosophy*, Philosophical Library, 1950.

Madden, Ward, *Religious Values in Education*, Harper & Brothers, 1951.

Pratt, J. B., *Naturalism*, Yale University Press, 1945.

Randall, J. H., Jr., and Buchler, J., "The Broader Conception of Nature," in *Philosophy: An Introduction*, Barnes and Noble, Inc., 1942.

Santayana, G., *Reason in Religion*, vol. 4 of *The Life of Reason*, Charles Scribner's Sons, 1905–1906.

Santayana, G., *The Realm of Matter*, Charles Scribner's Sons, 1930.

8

THEISM

The world is charged with the grandeur
  of God.
It will flame out, like shining from shook
  foil.

—G. M. HOPKINS

"THEISM" refers to that metaphysical position which
asserts the existence of God as an actual being. We have
seen that some naturalist philosophers use the word "God"
to mean a concept which binds human values or goals into
a unity. But this position is not usually considered a form
of theism, since God is here treated as an ideal rather than
as a "real" being. A very large part of the traditional philosophy of the West is theistic. Those metaphysical systems
which developed within the religious traditions of Judaism,
Christianity, and Islam unanimously took as their point of
departure the existence of a God who had created the
world and who was distinct from it. Although early Greek
philosophy and the atomist school that developed from it
represented a frank naturalism, the dominant metaphysical
tradition—that of Plato and Aristotle—was theistic. In
modern times, despite the rise of naturalism, many systems
of theistic metaphysics have been formulated. Modern
theistic doctrines have been marked by increasing degrees
of individualism and a lessening reliance on the presuppositions of the religious traditions.

Theology has been defined as that division of metaphysics which treats of the existence and nature of God and his relation to the world. We should take note of the traditional distinction between "natural" theology and "revealed" or "sacred" theology. In the religious culture of the Middle Ages it was generally assumed that there were two main sources of reliable knowledge, revelation and human reason. Medieval theologians held that, while the richest source of theological knowledge was to be found in revelation, it was perfectly possible to acquire knowledge about God "by the light of natural reason." Later, philosophers came to refer to any inquiry into the existence and nature of God without the aid of Scriptures, faith, tradition, a teaching church, etc., as "natural theology," "natural religion," "theodicy," or (as in the case of Kant) simply "theology." Our present inquiry is concerned, not with "revealed," but with "natural" theology.

CLASSICAL ARGUMENTS FOR THE EXISTENCE OF GOD

In the course of Western philosophy, a number of interesting arguments for the existence of God have been developed. It is somewhat misleading to refer to these arguments as "proofs," for many theologians have offered them not as proofs but as ways of showing that belief in God (primarily a matter of faith) could be seen to be reasonable. Be that as it may, we shall proceed to consider the three best-known classical arguments for the existence of God together with certain of their variations. These arguments are usually labeled: (1) the cosmological argument; (2) the ontological argument; (3) the teleological argument.

The Cosmological Argument

This argument has at least three forms. The proof from *motion* as set forth by Aristotle and reproduced in various ways in traditional philosophy runs this way: The world is composed of things which move or change. Of these, none has the power to move itself. All things are moved by others. But these other things also lack the capacity of self-movement and are themselves moved by others, which in turn are moved by still other agents. Now, unless we are to conclude that the world is an *infinite series* of moving things, none of which has the power of self-motion, we must conclude that it is ultimately moved by a mover which is itself unmoved. "It is evident," says Aristotle, "that the first mover must be something that is one and eternal."[1] This unmoved mover is God.

Of course, many things "move themselves." Animals, for instance, have the power of locomotion. In the context of the argument, however, the word "move" may be taken in a broad meaning akin to "cause." If we substitute "cause" for "move," we may obtain that variation of the cosmological argument which is known as the proof from *causality*. This argument goes as follows: Experience tells us that nothing which exists has brought itself into existence. That is, everything that exists has a cause or causes. But the causes of things are themselves caused, and those causes in turn are the effects of still other causes. It is evident, then, that the world is composed of things none of which has the power to cause itself; hence the world cannot be its own cause. Therefore it is concluded that the world is caused by some cause other than itself, a cause which is uncaused. This uncaused cause is God.

[1] Aristotle, *Physics*, 259a15.

A third variety of the cosmological argument is the argument from *necessity and contingency*. It is found in the writings of Thomas Aquinas in this form:

If everything is possible not to be, then at one time there could have been nothing in existence. Now if this were true, even now there would be nothing in existence, because that which does not exist only begins to exist by something already existing. Therefore, if at one time nothing was in existence, it would have been impossible for anything to have begun to exist; and thus even now nothing would be in existence —which is absurd. Therefore, not all beings are merely possible, but there must exist something the existence of which is necessary. . . . This all men speak of as God.[2]

In other words, a thing may be said to have *necessary* existence, if it *has* to exist. It has *contingent* or possible being only, if it *happens* to exist. Now experience tells us that nothing in the world *need* exist. That a table does not have to exist can be demonstrated by chopping it up. That a man need not be is attested by the fact of his death. The world as a whole, then, is a contingent rather than a necessary being, since it is composed of contingent beings. But if the world is contingent, there is no reason why there should be a world in the first place. The alternative is to assume the existence of a being who *has* to exist, who is a *necessary* being, who is the "reason" for the existence of the world. This is God.

Comment on the Cosmological Argument

The reader may care to sharpen his skill in analysis by subjecting the cosmological argument (as well as those proofs

[2] Aquinas, *Summa Theologica*, Part 1, Q. 2, Art. 3; Fathers of the English Dominican Province (trans.), Burns Oates and Washbourne, Ltd., London, 1924, p. 26.

we have yet to examine) to his own criticism. Here are a few well-known objections to the cosmological argument set down without further development:

1. The Aristotelian proof from motion rests upon an erroneous physical cosmology in which the earth was thought to receive motion transmitted by relatively immutable heavenly bodies which in turn were moved by the Unmoved Mover. Further, Aristotle's argument assumes that an infinite series of movers is impossible. But there is nothing about an infinite series, as such, which is self-contradictory. It is possible to construct such a series in arithmetic.

2. The argument from causality does not answer the child's question "Who made God?" Those who defend this argument deny self-causing power to Nature but attribute it without hesitation to God. But, when we make God, rather than Nature, the exception to causality as ordinarily experienced, we evade rather than solve the difficulty of accounting for the world. What we have done is simply to set the difficulty back one stage, by postulating a cause outside of Nature which is unlike other causes.

3. It may be admitted that nothing in Nature contains its own reason for being, and that therefore things and events are indeed contingent. But to infer from the contingency of things and events, taken individually, that Nature as a whole is contingent, and thus dependent upon another being, is to commit the fallacy of composition. This fallacy consists in arguing from the properties of the parts, taken separately, to a property of the whole, taken together. Because sodium and chlorine are poisonous, it does not follow that table salt, which is composed of these elements, is equally poisonous. Although any part of Nature, taken singly, may be contingent or dependent for its existence

on something else, it does not follow that Nature, taken as a whole, is also contingent. In other words, there is no reason why Nature cannot be considered to be the ultimate ground of all existence, even though its parts depend for their existence on other parts.

The Ontological Argument

This argument, which has many interesting and subtle variations, is associated with the name of St. Anselm, a theologian of the eleventh century. It was popular with the Continental rationalists of the seventeenth century and may be found in the writings of Descartes, Spinoza, and Leibniz. The Anselmian form of the argument may be freely paraphrased thus: Let us conceive of a perfect being (*ens realissimus*). Now such a being will contain all the attributes of perfection. Existence is one of these attributes, for, of two supposed "perfect beings," one of which exists and one of which does not exist, the former will possess something that the latter lacks, and hence alone will be the "perfect being." Now to say that the perfect being includes the attribute of existence is simply another way of saying that he (God) exists. From the very conception of God, therefore, his existence may be inferred.

But, it will be objected, by means of such an argument it would be possible to prove the existence of all manner of fictitious beings. This difficulty was actually offered to Anselm himself by a monk named Gaunilon, who observed that, although he could think very hard of a perfect island, this perfect island was not on that account brought into existence. Defenders of the ontological argument, however, deny the validity of the comparison between the conception of God and that of an island or any other created thing. For God, they say, is a *necessary* being. His essence (what he is) and his existence (that he is) are one and the same. Therefore God *must* exist. In created things, on the other hand, essence and existence are *not* the same. A particular flower has essence, for it may be described; it has existence, for there it is. But that the flower's essence and existence are two different things is proved by the flower's dying. After the flower's existence ceases, its character may be described in a poem. But its character did not suffice to hold the flower in existence. So with all created things. In God, however, essence and existence are identical. If they were not, if God did not *have* to exist, he would be just like a created thing and subject to passing out of existence like the flower. But such a God would not be a God at all. Now if in God essence and existence are one and the same, merely to define him—indeed, merely to *conceive* of him (as a perfect being, for example)—is to show that he exists. Or, as Descartes puts it, the existence of God follows from the idea of God just as the property of 180 degrees follows from the idea of triangle.

Comment on the Ontological Argument

The ontological argument has been rejected by a variety of philosophers, including Thomas Aquinas and Kant. Aquinas interprets the argument as asserting that the existence of God is *self-evident*. But, he says: "No one can mentally admit the opposite of what is self-evident; as the Philosopher [i.e., Aristotle] states concerning the first principles of demonstration. But the opposite of the proposition 'God is' can be mentally admitted: *The fool said in his heart, There is no God* (Ps. lii 1). Therefore, that God exists is not self-evident."[3] To put Aquinas in modern terminology, he is saying that the proposition "God exists" is not a tautology or an analytic statement like "A triangle has three sides," which is true *by definition*. "God exists" is to him a synthetic or factual statement whose truth cannot be established merely by examining its syntactical structure.

Kant sees in the ontological argument the confusion of a *logical* kind of existence with a *real* kind. Actual existence is not an attribute in the sense that "blue" and "perfect" are attributes. When we assert that the concept of God includes the attribute of existence, such existence can never be anything more than *possible* being. What happens in the ontological proof is that at the outset we covertly assert the actual existence of God. We can no more prove the actual existence of anything from its possibility than we can increase our bank balance by adding merely possible dollars to it.

Critics of the ontological argument agree that it commits the fallacy of begging the question—that is, of assuming as true what is to be proved. What should be established is that God exists; but this is taken for granted, under the counter, as it were, in the premises of the argument. All that the ontological argument asserts amounts to no more than this: if there *were* a perfect being, then he *would* actually exist; if there *were* a necessary being, then in him essence and existence *would* be identical and he would necessarily exist. What the argument fails to do is to "catch" the perfect or necessary being by showing that there actually *is* such a being.

[3] *Ibid.*, p. 20.

The Teleological Argument

This argument is sometimes known as the proof from design. It has two closely related forms. One points to the apparently purposive character of natural objects, citing such examples as the marvelous coördination of the parts of the human or animal eye or the wonderful instances of adaptation which abound in the world of plants and animals. Such purpose in Nature, it is argued, cannot be the result of mere chance, but must be the work of an intelligent author of Nature, who is God. A more general form of the argument appeals to the uniformity and order of physical Nature, taken as a whole. This argument interprets the order of Nature as evidence of intelligent design, and proceeds from this to infer the existence of God as the designer.

The notion that the ultimate cause of the order of physical Nature is something akin to mind or intelligence is as old as Anaxagoras, and is considerably developed in the philosophies of Plato and Aristotle. Cicero uses the argument from design in his *De Natura Deorum*. Medieval theologians employed the teleological proof in their writings, although they tended to give more prominence to the cosmological argument. The rise of the physical sciences in modern times produced among educated men a heightened admiration for the complex harmony of Nature. This in turn increased the popularity of the teleological proof. The argument from design was a particular favorite of the eighteenth-century deists—men who preferred a minimal "natural religion," based on reason and experience, to one founded on revelation or a teaching church. The deists liked to think of the universe as a wonderful machine (its laws so brilliantly revealed by the incomparable Newton) which God had created and then left to run according to its own laws without interference on his part.

The proof from design was popular with eighteenth-century English churchmen. William Paley, Archdeacon of Carlisle, argued in his *Natural Theology* for "the necessity, in each particular case, of an intelligent designing mind for the contriving and determining of the forms which organized bodies bear." Paley used the famous "watch" illustration, which he borrowed from the Dutch philosopher Nieuwentyt. If we should find a watch on an uninhabited island, argues Paley, we would naturally infer that this clever mechanism was the work of an intelligent craftsman rather than the product of chance. Now the universe is a mechanism incomparably more wonderful than a watch. Do we not therefore have the right to conclude that the universe is the product of a mind of surpassing intelligence, and that this mind is God?

The teleological argument appeared with renewed vigor after the triumph of the theory of biological evolution in the nineteenth century. To be sure, the "tough-minded" Darwinians took the data of evolution as proof that organic life is the chance product of nonpurposive adaptation to the material environment. But others interpreted the impressive history of the development of living forms as evidence of a cosmic direction and purpose which could only be attributed to God or something like a God. Bergson's *Creative Evolution* is full of examples of the marvels of adaptation to be found in organic Nature, from which he infers the existence of a cosmic purposive force. In our own day, the biologist Lecomte du Noüy used probability calculus to demonstrate that the probability of a single protein molecule's having organized itself by chance is incredibly small—2.02 × 10^{-321}, to be exact.[4] In his popular book *Human Destiny*, Du Noüy states that any man with respect for the methods of science can only infer that there is an anti-chance factor at work in the universe. This is God.

Comment on the Teleological Argument

Critics of the teleological proof point out that the form of the argument which appeals to the *purposive character of natural objects* developed within a period in history which lacked the concepts and techniques of empirical science. The behavior of natural objects was interpreted, in those days, almost exclusively according to an Aristotelian principle of internal and purposive causality with little attention to the role of external physical causality. For example, the falling of a stone was explained in terms of a tendency within the stone itself to fall, rather than as the result of an influence external to the stone. This type of thinking produced an exaggerated teleology, of which Voltaire makes fun in his *Candide*. In that book Dr. Pangloss, professor of metaphysico-theologo-cosmolonigology, addresses his ingenuous pupil thus:

'Tis demonstrated . . . that things cannot be otherwise; for, since everything is made for an end, everything is necessarily for the best end. Observe that noses were made to wear spectacles; and so we have spectacles. Legs were visibly instituted to be breeched, and we have breeches. Stones were formed to be quarried and to build castles; and My Lord has a very noble castle; the greatest Baron in the province should

[4] L. du Noüy, *Human Destiny*, Signet Books, The New American Library, 1949, p. 35.

have the best house; and as pigs were made to be eaten, we eat pork all the year round; consequently, those who have asserted that all is well talk nonsense; they ought to have said that all is for the best.[5]

The more general form of the teleological argument—that based on the evidence of a world order—was vigorously attacked by David Hume. It is true, says Hume, that from the existence of a house we may infer the existence of a builder. We may do this because we have *experience* of houses *and* of architects who design them and builders who construct them. But, Hume points out, although the order of Nature is given to us in experience, the existence of a cosmic designer is not. Therefore the argument rests on a bad analogy. Further, says Hume, even if we grant the existence of an intelligence which is responsible for the world order, it does not follow that this intelligence is God. At best, the argument from design indicates the existence of a finite being of whom nothing more can be said than that it is the cause of the order of Nature. We cannot conclude that this being is a God, who is infinite, omnipotent, all-good, etc. The very most the argument can support, says Hume, is the inference that "The cause or causes of order in the universe probably bear some remote analogy to human intelligence."[6]

Du Noüy's use of probability calculus to demonstrate the existence of an anti-chance factor in the cosmos is open to the following objection. When we say the probability of a penny's turning up heads on any given throw is ½, we are making an assumption concerning the behavior

[5] Voltaire, *Candide*, The Modern Library, 1930, p. 4.
[6] D. Hume, *Dialogues Concerning Natural Religion*, E. D. Aiken (ed.), Hafner Publishing Co., 1948, p. 94.

of pennies, namely, that it is equally likely that they will turn up one of two ways on any given throw. Assumptions of this kind do no harm in the case of simple objects like pennies and dice but may be very misleading when applied without care to more complex situations. We have no assurance that considerations of mathematical probability (the theory of which is still under development) may safely be applied to such complicated and inclusive areas as organic life or the cosmos taken as a whole.

RELATION OF GOD TO THE WORLD

Causality of God; Creation

In traditional theism the world is considered to be related to God as effect to cause. Does this mean that all forms of classical theism take God to be the creator of the world? Not if we mean by "creator" a being who makes the world from nothing (*ex nihilo*). In the theology of the Greek philosophers, for example, we find no notion of a God who creates from nothing. The Greeks had two different conceptions of the manner in which God and the world are related, neither of them involving "strict" creation. One of these we may call *transformation*, the other *emanation*.

In most Greek theologies matter is eternal. What God does is to give *form* to this matter. In his *Timaeus*, Plato explains the creation of the world by means of a poetic myth. God, gazing upon the eternal Forms, takes in hand the formless flux of matter and molds it according to the timeless patterns he sees before him. God fashions the world as a sculptor who, with his eyes on a fair model, gives form to the imperfect clay that is the only material available to him. Aristotle's account is hardly less poetic. God, the

Unmoved Mover, is absorbed in self-contemplation and has no knowledge of anything beyond himself. The effect of his presence, however, is such as to induce form within the eternal matter. Like a magnet unaware of the iron, God has from all eternity drawn matter toward him, the matter acquiring form as it moves toward "the object of its appetition." Because of the ever present influence of God, matter has always had some degree of form. Hence the world is eternal.

Later Greek philosophers, called Neoplatonists, explained the creativity of God in terms of emanation rather than transformation. According to Plotinus, God—"the One"—is Being itself. In the plenitude of his being (and in his wish to share it), God "spills over" being like wine from a brimming cup. Or, to change the metaphor, God *radiates* being, as the sun pours forth light and heat. These radiations or *emanations* assume the form of a hierarchy of stages of being, ranging from higher to lower. The world is one of the lower stages of this graduated system of emanations. Matter—which the Greeks regarded as the principle of imperfection—arises at that stage of the emanation process which is farthest from God. The imperfection of matter (communicated to the world, which is partly matter) is not to be explained by any original limitations within God. Rather, matter is the poor stuff it is, because it is the last in the series of emanations, and is therefore, metaphysically speaking, at the greatest distance from the creative source.

The notion that God creates the world *from nothing* (*ex nihilo*) is Judaic rather than Greek and arises from considerations of the story of creation as given in Genesis. This Biblical document gives a curious double account of creation, one aspect of which can be interpreted as a type of transformism. Historically, there was considerable debate among both Jewish and Christian theologians as to whether the world was formed by God's creative energy operating on a primordial chaos or material substratum, or whether God simply created the world from nothing. In general, traditional theologians tended to agree that revelation indicated that the world was created from nothing, but that this could not be proved from "natural reason." We shall see that the manner in which God is conceived to have created the world has some bearing upon the question of the attributes of God and upon what is called the problem of evil.

The Attributes of God

In the traditional theology of the West God was represented as having a number of attributes or qualities. Jewish and Christian philosophers went to great lengths to avoid the charge of what today we call *anthropomorphism*—the attributing to God of human qualities. God, they agreed, is to a large extent beyond human knowledge. Therefore, strictly speaking, we can say nothing about his nature which will adequately represent that nature. Yet in seeking to avoid the Scylla of anthropomorphism theologians feared to fall into the Charybdis of *agnosticism*, the position that God is unknowable and that nothing at all can be said about him. Various attempts to avoid this dilemma were devised. The Jewish philosopher Maimonides recommended the *vis negativa*. While we cannot attribute positive qualities to God, we can indirectly describe his nature by making negative statements. We cannot say, for example, that God is wise, but we can say that he is not unwise. Thomas Aquinas suggested the doctrine of *analogy*. We cannot apply to God attributes like "wisdom" or "goodness" *in the same sense* in which these words are applied to things of the created order. Such attributes can only be predicated of God *analogically* in a way which admits the need for correction.

Traditional theologians agreed that God had in *some* sense attributes such as infinity (that is, God is without limitations), goodness, omnipotence, omniscience, etc. While certain of the early fathers had difficulty in conceiving of God as something immaterial, it was generally held that God was a spiritual rather than a corporeal being. It was also agreed that God *thought* or was a mind; that in the work of the creation of the world he proceeded in a fashion not wholly different from that of a rational creature who carries a plan or design into effect and knows what he is doing.

The Problem of Evil

The traditional doctrines of the creativity and attributes of God produced many difficulties. One of the best known of these is the so-called problem of evil. The problem may be stated in this way: While there is in the world evidence of much that is orderly, good, and rational, there is even more compelling evidence of all-pervasive evil. There are physical evils, such as famine, earthquakes, and other natural catastrophes. There is pain, sickness, and death. There are moral evils—injustice, sin, the wickedness of men. There is war, which is a pandemonium of evils, both physical and moral. Now, if God *cannot* prevent evil in the world, it would seem that he is not all-powerful, and if he *will not* prevent evil, it would seem that he is not all-good.

Consider these two alternatives: (1) God is not all-powerful; (2) God is not all-good. The Greek philosophers tended to favor the first alternative. To them, *matter* is the principle of limitation and disorder, hence indirectly the source of all evil. God did not create matter. It coexists with God from all eternity. God is not an absolute lord over matter. Plato explicitly admits that God is *limited* by something outside himself which he calls "necessity." Indeed it is only by "persuasion" that his God can elicit a partial order within the material flux from which the world is formed. On the other hand, *Manicheism*, a religion which at one time nearly defeated Christianity in the West, was more receptive to the alternative of divine ill will. The Manicheans taught a *theistic dualism* in which two Gods, one of Light or Good, the other of Darkness or Evil, eternally coexisted. The order and harmony of the world was attributed to the God of Light, the disorder to the God of Darkness.[7]

Neither of these alternatives, however, was acceptable to traditional Christian theology, which attributed *both* infinite goodness and power to God. God is absolutely without limitation and he is all-good. Hence, other solutions to the problem of evil were formulated, none of which is completely satisfactory. One of the classic solutions, first developed by St. Augustine, suggests that evil is not something positive, but rather a privation or lack of an order which "ought to be there." Thus blindness is an absence or derangement of the physiological order which would nor-

---

[7] The doctrine preached by the prophet Mani had its origin in ancient Persia, which seems to have been the home of theistic dualism. A notable example is the Persian fire cult we call Zoroastrianism, which taught the coexistence of a God of Light (Ormuzd or Ahura Mazda) and a God of Darkness (Ahriman).

mally permit sight. In the moral realm, sin is the lack of a spiritual order proper to the soul. Now if evil is a privation or lack rather than a positive created thing, then God cannot be said to have created it.

The obvious objection to this answer to the problem of evil is that an all-powerful God could *prevent* the occurrence of this lack or privation. To which Augustinian theology would perhaps invite our attention to a more general way of taking evil as the result of privation. God himself is complete and infinite Being. Now created things, in virtue of the very fact that they *are* created, cannot possess complete being. They are not necessary beings, but contingent only. Because of this, created things have a tendency to slip away from being toward non-being. This *finitude* of things implies limitation and imperfection. To demand of God the removal of finitude from creatures is to ask that he make them God. No reasonable man would demand this. But it is from this finitude of things, from the contingency and dependence of the created order, that evil arises.

Interesting as these metaphysical considerations of evil may be, we should note that Augustine and other Christian theologians based their *primary* explanation of the presence of evil in the world upon certain historical events described wholly within the bounds of Scripture. According to this account, man brought his troubles upon himself. There was a certain primal fault committed by man, a fault so serious as to turn God away from him.[8] As a result of this break between man and his creator, there was a fall from man's once blessed estate. The consequence of this fall was a shattering of man's nature and the appearance of suffering and

[8] The doctrine of a primordial fault and a fall occurs in religions and philosophies of various cultures. The notion is present in Indian metaphysics. It is elaborated in mythopoeic language in Plato's *Phaedrus*.

death. Why did God permit man to commit this primal fault? Why does he allow his creatures, over whom he has domination, to choose evil instead of good? Theologians may reply that, since God created man in his image, he created him a *free* being and not merely a good-doing automaton. Since man is free, the choice between good and evil is open to him.

Certain philosophers have not been content to allow the problem of evil to rest within the context of religious faith but have striven to work out a solution consistent with the Christian view in terms of a "natural theology." Leibniz, for example, maintains in his *Theodicy* a position which has been called *cosmological optimism*. According to Leibniz, God has created the world according to the best possible plan. But the best plan, says Leibniz, "is not always that which seeks to avoid evil, since it may happen that *the evil is accompanied by a greater good*."[9] Since experience tells us that evil frequently brings about good (an illness, for example, may give a man time to reflect on a misspent career and thus lead him to a nobler life), it may be concluded that all evil serves some higher good of which we may not have knowledge. Leibniz' reasoning on this problem has rarely been found convincing. His doctrine that "this is the best of all possible worlds" is mercilessly satirized by Voltaire.[10]

GOD AS THE WHOLE

Spinoza's Concept of God

As Western thought gradually broke away from the framework of traditional religion within which it had operated

[9] G. W. F. Leibniz, *Selections*, P. P. Wiener (ed.), Charles Scribner's Sons, 1951, p. 510.
[10] See the excerpt from *Candide* on pp. 273–274.

for sixteen hundred years, the character of metaphysical systems became increasingly independent and individualistic. Some philosophers, like Descartes, tried to tie their new systems to traditional theology. Others, like the seventeenth-century Dutch philosopher Baruch Spinoza, sharply criticized the traditional concept of God and put forward their own. Spinoza's theology is particularly interesting because in it is broken down the traditional distinction between God and Nature. God and Nature are one and the same, he says, but Nature is *more* than the physical universe. This is puzzling, and Spinoza has been called everything from a "God-intoxicated man" to a "forerunner of contemporary Naturalism." Some years ago, when Albert Einstein was questioned by newspaper reporters as to his belief in God, he replied, "My God is the God of Spinoza." This left the reporters little wiser than before.

According to Spinoza, God, while not identical with the physical universe, is inseparable from it. To God, Spinoza gives the impersonal name of *Substance*. The traditional definition of substance is "any independently existing thing." Applying this definition with rigorous exactness, Spinoza states that there can be but one *absolutely* independent thing. This is God, upon whom everything else depends. All other beings, says Spinoza, including the physical universe and everything in it, are *modes* or aspects of this infinite Substance. These modes follow from the nature of Substance by the same inexorable necessity by which the properties of a geometrical figure follow from the figure itself as given. The world, therefore, *proceeds* from God by *necessity*. The world is a necessary consequence of the nature of God and it is part of that nature.

An analogy may be drawn between the Spinozistic relation between God and the world, and that which exists between the premises and the conclusion of any syllogism:

Men are rational.
Greeks are men.
Therefore, Greeks are rational.

The premises of this syllogism imply or "contain" the conclusion, which is, of course, *part* of the total syllogism. The conclusion itself "follows" from the premises necessarily. In an analogous fashion God or Substance "contains" the world which is a *part* of God and *follows necessarily* from the nature of God. Now if the physical universe is a necessary consequence of God's nature, it would seem that God must implicitly contain *matter*. This Spinoza readily concedes. The infinite Substance contains not only the infinite attribute of *thought* or mind (which traditional theologians had always ascribed to God) but also the infinite attribute of matter, or *extension*, as Spinoza puts it.

The consequences of Spinoza's concept of God show certain radical differences between this God and the God of traditional theology. First, orthodox theologians held that God was spirit only. Spinoza maintains that God is matter as well as mind. Second, the traditional God produced the world by a free creative act according to a certain plan or design in his mind. Spinoza denies that God creates in this quasi-human and arbitrary manner. The world has existed from all eternity as a mode or aspect of infinite Substance, and it is a necessary consequence of that Substance's nature. Third, the traditional doctrine of the relation of God to the world emphasized the *transcendence* of God. That is, God is a causal power who is apart from and beyond the world which is his effect. Now Spinoza *denies the separation* between God and the world. To him, God is an *immanent* rather than a transcendent cause—an indwelling or inseparable cause with which the effect (the world) is continuous. But God does not dwell within the physical universe as a part lies within a whole. Rather the reverse. The world, which is the part, dwells within God, who is the Whole. Now, while the terms "God" and "Nature" are interchangeable, God is not identical with *physical* Nature; rather does he include or contain the physical universe. That is why Spinoza approves the saying of St. Paul, "In Him we live and move and have our being."

Spinoza then proceeds to the following conclusion: Since all that exists in the universe is a necessary consequence of God's nature, there is no freedom in the world. Every event in the universe, from the fall of a stone to the act of a man, is inexorably determined by the necessity of God's nature. Only that man can be called "free" who *understands* that God alone is a free cause, and that all else follows from God by necessity.

God as Immanent and Transcendent Cause

The concept of God as the immanent or inseparable cause of the world is not peculiar to Spinoza, although his particular metaphysical system is unique. In the religious traditions of the West we may distinguish two different lines of emphasis on the relation of God to the world. One line is that of those theologians who have endeavored to interpret the meaning of God in highly rational or "scientific" terms. The result is "the God of the philosophers," the Infinite Cause of the cosmos, the creator and foundation of the total hierarchy of being. In this context the stress is nearly always on the *transcendence* of God, his distinctness or separation from the world, rather than on his *immanence* or indwellingness. But the God of the Western religious traditions is not only the impersonal First Cause of the world. He is also a God of Love who cares for man. According to Christian doctrine, the love of God for his creatures is so great that he *came into the world* as Jesus, the Son of God, the second person of the Trinity; and *remains with* the world in the form of the Paraclete, the Holy Spirit, the third person of the Trinity.

Devout Christian writers, absorbed with the God of Love, rather than with the infinite First Cause, invariably emphasized God's *closeness* to the world. The mystics—of whom the Christian tradition includes Theresa of Avila, John of the Cross, Ruysbroeck, Eckhart, and Jacob Boehme —particularly stressed the immanence of God, the unity of all things within the Divine. But orthodox theologians were fearful of pushing the concept of God's immanence to extremes. Although a large measure of truth was conceded to the mystics, the balance of orthodoxy tipped toward transcendence. Excessive emphasis on God's immanence was regarded with suspicion. Later, this was to be called "pantheism."

Pantheism

"Pantheism" is a word which seems to have been used first by John Toland in 1705 and means literally "All is God." The illustrious Dr. Johnson defined a pantheist as "one who confused God and Nature" and referred to the followers of Spinoza as pantheists. Spinoza is, of course, a pantheist by definition, if we take "pantheism" to mean (1) God is inseparable from Nature or (2) God is the infinite Whole, and everything which exists is a part or "mode" of that

Whole. We frequently hear the word "pantheism" applied to certain poetry in which the poets sing of the unity of all things within the Divine. Goethe, who admired Spinoza, tells us in his poem "One in All" that the best way to find oneself is to lose oneself in the Infinite. We have it didactically from Pope that:

> All are but parts of one stupendous whole,
> Whose body Nature is, and God the soul.[11]

Or in Emerson, under the spell of Indian mysticism:

> They reckon ill who leave me out;
>   When me they fly, I am the wings;
> I am the doubter and the doubt,
>   And I the hymn the Brahmin sings.[12]

The indwellingness of Deity in Nature is a theme of Edna Millay's *Renascence*:

> God, I can push the grass apart
> And lay my finger on thy heart![13]

Of all poets, Wordsworth is most absorbed with the immanence of the Divine in Nature:

>   . . . And I have felt
> A presence that disturbs me with the joy
> Of elevated thought; a sense sublime
> Of something far more deeply interfused,
> Whose dwelling is the light of setting suns,
> And the round ocean and the living air,
> And the blue sky, and in the mind of man:
> A motion and a spirit, that impels

[11] A. Pope, *Essay on Man.*
[12] R. W. Emerson, "Brahma."
[13] E. Millay, *Renascence*, Harper & Brothers, 1917.

All thinking things, all objects of all thought
And rolls through things.[14]

God as All-Soul or All-Mind

The same generic concept of God, which in some settings
we label "pantheism," occurs again in the doctrine of the
All-Soul or All-Mind—an idea of God both ancient and
modern. The philosophers of ancient India held that the
individual soul (atman) is but a particularization of the
infinite all-encompassing soul which is God (brahma). In
the West, the Stoics regarded individual minds as parts of
an all-containing Universal Reason. Certain commentators on Aristotle, such as Alexander of Aphrodisias, interpreted the master's puzzling doctrine of the immortality of
the "active intellect" to mean that individual minds are related to the Divine as sparks to a flame. It was the preference of medieval Arabian philosophers for this interpretation of Aristotle that caused Christian philosophers to
condemn Moslem theology for what today we would call
"pantheism." The All-Mind occurs in Yankee dress in New
England transcendentalism; Emerson's "oversoul" owes
much to atman and brahma. A contemporary version of
the All-Soul is offered by Dean Inge: "The entire cosmic
process is the life-frame of the universal Soul, the Divine
Logos. With this life we are vitally connected, however
brief and unimportant the span and the task of an individual
career may seem to us. If my particular life-meaning passes
out of activity, it will be because the larger life, to which
I belong, no longer needs that form of expression."[15]

[14] W. Wordsworth, "Lines Composed a Few Miles Above Tintern
Abbey."
[15] W. R. Inge, *Outspoken Essays* (First Series), Longmans, Green and
Co., London, 1924, p. 273.

John Steinbeck in his story *The Grapes of Wrath* has Casey, the preacher, say, "I guess there's just one great big soul and we're all little pieces of it." In Thomas Mann's great dialectical novel, *The Magic Mountain*, the All-Soul is evoked with dramatic effect. At a critical point in that work the tubercular hero, Hans Castorp, has a strange and terrible dream in which he chooses between life and death. On waking, he says to himself: "Now I know that it is not out of our single souls we dream. We dream anonymously and communally, if each after his fashion. The great soul of which we are a part may dream through us, in our manner of dreaming, its own secret dreams. . . ."[16]

Is the Absolute God?

Not unrelated to the concept of God as All-Mind is the Absolute of the idealist philosophers. It is not easy to say just what the Absolute is, since various absolute idealists speak of it in somewhat different ways. They agree, however, that the Absolute is the ground of all being; that upon the Absolute all things depend. Hence the Absolute fulfills the primary role of the God of traditional theology. The Absolute is the Whole, of which everything is a finite fragment. It is the one reality, and all else is appearance. The Absolute is something like an all-pervasive thought which reveals itself through Nature and through all things—these being but *aspects* of the Absolute. Hegel tells us that the Absolute is "not just the Supreme Being," transcending the world and distinct from it: "Common fancy puts the Absolute far away in a world beyond. The Absolute is rather directly before us, so present that so long as we think, we

[16] T. Mann, *The Magic Mountain*, Alfred A. Knopf, Inc., 1927, p. 624.

must, though without express consciousness of it, always carry it with us and always use it."[17]

According to Josiah Royce, the Absolute is that "larger Self" which includes all individual selves. He tells us that the Absolute is at the very least a person and more definitely conscious than we are. All the problems of the world are solved within the Absolute; the darkest mysteries are known to it. Nor can we escape the Absolute, for: "Flee where we will, . . . the net of the larger Self ensnares us. We are lost and imprisoned in the thickets of its tangled labyrinth. The moments are not at all in themselves, for as moments they have no meaning; they exist only in relation to the beyond. The larger Self alone is, and they are by reason of it, organic parts of it. They perish, but it remains; they have truth or error only in its overshadowing presence. . . . There is, then, at last, but one Self, organically, reflectively, consciously inclusive of all the selves, and so of truth."[18]

F. H. Bradley sees the Absolute not as a larger Self or Person, but as "superpersonal." The Absolute is the foundation of all reality, it *is* reality, but it is not the God of the traditional religions. "God," says Bradley, "is not God, till he has become all in all, and . . . a God which is all in all is not the God of religion. God is but an aspect, and that must mean but an appearance of the Absolute."[19]

In any metaphysical system in which God or the Absolute is taken as the Whole—everything else being an aspect

[17] G. W. F. Hegel, *Logic* (rev. ed.), Wm. Wallace (trans.), Clarendon Press, Oxford, 1892, p. 50.

[18] J. Royce, *The Spirit of Modern Philosophy*, Houghton Mifflin Co., 1892, p. 379.

[19] F. H. Bradley, *Appearance and Reality* (1893), Clarendon Press, Oxford, 1946, p. 433.

or part of that Whole—the problem of evil is there to be reckoned with just as an orthodox theology. For if God or the Absolute contains all, it must contain evil as well as good. Some absolute idealists endeavor to meet this difficulty by saying that evil is conflict and disharmony on the scale of the *part*, but within the *whole* all conflict is resolved. In the Absolute, evil disappears. As in Meredith's poem:

> Stop a moment: I seize an idea from the pit.
>   They tell us that discord, though discord alone,
> Can be harmony when the notes properly fit:
>   Am I judging all things from a single false tone?[20]

According to Bradley, we may say that the Absolute *has* evil, since it contains a province of which evil is a partial element. But we cannot say that the Absolute *is* evil on the basis of the character of one of its "fragmentary and dependent details." It was possibly argument of this sort William James had in mind when he said "Damn the Absolute!"

GOD AS FINITE

Concepts of God fall into two kinds: (1) God as *infinite;* God is the ultimate metaphysical factor, the foundation of everything, the cause of all being. God, as infinite, is not limited by anything outside himself. (2) God as *finite;* he is one of the ultimate cosmic factors, but he is not the only one. God is *limited* by something other than himself. Greek philosophers, like Plato, hesitated to make God responsible for *everything*—for they had in mind the presence of imperfection and disorder in the world. Accordingly, they made matter or necessity a cosmological factor coeternal

[20] G. Meredith, "Martin's Puzzle."

with God. Thus conceived, God is finite—in the sense of being limited by something other than himself, something beyond his complete control. The God of traditional Judaeo-Christian theology, on the other hand, is infinite, for he is unlimited by anything outside himself. He is the Supreme Being, the single, ultimate, metaphysical fact, upon which everything else depends.

Modern concepts of God may be classified in the same way. Spinoza's God is infinite, the one self-caused Substance of which everything else is but a mode. The Absolute of the idealists is very much like Spinoza's God in this respect. The Absolute, too, is unlimited by anything other than itself. It is the sole reality, containing within itself the whole complex system of appearances which is our world. The Absolute is the ultimate ground of all being.

But despite Spinoza and the Absolute idealists, modern theism shows an emphatic trend in favor of a *finite* deity. This limited God plays an important role in the cosmos, but he is circumscribed, even thwarted, by other metaphysical elements. Alexander's Deity has not yet emerged from the womb of the cosmos. Whitehead's God can persuade but cannot compel. Bergson's vital force is struggling through matter. James' wider self is partially dependent for his very existence upon our belief in him. In this final section of our brief theological survey we shall examine these restricted deities in further detail.

Evolutionary and Emergent Deity

One effect of the concept of evolution upon the generation of philosophers preceding our own by one or two was to stimulate the production of natural theologies of an evolutionary type. These philosophers saw the state of present living forms to be but a stage in a vast biological process of transformation and development. The physical universe itself they accepted as a mere moment in the stupendous scheme of cosmic evolution. But what, they asked, is the force behind all this? It is God. But it is God conceived as a power not so much outside the cosmic process as within it, at its heart. God is part of the evolutionary process. Deity itself evolves. It may be that God is at this moment "hatching out" from the mighty universe, emerging gradually as from a cosmic womb, to transcend the process of which he is the immanent cause. Says W. P. Montague: "We are confronted with a God, or something very like a God that exists . . . as an ascending force, a nisus, a thrust toward concentration, organization, and life. This power appears to labor slowly and under difficulties. We can liken it to a yeast that, through the aeons, pervades the chaos of matter and slowly leavens it with spirit."[21]

In his *Creative Evolution*, Bergson conceives of God as a vital force, the *élan vital*, the primal source of creative energy. Like Plotinus' One, this pure and undifferentiated Life finds itself thwarted and blocked by *matter*, which has come into being as an indirect and unwanted by-product of itself. The *élan vital* is like a fountain surging upward or a rocket shooting toward the sky. Matter is like the drops which fall back against the upswelling thrust of the fountain or the dead ashes that drop earthward from the rocket. Its free creative play hindered by matter, the *élan* plunges into the inert stuff that resists it, and the marvelous multiplicity of living forms arises. The story of evolution is the history of the attempts the life force has made—and is still making—to overcome the matter into which it has entered,

---

[21] W. P. Montague, *Belief Unbound*, Yale University Press, 1930, p. 74.

to regain its original undifferentiated one-ness, to win through to its primordial freedom.

Another form of evolutionary theism is the doctrine of *emergent evolution*, associated with C. Lloyd Morgan and S. Alexander. According to the emergent evolutionists, cosmic evolution is not just a mechanistic regrouping of atoms but an organic process in which we may discern the emergence of qualitatively different levels of being: "Within the all-embracing stuff of Space-Time, the universe exhibits an emergence in Time of successive levels of finite existences, each with its characteristic empirical quality. The highest of these empirical qualities known to us is mind or consciousness. Deity is the next higher empirical quality to the highest we know. . . ."[22] That is, within *Space-Time*, the primordial matrix of things, the cosmic womb from which all successive orders of being emerge, there is at work a creative *nisus* or upward thrust which pushes to the surface, as it were, a succession of qualitatively different emergents. *Matter* represents but one stage in the emergent process—the comparatively primitive level of physical, inorganic being. From matter there arises a new and relatively independent level of being—*life*. From life emerges *consciousness*, a still more highly organized state of things. From within consciousness *mind* separates out to form the next higher autonomous realm of being. *Value*, according to Morgan, is an emergent level higher still. Finally, there is *deity*, the creative nisus itself, which has been slowly driving upward and outward these various strata of being. Deity has not yet emerged but is in the process of emerging from the cosmos. As yet we can but faintly sense its "numinous" presence. In the diagram given,

[22] S. Alexander, *Space, Time, and Deity*, Macmillan and Co., London, 1934, vol. 2, p. 345.

deity forms the apex of the cosmic pyramid, and it is represented by dotted rather than solid lines to show that it has not yet emerged:[23]

To Alexander the infinite God of traditional theism is not actual but ideal. God, thus conceived, has not yet *become*

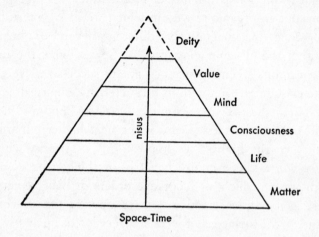

actual. The actual God is the universe viewed as *tending toward* deity. The universe is God's *body* and includes all the gradations of being which have emerged up to this time. The quality of deity, straining to the cosmic surface, is the *mind* of God. Deity is both created and creating, immanent and transcendent. "God," says Alexander, "is immanent in respect of his body, but transcendent in respect of his deity."

Whitehead's God

We know that to Whitehead the world is a process in which we may discern a vast interrelated scheme of actual

[23] See C. Lloyd Morgan, *Emergent Evolution*, Henry Holt and Co., 1927, pp. 9–14.

events—a table, a rainbow, the life of a man, the explosion of a star—no one of which can be adequately understood apart from its relation to other events. Now these actual happenings which constitute the world are only *part* of what Whitehead calls "the total metaphysical situation." Over and above the *actual* lies the vast domain of the *possible*, a realm which comprises all the things that *could be*. But the two spheres are not cut off from each other. Since any event is, so to speak, an *actualized possibility*, the realm of the possible must have an area of contact with the actual. The possible enters into the actual; it has *ingress* into the spatiotemporal world.

Now a puzzling question arises. How does the world come to have the particular character it possesses? How is it that, out of the boundless stock of possibilities, *this* particular set has been actualized? Why *this* world rather than another? To answer this question, Whitehead feels it necessary to introduce a metaphysical factor which is responsible for this particular crimp in the nature of things. He postulates an agent which causes to emerge from the timeless domain of possibilities that particular, concrete system of patterns which is the actual cosmos. This agent is God, whom Whitehead calls "the Principle of Concretion." God's function is to impose a *limit* upon the limitless system of possibilities. God determines an actual course of events which, "metaphysically speaking, might have been otherwise."

Why is it that God makes concrete or actual *this* set of possibilities which is our world? If, metaphysically speaking, it might have been otherwise, what *reason* can be offered for God's having selected *this* world to actualize rather than another? Whitehead's answer is that no reason can be assigned. That is why we must say that God's exist-ence is the ultimate *irrationality*. "No reason can be given for the nature of God," says Whitehead, "because that na-ture is the ground of rationality."[24]

But God, thus conceived, appears as remote from the human heart as Aristotle's Prime Mover—to which White-head's Principle of Concretion bears some resemblance. Thus, Whitehead is faced with the old problem of the two Gods. One is the cosmic force, the impersonal, metaphysical Deity of the philosophers. The other is the God of Love, who is close to us, embracing all things in his tender care. In the history of theism, says Whitehead, these two Gods have never satisfactorily been reconciled. He himself at-tempts a reconciliation by suggesting that the nature of God is *dipolar*, that is, it has a double aspect. One aspect of God is his *antecedent* nature, the other is his *consequent* nature.

In his antecedent nature God is the Principle of Concre-tion, the cosmic factor which elicits actuality from possi-bility. But God, taken as the Principle of Concretion, is more *conceptual* than he is *actual*. This is a supreme meta-physical paradox. For, although God is the Principle of Actuality, he is himself deficient in actuality. Conceived as the metaphysical agent which presses the actual out of the possible, God is not quite a "real" being. In this respect, Whitehead's God is a little like Alexander's Deity, who, as creative nisus, is responsible for the emergence of all the various levels of being in the cosmos, yet is himself not yet actual.

But Whitehead's God has also a consequent or derivative

[24] A. N. Whitehead, *Science and the Modern World*, The Macmillan Company, 1931, p. 257.

nature. This is God as he is here and now related to and affected by the world he has brought into existence. In this aspect of God's nature we find the God who is the object of religious worship. This is the God who dwells in the world and in whom the world dwells. This is the God who is near to us, whom we love, and who loves us: "The image under which this operative growth of God's nature is best conceived, is that of a tender care that nothing be lost. . . . He does not create the world, he saves it; or, more accurately, he is the poet of the world, with tender patience leading it by his vision of truth, beauty, and goodness."[25]

What about evil? If God is conceived, as in traditional theism, as a supreme and all-powerful creator, or as the Absolute, the infinite ground of all being, then such a God must be held responsible for the evil as well as the good. "He is then," says Whitehead, "the supreme author of the play, and to Him must therefore be ascribed its shortcoming as well as its success."[26] But God, as conceived by Whitehead, is not the foundation of the total metaphysical situation. He is but *one* of the cosmological factors, his function being to lure the possible over into the actual. In his consequent nature, God is a power which bends the world by persuasion toward the good. With Plato, Whitehead says, "God is the author of good things only."

The ultimate source of evil lies not in God but in the nature of things. The basic character of the cosmos is process, change, passage. In the actual world there is nothing which can escape this transiency; there is nothing which abides forever. God cannot prevent the passingness of things. "The ultimate evil in the temporal world," says Whitehead, "lies

[25] A. N. Whitehead, *Process and Reality*, The Macmillan Company, 1929, pp. 525, 526.
[26] *Science and the Modern World*, p. 258.

in the fact that the past fades, that time is a 'perpetual perishing.' "[27] There is another reason for the presence of evil in the world. Whenever any given possibility is actualized, the realization of certain other possibilities is thereby excluded. One of life's tragedies is that we must choose between beautiful things. Acceptance of one desired object all too often entails the rejection of others. To try to hold on to two incompatible goods is to risk catastrophe. We cannot eat our cake and have it. Or, as Whitehead puts it, "The nature of evil is that the characters of things are mutually obstructive."[28]

A Modern Fideist Approach; William James

All this philosophizing about God is quite repugnant to William James, who has himself had considerable influence on modern religious thinking. To James, natural theology is an abomination of desolations. For just about all such rationalistic speculations can show for their trouble is some kind of metaphysical deity whose dubious existence is of little interest to anybody besides theistically inclined metaphysicians. James' approach to the problem of God is quite different. It is *fideistic* rather than rationalistic. That is, for James, God is not primarily an object of knowledge. He is an object of faith: "There is one element of our active nature which the Christian religion has emphatically recognized, but which philosophers as a rule have with great insincerity tried to huddle out of sight in their pretentions to found systems of absolute certainty. I mean the element of faith."[29]

[27] *Process and Reality*, p. 517.
[28] *Ibid.*
[29] W. James, *The Will to Believe*, Longmans, Green and Co., 1912, p. 90.

To many critics, James' emphasis on the primacy of faith suggests a modern return to what the fathers of the church considered the only direct way to God. *Credo ut intellegam!* First, we must *believe*, and then understanding will be added. But James attributes a power to faith which the old fathers would never have dared to claim for it—the power *to bring God into existence*, or at least to sustain and increase his being. "I firmly disbelieve," says James, "that our human experience is the highest form of experience extant in the universe."[30] In religious experience, he tells us, we are conscious of a continuity between ourselves and "a wider self through which saving experiences come."[31] Between this wider self and our individual selves there exists a relation of mutual dependence: "I do not see why the very existence of an invisible world may not in part depend on the personal response which any one of us may make to the religious appeal. God himself, in short, may draw vital strength and increase of his very being from our fidelity."[32]

Pragmatism teaches that there is no complete separation between beliefs and facts. Within the moral and religious realm, James seeks evidence to support his pragmatism. In a famous illustration, he tells us how a belief can create a fact. A man, fleeing for his life, finds himself on the brink of a chasm. It is just possible to jump it. A successful leap will take the man to safety. A miss means death. Now if the man believes with every fiber of his being that he can jump the chasm, the chances are he will be successful. If he

[30] W. James, *Pragmatism*, Longmans, Green and Co., 1928, p. 299.

[31] W. James, *Varieties of Religious Experience*, Longmans, Green and Co., 1908, p. 515.

[32] W. James, *The Will to Believe*, p. 61. An unkind critic once compared James' notion that our belief in God contributes to his existence to that of Peter Pan who tells us that our belief in fairies keeps them alive.

entertains doubts and hesitations, he will fail. So it is with judgments of the moral and religious order. We have no final assurance of God's existence. If we had such assurances, faith in God would not be a primary element of religion. Religious faith is positive commitment in regard to a situation the outcome of which is not assured.

On pragmatic principles, says James, if the hypothesis of God *works* satisfactorily, in the widest sense of the word, it is true. Does it make a difference, he asks, whether God exists or not? James believes that it does. If the materialist is right, he says, then the things that matter most are at the mercy of the things that matter least. If, however, there is a being which is the deepest power in the universe, a power conceived under the form of mental personality and which works for good, then life becomes immeasurably richer and more meaningful; an incomparable vista of values opens out before us. Is not the second alternative worth believing in? Should we shrink from it because we *may* be in error? To James (as to Pascal) belief in God represents the choice of a live option, a momentous choice well worth a gambler's risk.

Conclusion

The English philosopher John Wisdom tells a now famous story about two people who return to their long-neglected garden and find flowers growing among the weeds. One says to the other, "There must be a gardener who comes and tends this garden." The other says no, the flowers just happened to grow without tending. But the first man says, "Look at the way those flowers are arranged. There's a purpose and feeling for beauty here." The other shakes his head; a gardener would have done something about those weeds. The two people make inquiries, but they can find no one who has seen a gardener come. They return to the garden and look at it more closely. Both see the same garden. Both examine the same evidence. But each interprets it differently. "I still believe a gardener comes," says the first man. But the second says, "There is no gardener." Which is right?

FURTHER READINGS

Alexander, S., "Deity," in *Space, Time, and Deity*, Macmillan and Co., London, 1934, vol. 2, book 4.

Aquinas, Thomas, "The Existence of God," in *Summa Theologica*, Fathers of the English Dominican Province (trans.), Burns Oates and Washbourne, Ltd., London, 1924, Part 1, Question 2.

Aquinas, Thomas, *Basic Writings of St. Thomas Aquinas*, Anton Pegis (ed.), Random House, 1945.

Aristotle, *Metaphysics*, in *The Basic Works of Aristotle*, R. McKeon (ed.), W. D. Ross (trans.), Random House, 1941, Book 12.

Baldwin, R. C., and McPeek, J. A. S., "In Search of God," in *An Introduction to Philosophy Through Literature*, The Ronald Press Co., 1950.

Bergson, Henri, *Creative Evolution*, A. Mitchell (trans.), Henry Holt and Co., 1911.

Du Noüy, Lecomte, *Human Destiny*, Signet Books, The New American Library, 1949.

Hume, David, *Dialogues Concerning Natural Religion*, E. D. Aiken (ed.), Hafner Publishing Co., 1948.

James, William, *The Will to Believe and Other Essays*, Longmans, Green and Co., 1912.

Kant, Immanuel, "The Ideal of Pure Reason," in *Critique of Pure Reason* (rev. ed.), F. Max Müller (trans.), The Macmillan Company, 1922, pp. 459–516.

Laird, John, *Theism and Cosmology*, Allen and Unwin, London, 1940.

Leibniz, G. W. F., *Theodicy* (abridgment), *Leibniz: Selections*, P. P. Weiner (ed.), Charles Scribner's Sons, 1951, p. 510.

Montague, W. P., *Belief Unbound*, Yale University Press, 1930.

Morgan, C. Lloyd, *Emergent Evolution*, Henry Holt and Co., 1927.

Plato, *Timaeus*.

Randall, J. H., Jr., and Buchler, J., "Supernaturalism," in *Philosophy: An Introduction*, Barnes and Noble, Inc., 1942.

Spinoza, Baruch (Benedict), *Ethics*, R. H. M. Elwes (trans.), Tudor Publishing Co., 1934, Part 1.

Turner, Vincent, S. J., "The Preliminaries of Theism," *The Dublin Review*, Spring, 1951.

Whitehead, A. N., *Science and the Modern World*, The Macmillan Company, 1925, chap. 11.

Whitehead, A. N., *Process and Reality*, The Macmillan Company, 1929, chap. 3, sec. 1.

Wisdom, John, "Gods," in *Essays on Logic and Language*, A. G. N. Flew (ed.), Basil Blackwell, Oxford, 1951.

PART IV

PROBLEMS OF VALUE

9

ETHICS

ETHICS may be tentatively defined as the study of those principles by which we determine what actions are *right* and what ends are *good*. Ethics is sometimes called "moral philosophy," that is, the study which inquires into the principles of morality. Both "ethics" and "morals" derive from words meaning *custom*. Some analysts of human behavior say that morals are nothing but customs or "folkways." Others say that the foundations of morality are more than customs, that ethics deals with human conduct as it *ought* to be rather than as it *is*. We often use "ethics" in the narrow sense of "rules for professional conduct." Thus we say that a physician who tries to take a patient away from a colleague is violating the ethics of the medical profession. In its broader sense, ethics is said to be concerned with the rules for conduct generally, with a view to inquiring what may be the nature of those principles upon which the rules are based. Some moral theorists prefer to begin ethical inquiry with the generic question "What is the good?" All men want what is good, they say, but "good" denotes a property which may be found in other things as well as in human conduct.

Ethics and Politics

The Greeks commonly regarded ethics as a subclass of *politics*. Ethics treats of the good of the individual person only, while politics attends to the good of the corporate entity of which the individual person is a member. Plato felt that the crucial question "What is justice?" could not be answered satisfactorily if the problem was restricted to the conduct of men taken individually. In his famous political treatise *The Republic*, Plato expands the framework of the problem of justice so that it includes the state, which Plato regarded as the individual person "in capital letters."

Something of the Greek distinction between ethics and politics remains today in the common practice of dividing ethics into *individual* and *social* ethics. But our conception of the relation between the individual person and the state is somewhat different from that of the Greek theorists. For they thought that the state was prior in importance to the individual person. Moreover, for certain historical reasons— one of which is the split between political and moral theory, dating from the Renaissance, and not yet completely closed —it is more difficult for us than it was for the Greeks to bring politics and ethics into sharp focus within the same frame. Nearly everyone today, however, would agree that a closer union between personal morals and the conduct of politics would be a very good thing.

Religious and Autonomous Ethics

If we have been brought up within a religious tradition, we naturally think of the distinction between right and wrong as having ultimately a religious foundation. Western theologians have generally maintained that all particular good proceeds from God, who is the source of the right and identical with the good. It is true that we live in a secular age. But the continuity between the ideas of our time and the ages of faith (which take up about sixteen hundred years of Western culture) is still not wholly broken. This situation frequently produces in us a *dual* attitude toward moral principles. Sometimes we grant them authority in their own right; sometimes we appeal to their religious origin. This dual attitude is illustrated by the remarks of President Truman in an address he made to a group of law enforcement officers in 1950. "We must teach that we should do right because it is right," said Mr. Truman. Yet he coupled this assertion with the further statement that the fundamental basis of "right" as embodied in the nation's law "was given to Moses on the Mount," that it "comes from the teaching we get from Exodus and St. Matthew, from Isaiah and St. Paul."[1]

Consider for a moment the notion of "human dignity." This vague but important belief that there is in each human person a fundamental worth or value which may not rightly be ignored is probably one of the basic presuppositions of Western society. In what does this dignity consist? What is its foundation? To those who still live within one of the religious traditions of the West, the answer to this moral question is not difficult. The foundation of human dignity, they say, lies in the fact that God created man in his image, that all men regardless of condition are equally dear to God. Or, in the words of Mr. Truman on another occasion, "We believe that men are equal because they are all created by God. . . . Because of that relation between God and man, we believe that each man in himself has dignity and indi-

[1] Reported in *The New York Times*, February 16, 1950.

vidual worth."[2] This answer to the problem of the foundation of human dignity is a simple version of that offered by
traditional theologians.

Now many philosophers today take exception to this
traditional position on "human dignity" because (being
naturalists) they object to making the validity of ethical
concepts depend on a supernaturalist metaphysics. John
Dewey, for example, finds that "the assertion that the rights
and freedom which constitute democracy have no validity
or significance save as they are referred to some center and
authority outside nature" reflects an "intrinsically skeptical,
cynical and pessimistic view of human nature." "The fact
of the case," says Dewey, "is that naturalism finds the
values in question, the worth and dignity of men and
women, residing in human nature itself."[3]

As far as the purposes of our ethical survey are concerned, no issue need be raised in terms of naturalism or
supernaturalism. Whether their backgrounds be religious
or not, most moral philosophers have agreed that an ethical
doctrine can be constructed at least without immediate
reference to a religious framework. Kant, for example, was
a pious Lutheran, yet he produced an ethical system which
he put forward as independent of particular religious traditions, holding it to be a practical basis of moral doctrine to
which all reasonable men could agree. Outright disbelief in
the metaphysical assumptions of the Judaeo-Christian tradition has not prevented modern philosophers from writing
valuable books on ethics. Indeed, long before there was a
Judaeo-Christian tradition in the West, the pagan Aristotle

---

[2] Reported in *The New York Times*, May 15, 1950.
[3] J. Dewey, "Anti-Naturalism in Extremis," in *Naturalism and the
Human Spirit*, Y. Krikorian (ed.), Columbia University Press, 1944,
pp. 8, 9.

had written a naturalistic ethical treatise marked by such shrewdness and common sense that the theologians of later times incorporated his views in their own writings on ethical questions. To an important extent it was the study of Aristotle's ethical writings which convinced these theologians that the science of ethics possessed a relative but none the less real autonomy. All men by the light of "natural reason," they conceded, could know the principles of ethics, the science which pertains to man's natural, if not his supernatural, end.

In this brief inquiry into ethics we shall examine a few classic and modern types of ethical theory together with the views of the philosophers who support them. If the reader has never troubled to formulate his own moral "first principles," this survey may stimulate him to the attempt.

REASON AND SELF-REALIZATION; ARISTOTLE AND DEWEY

An ethics of *reason* (ethical rationalism) holds that moral acts must be defined in terms of intelligent choice. An ethics of *self-realization* maintains that the good life for man consists in the harmonious development of all his capacities. An examination of the ethics of Aristotle and John Dewey will show us how an ancient and a modern moral doctrine incorporate these elements, together with strong emphasis on the inseparability of the good life from *social* relations.

Aristotle and the Good

According to Aristotle, the good is that at which all things aim. The good for man is what we desire for itself, that for the sake of which everything else is done. Happiness is this good.[4] Now happiness is not a passive state, but activity in accordance with virtue. We are not *endowed* with virtues. We acquire them by learning, habit, and practice. Virtues are of two kinds: intellectual and moral. The highest intellectual virtue is *wisdom*. The moral virtues are many, and may be defined in terms of a mean between an excess and a defect. Courage, for instance, stands between rashness and cowardice, and generosity between prodigality and meanness: "Virtue must have the quality of aiming at the intermediate. . . . Hence it is no easy task to be good. For in everything it is no easy task to find the middle, e.g. to find the middle of a circle is not for everyone but for him who knows; so, too, any one can get angry—that is easy—or give or spend money; but to do this to the right person, to the right extent, at the right time, with the right motive, and in the right way, *that* is not for every one, nor is it easy; wherefore goodness is both rare and laudable and noble."[5]

A necessary ingredient of the moral act is the element of *choice*. Actions in which choice is present form a subclass of voluntary actions. Choice, however, is distinct from other voluntary actions in that it reflects the element of reason or intelligence in man's nature. Moral acts are *free* and *reasonable* acts.

According to Aristotle, the complete development of anything is its highest good. Development requires the transformation of potentialities into actualities. Development means capacities realized. The end or goal of a sapling

----

[4] Aristotle's ethical theory is sometimes classified as *eudaemonism,* a name given to any moral doctrine which identifies the good with *happiness.*

[5] Aristotle, *Nichomachean Ethics,* W. D. Ross (trans.), Book 2, 1106b14, 1109a20.

is to be as much of a tree as possible. In man's case, his end is to be as much of a man as possible. Now man is a rational animal. Those capacities which he shares with other animals (for instance, eating and reproducing) should be realized, since he *is* animal. But he is a *rational* animal. It follows that those capacities which man does not share with other animals—those powers which set him apart *as a man*—should be fulfilled in such a way that they will have priority and control over the development of man's animal capacities.

A good man, then, will act according to that aspect of his nature which marks him off from the other animals. The moral life will be of a specifically human character. Life conceived only in terms of eating, bodily comfort, fighting, and sexual pleasure is a life open to irrational animals. Such a life is not characteristically *human*, and therefore it is not good *for a man*. Aristotle does not mean that eating, sexual activity, and the rest are *bad*. They are good, provided that they operate under the control of activities which are specifically human. Thus the good life may be defined in terms of the development of all our capacities under the control of reason or intelligence. The highest of the rational capacities, Aristotle thought, is that of contemplation, a theoretical and disinterested knowledge of things which only a few men can achieve. But all this is only a partial definition of the good life, since it omits the *social* or, as Aristotle would say, the *political* element. Human capacities cannot be realized in isolation. They can come to fruition only within the larger frame of relations between man and his political community. A man who attempts to live apart from the social environment which is natural to him is not living as a human: "Man is by nature a political animal. . . . The individual, when isolated, is not self-sufficing; and therefore he is like a part in relation to the whole. He who is unable to live in society or who has no need because he is sufficient for himself, must be either a beast or a god."[6]

Moderation and Reason

Aristotle's definition of moral virtue in terms of a *mean* brings his teaching within the group of ethical creeds which hold up *moderation* as an ideal of conduct. This includes the Stoic tradition from which we derive the tags *Nihil nimis* ("Nothing too much") and *In medium virtus stat* ("Virtue stands in the middle"). Classical Chinese philosophy also taught a doctrine of the mean. Confucius' "superior man" always took hold of extremes of doctrine, determined the mean, and employed it in the government of the people. Some critics say that moderation is a characteristic ideal of *naturalistic* ethical doctrines in contrast to the ideal of complete commitment and self-abandonment found in the ethics of *religious* teaching. This generalization is probably worth very little, even though one would have to admit that it is as difficult to imagine Aristotle and Confucius exhorting their disciples to sell all they had and give the money to the poor as it is to imagine Jesus defining virtue as a mean between an excess and a defect.

Emphasis on the role of reason in moral acts enables us to classify Aristotle's doctrine as an example of *ethical rationalism*. The common denominator of the various forms of ethical rationalism is the belief that a truly moral act must in some way be a reasonable act. There are comparatively few moral philosophers who are not in some sense ethical rationalists. The Greeks, who did not make the sharp

[6] Aristotle, *Politics*, B. Jowett (trans.), Book 1, 1253a1, 27.

distinction between "intellect" and "will" later emphasized by the Christian tradition, tended to think of moral goodness as a *species of wisdom.* Socrates has traditionally been credited with teaching that knowledge is virtue. The Stoics, who believed that everything in Nature proceeded according to the metaphysical principle of universal reason, quite naturally regarded rationality as a criterion of moral acts. Spinoza considered reason, not only as the means by which we can control natural forces, but also as the instrument of analysis by which the passions which hold us in bondage can be mastered. Even Kant, who held that right acts proceed from the *will* rather than from *knowledge*, believed that in ethical matters reason had the function of guiding the will according to rational principles. The truly good will, says Kant, is a rational will. John Dewey, as we shall see, holds that reason plays the dominant role in moral acts, if "reason" be interpreted as "intelligent insight into complete and remote consequences of desire." In practical life, we are all ethical rationalists to a degree. It is a presupposition of society that reason guides us in matters of right and wrong. In law, the actions of a defendant in certain circumstances are considered in the light of what a "reasonable man" would do in similar circumstances.

Moral Ideas as Practical Instruments; Dewey

Like Aristotle, Dewey believes that intelligence plays a dominant role in moral acts and that the good life consists in self-realization within a system of social relations. It is in Dewey's *instrumental* conception of the nature of moral acts that we see a distinctively modern emphasis. According to Dewey, there is no fixed eternal good to which all men by nature aspire. There are *goods*—natural goods such as health, wealth, friendship, and aesthetic appreciation; moral goods, such as justice, temperance, and benevolence. But even these goods are too generic to be sought *as such*. For practical purposes, the good always lies in a particular situation. "Every moral situation," says Dewey, "is a unique situation having its own irreplaceable good."[7]

Moral acts are not directed toward the achievement of goals or ends which are established and permanent. Goals or ends are *instruments* we use in intelligent solutions of problems raised by our natural and social environment. "Why have men become so attached," asks Dewey, "to fixed, eternal ends? Why is it not universally recognized that an end is a device of intelligence in guiding action, instrumental to freeing and harmonizing troubled and divided tendencies?"[8] Scientific method is concerned with the control of our natural environment. Methods in morals help us meet those problems which arise from our relations to other men. Yet the two methodologies are not cut off from each other. Rather, they interpenetrate. Science has enormous moral potentialities; for it has the power to better the human condition. Morals progress by the application of scientific method; for a moral problem is a situation of blocked action calling for reflection, hypothesis, intelligent choice, and confirmation in experience. Like other ends, moral ends are instruments by which we remove obstacles to practical action. That is, they are ends which are at the same time means.

Man's proper business is practical activity, says Dewey. Aristotle was wrong in fixing on contemplation as the ful-

[7] J. Dewey, *Reconstruction in Philosophy* (1920), A Mentor Book, The New American Library, 1950, p. 132.
[8] J. Dewey, *Human Nature and Conduct*, The Modern Library, 1930, p. 231.

fillment of the highest capacity of man, even though he limited it to a knowledgeable few. Esteem of the contemplative life arises from a false "spectator" theory of the relation of man to Nature. Since contemplation affects nothing, it is worth nothing. "While saints are engaged in introspection," says Dewey, "burly sinners run the world."[9] Practical activity involves the attainment of ends which are relevant to the solution of problems which our ever developing natural and social environment poses to us. An ethical act derives its moral content, not from an eternal moral law externally imposed from above, but rather from its relevance to the practical situation at hand.

Moral Conduct as Intelligent Choice

Like Aristotle, Dewey holds that a moral act must contain the factor of *choice*. "Only deliberate action," says Dewey, "conduct into which reflective choice enters, is distinctively moral, for only then does there enter the question of better or worse."[10] Like Aristotle too, Dewey emphasizes the critical role of reason in the moral act. But the "reason" which guides moral conduct is not a divine endowment as the Greek philosopher sometimes seems to suggest. Rather, "reason" is a set of habits which enables us to discriminate among possible alternatives of action. Reason in morality is intelligent choice in a practical situation. It is the ability to foresee imaginatively the consequences of a proposed act; it is the capacity to compare and to evaluate those alternative consequences in the light of the goals we wish to achieve; it is competence in assessing the claims of others who may be affected by those consequences. "Moral in-

[9] J. Dewey, *Reconstruction in Philosophy*, p. 154.
[10] J. Dewey, *Human Nature and Conduct*, p. 279.

sight, and therefore moral theory," says Dewey, "consist simply in the every-day workings of the same ordinary intelligence that measures dry-goods, drives nails, sells wheat, and invents the telephone."[11]

Suppose a man, after many years at a particular job, becomes dissatisfied and wishes to change his vocation. This moral situation, like all others, begins with an unsettled, troubled state of affairs in which the routine of daily living is disturbed by doubts and uncertainty. Sound moral decision resolves doubts, restores equilibrium, and clears the way for action. The man who is considering changing his job can make a sound moral decision only by intelligent reflection. This will involve formulating his desires within his own mind more clearly; consideration of the alternative consequences of this or that choice; attention to the claims of others, such as members of his family who may be committed by his decision. No all-binding moral law will help here. This moral situation, like most, simply cannot be abstracted from particular circumstances. Successful solution will be just as specific, and will depend upon the quality of intelligent insight the man can bring to bear on the probable net results of each of the alternatives between which he must choose and their relevance to the ends he desires to attain.

Self-Realization within Democracy

In Dewey's ethical doctrine we find an emphasis on the social nature of moral acts which is kindred to Aristotle's. The American philosopher admires the Greek's "profound insight into the relation of man to society, and the dependence of the individual upon the social body." But Dewey

[11] J. Dewey, *The Philosophy of John Dewey*, J. Ratner (ed.), Henry Holt and Co., 1928, p. 310.

sees moral acts deriving their meaning with reference to a *modern* social structure, which in complexity far transcends the democracy of the tiny city-state within which Greek life was so tightly contracted. Modern democracy, Dewey believes, is the widest and most inclusive category of social adaptation. It is by no means "prior to the individual," as the Greeks thought their state was. Democracy has emerged "as a kind of net consequence of a vast multitude of responsive adjustments to a vast number of situations, no two of which were alike, but which tended to converge to a common outcome." Men are best able to realize their individual capacities within a democratic society, for:

. . . All social institutions have a meaning, a purpose. That purpose is to set free and develop the capacities of human individuals without respect to race, sex, class or economic status. And this is all one with saying that the test of their value is the extent to which they educate every individual into the full stature of his possibility. Democracy has many meanings, but if it has a moral meaning, it is found in resolving that the supreme test of all political institutions and industrial arrangements shall be the contribution they make to the all-around growth of every member of society.[12]

The significant word here is "growth." The metaphor is biological. Aristotle defined the good of anything as its highest development. The goal of an organism is maturity. So, in the case of man, Dewey sees his good, not in fixed results to be attained, but in continuing improvement and progress. Creative development of individual capacities within a democratic society is the highest good. "Growth itself," says Dewey, "is the only moral 'end.' "[13]

[12] J. Dewey, *Reconstruction in Philosophy*, p. 147.
[13] *Ibid.*, p. 141.

THE GOOD AS PLEASURE AND UTILITY

Hedonism

There is a classic theory concerning the nature of the good which asserts that all good (including moral good) is *identical with pleasure;* that the greatest good for man is to be defined negatively as the avoidance of pain, positively as the attainment of maximum pleasure. This theory is known as *Hedonism* (from the Greek ἡδονή—pleasure) and was held by certain ancient ethical schools such as the Cyrenaics and the Epicureans. Tradition has assigned the tag "Let us eat, drink, and be merry, for tomorrow we die" to the Epicureans, but there is no evidence that Epicurus himself or any of the philosophers of his school identified the good with an earthly paradise of sensual delights. Rather, Epicurus esteemed the pleasures of the mind as superior to those of the body and held that "the painless state" (ἀπαθία) in which the gods dwelt was most nearly approached by the serene and detached contemplation of the philosopher.

Utilitarianism; Kinds of Pleasure

A more modern and very influential version of hedonism was promulgated under the title of *utilitarianism* by the English philosopher John Stuart Mill. "Utilitarianism" was the name given by Mill to a doctrine first expounded by Jeremy Bentham, in whose teachings Mill was rigorously indoctrinated by his father, James Mill. According to the younger Mill, utilitarianism, "The creed which accepts as the foundation of morals utility, or the greatest happiness principle, holds that actions are right in proportion as they tend to promote happiness, wrong as they tend to produce the reverse of happiness. By happiness is intended pleasure and the absence of pain: by unhappiness, pain and the privation of pleasure."[14] The first part of this statement has nothing directly to do with hedonism. It is the second part, in which happiness is identified with pleasure, that interests us here. Bentham took pleasure as something *quantitative*, something which is open to measurement. *More* pleasure is simply the heightening of pleasure and this increase is at least theoretically capable of being calculated. Now Mill modifies this Benthamist hedonism in an important respect. While he identifies happiness with pleasure, he distinguishes between *kinds* of pleasure. There are *qualitative* differences in pleasures. Some pleasures are "lower" or "grosser," others are "higher" or "nobler," the former generally being bodily pleasures, the latter intellectual. "It is quite compatible with the principle of utility," Mill thought, "to recognize the fact that some kinds of pleasure are more desirable and more valuable than others."[15] He quickly saw that to maintain hedonism in a purely quantitative form would lead to awkward conclusions. For, if pleasure were merely quantitative, if all pleasures were qualitatively alike, then there would be no reason to suppose that the human ideal of happiness would be on a different level from that of a pig. Mill rejects Bentham's undifferentiated hedonism because he is convinced that "It is better to be a human being dissatisfied than a pig satisfied; better to be Socrates dissatisfied than a fool satisfied."[16]

Now, if we are to distinguish between "higher" and

[14] J. S. Mill, *Utilitarianism*, The Liberal Arts Press, 1949, p. 7.
[15] *Ibid.*, p. 8.
[16] *Ibid.*, p. 10.

"lower" pleasures, the former to be pursued rather than the latter, the question arises: How are we to know which pleasure is higher and which lower? A loyal empiricist and suspicious of anything savoring of "mysticism," Mill sternly rejects any attempt to settle this question by an appeal to *intuition*, by which Mill understood a form of direct knowledge independent of empirical reference or public confirmation. He prefers to point to those who have had experience of *both* "higher" and "lower" pleasures, with the claim that by far the greater number of these men have shown by their actions that the "higher" pleasures are to be desired. "Of two pleasures," says Mill, "if there be one to which all or almost all who have experience of both give a decided preference, irrespective of any feeling of moral obligation to prefer it, that is the more desirable pleasure."[17]

Altruism in Utilitarianism

There is another way in which Mill is forced to modify Bentham's hedonism, and this stems partly from the importance Mill attaches to man's *social* character. Like Aristotle, Mill believed that man is a social animal and cannot live the good life apart from society. "The social state," says Mill, "is at once so natural, so necessary and so habitual to man, that, except in some unusual circumstances or by an effort of voluntary abstraction, he never conceives himself otherwise than as a member of a body."[18] Now Bentham believed that men who constitute society are motivated by their own selfish interests. Mill, however, amends this egoism to the point of admitting that men frequently desire to bring about happiness *for others*, and that this is a good

[17] *Ibid.*, p. 9.
[18] *Ibid.*, p. 33.

thing. For, in order to bring about the greatest amount of *total* happiness, there will be times when we must sacrifice our particular pleasure for that of others. A nurse who stays to die at her post in order that her patients may live is a case in point.

Because of his inclusion within utilitarianism of the element of sacrifice of personal happiness for the good of others, Mill's doctrine has been labeled *altruistic hedonism*. Mill derives his altruism, however, from frankly naturalistic premises. In animals, he says, we find not only the drive of *self-preservation* or self-defense but also the instinct of *sympathy*. In the animal kingdom this sympathy rarely reaches beyond the immediate offspring, but in man it may be extended to include all men. As he develops this argument, Mill turns it back in the direction of egoism. Due to his superior intelligence, Mill says, man can discern that his own personal welfare is bound up with that of the community, so that when he sees that community imperiled in any way he feels his own security threatened.

Is Pleasure the Good?

Mill's utilitarianism, whose first principles we have only briefly sketched, provides much valuable analysis of ethical questions. But many critics have claimed that Mill's insistence on identifying his utilitarian theory of happiness with *the pleasure principle* weakens the foundation of his doctrine. Suppose we consider the following objections, the first of which applies to hedonism in general, the other two referring more particularly to Mill's version of it:

1. In its ordinary meaning, pleasure refers to a relatively brief response, a short period of exalted good feeling. If the hedonist's claim that pleasure is the good and *the only good*

(for, of course, one need not be a hedonist to hold that pleasure *is* good), then one need only to point to common experience to show that the lives of many "good" men are determined by goals other than pleasure in the usual sense. If, on the other hand, by "pleasure" is meant something more than a brief span of heightened good feeling—for example, the satisfaction which accompanies intellectual endeavor or activity in behalf of social welfare—then the word "pleasure" is inflated to cover large areas of experience to which it is not conventionally applied. The word "happiness" would fit as well, and perhaps better; for "happiness" is commonly used to designate a satisfaction which endures.

Mill himself admits this distinction between pleasure and happiness but claims that the happy life is the one with the fewest pains and the most pleasures. It is questionable, however, if the good men Mill admired defined their goals in terms of a life of maximum pleasure. Pleasure and, for that matter, happiness itself seem to be by-products, arising *per accidens*, as the philosophers say, from activities which are not aimed at pleasure or happiness *as such*.

2. When we admit, as Mill does, that there are *kinds* of pleasure, some "lower" and some "higher," do we not at the same time admit the presence of a factor *by virtue of which* these pleasures are "lower" and "higher"? But this factor by means of which we distinguish between the *qualities* of pleasures can hardly *itself* be a pleasure principle, unless "higher" pleasure means merely an increase in the *quantity* of pleasure—which Mill denies.

3. To assert, as Mill does, that there are some pleasures which are more *desirable* than others is subject to the preceding difficulty. In addition, Mill's use of the word *de-*

sirable ("ought to be desired") as a synonym for *desired* produces confusion. He states that (a) happiness (pleasure) is the only thing *desirable*, and supports this assertion by the claim that (b) happiness (pleasure) *is in fact desired*. But "desirable" and "desired" do not mean the same thing. The first, with its compressed "ought," refers to a criterion or standard by which actions are to be judged, and thus has a *normative* reference. "Desired," however, points simply to what in fact is, and thus has only a *positive* reference.

Is Social Utility the Good?

Let us forget about the hedonist element in utilitarianism and compress what remains into the following proposition: *The morally good is the same thing as the socially useful.* Such a definition of the good seems quite reasonable. Killing a man except in self-defense is morally wrong because such an action is not only harmful to the victim; it also imperils the welfare of the social group. Giving food and clothing to the poor is morally right because such charity not only makes the poor people happier; it also improves the condition of society as a whole. What is the end of human life but usefulness to others? Do we not send our children to good schools so that they will grow up to become useful citizens in a democratic society? Christian doctrine itself seems to make morality equivalent to helping others. Does not Jesus' teaching that we should feed the hungry and clothe the naked constitute (as Mill declares) "the ideal perfection of utilitarian morality"?

Can such a warm-hearted and altruistic definition of the good be criticized? Some critics object to the term "socially useful" on the grounds of vagueness. It is just as difficult to define what is "socially useful," they say, as it is to define what is "morally good." From a social-utility point of view, we might all agree that murder, being socially harmful, is properly considered morally bad, while ameliorating the condition of the poor, being socially useful, is morally good. But suppose the case under consideration were that of a man who proposes to enter a monastery, there to spend the rest of his life in prayer and contemplation. To reach agreement on the moral rightness of his act and the moral desirability of his goal would require a searching inquiry into the *meaning* of social utility.

Other critics hold that a definition of the good in terms of social utility can never be any more than secondary. For, they say, whenever we assert that the good is the same thing as the useful, we are forced to make an exception of that for the attainment of which the good *is* useful. That is, a thing can be said to be useful only if it helps to bring about a state of affairs other than itself. Thus, a hammer is useful in that it helps us drive nails through wood. Now what is that for which the socially useful *is* useful? If the aim of good schools is to produce useful citizens, what are the citizens to be useful *for?*

Mill, of course, would reply to this last objection that there is only one state of affairs which is *good in itself*, this being the maximum amount of general happiness; all other goods are to be defined in terms of their utility in bringing this about. John Dewey, on the other hand, would reply that both the objection and Mill's answer are wrongly conceived. For they both assume that any definition of moral good must be in terms of a single good-in-itself to which all other goods are instrumental and subordinate. Dewey, as we have seen, holds that there is no single good-in-itself, whether this be taken as maximum happiness, the welfare of the social group, or something else. To Dewey there is no good, there are only goods. There is no end, there are only ends. And ends are always *ends-in-view*. The only thing which qualifies for the title of *the* moral end is creative growth of the individual within a society—and this concept precludes fixed ends.

Some critics find an excessive emphasis on *altruism* in social-utility doctrines of the good. The "morally good," they say, cannot be quite the same thing as the "socially useful," because there are morally good acts which do not involve our relation to others. Not only does one owe moral obligation to others, says W. P. Montague; one owes it to oneself. "To say that Robinson Crusoe had no moral duties because he had no neighbors is to forget that one's nearest neighbor is one's own future self."[19] As for utilitarians and social-good theorists who support their doctrine by reference to the Christian ethic, is it possible that they assume the presence of an exaggerated altruism in the teachings of Jesus which may not be there at all? Says C. G. Jung:

The acceptance of oneself is the essence of the moral problem and the epitome of a whole outlook upon life. That I feed the hungry, that I forgive an insult, that I love my enemy in the name of Christ—all these are undoubtedly great virtues. What I do unto the least of my brethren, that I do unto Christ. But what if I should discover that the least amongst them all, the poorest of all the beggars, the most impudent of all offenders, the very enemy himself—that these are within me, and that I myself stand in need of my own kindness—that I myself am the enemy who must be loved—what then?[20]

[19] W. P. Montague, *Ways of Things*, Prentice-Hall, Inc., 1940, p. 149.
[20] C. G. Jung, *Modern Man in Search of a Soul*, Harcourt, Brace and Co., 1933.

MOTIVES AND INTUITION

Consequences or Intent

What makes an act morally right or wrong? Is it the consequences, the results of that act, or is it the motive, the intention of the doer? Here is a wealthy man who arranges that a slum dwelling be torn down, provides temporary shelter for the tenants, builds a clean new apartment house in which he houses the tenants at a rental no higher than they paid before. Who would deny that this is a morally good act? Yet we have made no inquiry into the man's motive for doing this. Perhaps no such inquiry is necessary; perhaps the morality of the act is sufficiently guaranteed by its beneficial consequences. On the other hand, people generally agree that motive or intention does have something to do with the rightness of an act. Giving money to a destitute man, let us concede, is a morally good act. Yet suppose a teacher, passing a beggar on the street, gives him some money, his motive being a desire to impress with his generosity some of his students standing about. The *results* of the act, as far as the beggar is concerned, are identical with the gift of the same amount of money by another man who offers it simply because he considers it his duty to help the poor. The dollar from the first man buys as much food as the dollar from the second. Yet if the students knew the motive of their teacher's act, they probably would not consider the act morally estimable.

Most of us would probably admit that motives have something to do with the morality of an act, yet we might hesitate to define morality wholly in terms of the intention of the doer. The wail of a child, "I didn't *mean* it," checks the upraised hand over the broken lamp. Yet to say of a man, "Poor fellow, he *means* well," is decidedly not a tribute of moral esteem. There is a saying that virtue is its own reward, but there is another which states that the road to hell is paved with good intentions. Perhaps both motives and consequences must be considered in any definition of a moral act. But where should we place the emphasis?

Ethical theories are sometimes classified according to whether their primary emphasis is on motives or consequences. True, there is no recognized moral theory which states that the moral content of an act lies *entirely* within the intent of the agent; nor is there any well-known ethical doctrine which judges morality *wholly* in terms of consequences. But moral theories do differ in respect to the stress they place on one or the other. Utilitarian and instrumental theories of the good, such as those of Mill and Dewey, tend to fall within the type of moral theory which stresses *results*. The classic example of a morality of *intent* is the ethical teaching of Immanuel Kant. According to Kant, true moral acts are done from *duty*, not from inclination or the sake of advantage. It may be that some things we do with a view to profit will happen to be in accord with duty. Such actions, however, although not morally bad, have no positive moral content. Let us look at Kant's moral theory in further detail.

Kant's Voluntarism

Voluntarism in ethical theory refers to an emphasis on the primary role played by the *will* in the moral situation. According to Kant, there are two principal faculties of man: (1) the *knowing* faculty and (2) the *willing* faculty. Knowledge makes *science* possible. But it is the *will* which is the foundation of morals, as well as the sole source of that which alone is good in itself. "Nothing can possibly be conceived in the world," says Kant, "or even out of it, which can be called good without qualification, except a *good will*."[21]

Now reason and will are not wholly cut off from each other, says Kant, for reason can and does guide the will according to its own rational principles. Yet man, as *willing*, man as a *moral* being, can penetrate to depths which are closed to *knowing* man, whose understanding is confined to appearances which derive their systematic order from the categories of the mind. To illustrate: Kant says that through reason we can never come to know the existence of God. To man, as a *knowing* being, God remains only a *possible* entity. Nevertheless, although we can never demonstrate that God is, our *will* directly acquaints us with the necessity of postulating his existence. We cannot prove God by pointing to the starry heavens above, but the moral law within our breast convinces us of him. Similarly, reason can tell us only of the possibility of immortality, but the will compels us to assert its actuality. For the *summum bonum* (the union of virtue and happiness) toward which the will strives cannot be reached in this life. Yet a good will is *worthy* of this highest good.

Kant's Intuitionism; Conscience; the Imperatives

By "intuitionism" in ethical theory we mean any view which holds that the basic principles of morality are directly recognized by us as valid without any need of proof or confirmation from external sources. According to Kant, we

---

[21] I. Kant, *Fundamental Principles of the Metaphysic of Morals*, T. K. Abbott (trans.), The Liberal Arts Press, 1949, p. 11.

can know for ourselves what is right and wrong, and this direct and immediate knowledge comes from an inner moral awareness. This internal apprehension of moral law men commonly name *conscience*. Now conscience, Kant tells us, acquaints us with the moral law in the form of a command or *imperative*. The imperative of conscience is known as the *categorical* imperative to distinguish it from a *hypothetical* imperative. Both categorical and hypothetical imperatives, when expressed, contain the word "ought"; but the categorical imperative is *unconditional*, while the hypothetical imperative refers to results which benefit the doer in some way. "It pays to tell the truth" and "You ought to be honest, because honesty is the best policy" are examples of hypothetical imperatives. But the categorical imperative simply commands, "Thou oughtst!" If we ask "Why?" we receive no reply beyond "Thou oughtst, because thou oughtst."

The categorical imperative, Kant tells us, may be formulated in a number of alternate ways. One is: "Act only on that maxim whereby thou canst at the same time will that it should become a universal law."[22] To test the morality of a proposed act the agent should ask himself, "Can I honestly will that which I am about to do should be generally done? Or am I making an exception in favor of myself?" We can see that this formulation of the categorical imperative is related to the "golden rule": "Do unto others as you would have others do unto you."[23] Another formulation of the categorical imperative is stated by Kant as: "So act as to

[22] *Ibid.*, p. 38.

[23] The golden rule is found in the Sermon on the Mount thus: "Therefore all things whatsoever ye would that men should do to you, do ye even so to them" (Matthew 7:12). The golden rule occurs in negative phrasing (but with positive import) in the Confucian teaching of reciprocity.

treat humanity, whether in thine own person or in that of any other, in every case as an end, never as a means only."[24]

Questions for Kant

In so far as it emphasizes the relevance of motive to moral conduct, Kant's ethical doctrine provides a powerful check to the potential one-sidedness of utilitarian ethics. When applied to the analysis of moral situations, Kant's scrutiny of intent serves as an admirable corrective for tendencies to focus exclusively on results. In practical life, both motives and consequences press their claims upon us, and any adequate ethical theory will take serious account of intent as well as outcome. It is impossible to give an adequate exposition of Kant's moral doctrine in a page or two; for this reason, critical evaluation should perhaps be postponed until the reader's interest has led him to a reading of Kant himself. Nevertheless, we can set down a few questions adapted from various critiques of Kant's theory, if only in order that they may be taken along to this future reading:

1. Kant's voluntarism seems to create an exaggerated dualism between the theoretical or "scientific" realm and the sphere of the moral or practical. Is such a radical dualism between man as *knowing* and man as *willing* defensible?

2. Is Kant's claim that a good will is the only conceivable good-in-itself consistent with his claim that the good will is *worthy of happiness?* (Would not happiness then be the good-in-itself?)

3. Kant seems to assume that a moral sense is something *innate*, a faculty with which man is endowed, rather than a capacity he acquires. Can this assumption be defended?

[24] I. Kant, *op. cit.*, p. 47.

4. From what source do the imperatives of conscience derive their authority?

5. Will any of the various formulations of the categorical imperative tell us what to do in any specific situation? If not, what function do they have?

The Good as Indefinable; G. E. Moore

A highly individual form of ethical intuitionism, very different from Kant's, is held by the English analytic philosopher G. E. Moore. Moore maintains that all ethical propositions are based on the notion of "good." Now we can know what "good" is only by direct acquaintance (intuition). For "good" is qualitatively unique. There is nothing else like it. It is *sui generis.* "Good" is something simple (that is, it has no parts) and therefore cannot be defined. We cannot set forth the *meaning* of "good" in propositions which do not include the notion of good:

> "Good," then, if we mean by it that quality which we assert to belong to a thing, when we say that the thing is good, is incapable of any definition, in the most important sense of that word. The most important sense of "definition" is that in which a definition states what are the parts which invariably compose a certain whole; and in this sense "good" has no definition because it is simple and has no parts. It is one of those innumerable objects of thought which are themselves incapable of definition, because they are the ultimate terms by reference to which whatever *is* capable of definition must be defined.[25]

"Good," says Moore, is unanalyzable in much the same way as the perceived quality "yellow" is unanalyzable. To be sure, yellow may be defined in terms of light vibrations.

[25] G. E. Moore, *Principia Ethica* (1902), Cambridge University Press, 1951, pp. 9, 10.

But it is not light vibrations we perceive when we experience yellow. What we do enjoy when we have the experience of yellow is just the unique, indefinable quality "yellow" and that is all there is to it. In the same way, "good," as experienced, is not explainable in terms of anything but itself.

But what about those ethical theorists who *have* explained "good" in terms of something else? Hedonists say the good is pleasure; utilitarians say it is the greatest happiness of the greatest number, etc. They are wrong, says Moore. Whoever defines "good" in terms of something other than good, such as pleasure or utility, is guilty of the *naturalistic fallacy*. Moore does not object to the proposition "Pleasure is good," or "Social utility is good." It is statements such as "Pleasure is the *only* good" and "Social utility is what we *mean* by good" that he refuses to accept. For the same reason, Moore rejects any attempt to define "good" by appeal to the descriptive sentences of the special sciences. The claim, for example, that "good" can be explained in terms of certain psychological states would be dismissed by Moore as another instance of the naturalistic fallacy.

Moore's claim that "good" is indefinable has reminded some of G. K. Chesterton's attitude to the quality "mean." According to Chesterton, you cannot explain what it is that constitutes meanness in a man. A mean man is just plain *mean*, and that's all. More seriously, some critics of Moore's position think he has failed to make an important distinction between two kinds of definition corresponding to the two kinds of knowledge—knowledge by acquaintance and knowledge by description.[26] Yellow is yellow, as Moore

---

[26] See footnote 6, p. 168.

says, and to state that yellow is light vibrations of such
and such a kind does not do justice to the *unique perceptual
quality* of yellow. Yet we may *understand* what yellow is,
we may know *about* yellow, by defining it in terms of its
wave length. Moore may well be right in claiming that,
when we know "good," the peculiar quality of this direct
experience is unanalyzable in terms of predicates other than
"good." But could it not be the case that we can *know
about* good by means of predicates which do not refer to its
unanalyzable quality? If so, it would seem that an attempt
to define "good" in terms of predicates other than good is
—in principle, at least—not fallacious. It does not follow,
of course, that defining "good" in predicates other than
good is necessarily acceptable when such definition involves
reductionism—as, for example, the statements "Good is
nothing but pleasure" and "Morality is nothing but conditioned reflexes."

ETHICAL STATEMENTS AS EXPRESSIONS
OF FEELING

Approval and Disapproval

Are ethical propositions reducible to statements concerning someone's feelings? This question has received considerable attention from recent "philosophers of language."
Some years ago, Bertrand Russell put forward the suggestion that ethical propositions are essentially implicit expressions of approval or disapproval. That is, when a person
says "*x* is good," or "*y* is morally right," he is expressing
approval of *x* and *y* and implicitly exhorting others to feel
the same way. Similarly, when a person says "*x* is bad," or
"*y* is morally wrong," he is expressing disapproval of *x*

and *y* together with his desire to persuade others to disapprove as well. This approach to ethical propositions has been taken by a number of contemporary philosophers who have subjected various types of ethical statements to linguistic analysis. For example, C. L. Stevenson offers the following schema as a "working model" suitable for the preliminary stages of analysis of ethical meaning:

(1) "This is wrong" means *I disapprove of this; do so as well.*
(2) "He ought to do this" means *I disapprove of his leaving this undone; do so as well.*
(3) "This is good" means *I approve of this; do so as well.*[27]

Ayer's Four Types of Ethical Propositions

A. J. Ayer claims that a large number of statements about moral matters are simply expressions of emotion. The statement "It was wrong to steal that money" amounts to no more than the exclamation "You stole!" uttered in a tone of disapproval. According to Ayer, four types of ethical propositions should be distinguished: (1) propositions which express the meanings of ethical terms, (2) propositions which express the phenomena of moral experience, (3) exhortations to moral virtue, and (4) actual ethical judgments, such as "It is wrong to steal." Now propositions of the first type only—that is, those in which the meanings of ethical terms are analyzed—properly belong to ethical philosophy. The second type, which describes the phenomena of moral experience and their causes, should be relegated to psychology or sociology. Propositions of the third type—exhortations to moral virtue—are not proposi-

[27] C. L. Stevenson, *Ethics and Language*, Yale University Press, 1945, p. 21.

tions at all, but ejaculations designed to make the reader or hearer act in a certain way. Propositions of the fourth type —actual ethical judgments such as "It is wrong to steal"— are not genuine propositions either. They are not analytic statements, nor are they descriptions of fact; they are pseudo propositions: "In saying that a certain type of action is right or wrong, I am not making any factual statement, not even a statement about my own state of mind. I am merely expressing certain moral sentiments. And the man who is ostensibly contradicting me is merely expressing his moral sentiments. So that there is plainly no sense in asking which of us is in the right. For neither of us is asserting a genuine proposition."[28]

Nothing but Feelings?

Many ethical philosophers strongly disagree with the opinion that ethical statements are no more than expressions of someone's feelings. They admit that analysis of the meaning of ethical terms should occupy a prominent place in moral philosophy. But they refuse to accept the claim that ethical judgments proper are nothing but expressions of approval or disapproval, or statements about somebody's emotions. Such a position consistently held, say the critics, leads to conclusions so strained and artificial that it can only be maintained in an academic sort of way. Consider a dispute between a Nazi SS officer and a protesting clergyman who holds, "It is wrong to gas these Jews." Can anyone sincerely accept the conclusion that this dispute is no more than a mutual exhibition of moral sentiments—of interest,

[28] A. J. Ayer, *Language, Truth and Logic* (rev. ed.), Victor Gollancz Ltd., London, 1948, pp. 107, 108.

perhaps, to a psychologist? To say that ethical statements are "merely" expressions of emotions is to commit the fallacy of reductionism.

According to the critics of this view, the statement that "strictly ethical" judgments are not propositions at all is, of course, *true by definition*, if the premise upon which it depends is granted, namely, that there are only two kinds of "genuine" propositions, analytic and "factual." But it is by no means self-evident that these are the only two types of "genuine" propositions. It is true that ethical statements of the type "*X* is right" and "*Y* is wrong" are not empirical statements of the kind "Ten thousand Jews were gassed." But it does not follow that statements of the former class reflect nothing but subjective feelings of approval or disapproval. Russell himself has doubts on the matter. He stoutly maintains that the good must be defined in terms of desire, and that a person who judges "*X* is good" is wishing others to feel certain desires. But, he asks:

What are "good" desires? Are they anything more than desires that you share? Certainly there *seems* to be something more. Suppose, for example, that some one were to advocate the introduction of bull-fighting in this country. In opposing the proposal, I should *feel*, not only that I was expressing my desires, but that my desires in the matter are *right*, whatever that may mean. As a matter of argument, I can, I think show that I am not guilty of any logical inconsistency in holding to the above interpretation of ethics, and at the same time expressing strong ethical preferences. But in feeling, I am not satisfied. I can only say that, while my own opinions as to ethics do not satisfy me, other people's satisfy me still less.[29]

---

[29] B. Russell, "Reply to Criticisms," in *The Philosophy of Bertrand Russell*, P. A. Schilpp (ed.), Northwestern University, 1944, p. 724.

ETHICAL RELATIVISM; POWER MORALITY

The Relativity of Morals

We have seen that some philosophers conclude, upon the basis of linguistic analysis, that there is no genuine difference between ethical statements of the type "X is wrong" and "X is right." A similar conclusion is reached by another type of argument, which asserts that the validity of all statements about moral matters is relative to the individual person or to the particular group to which the person belongs. The view that moral right and wrong are relative to the individual or to the group is a very old one. It appears to have been held by certain Sophists in ancient Greece and was vigorously attacked by Socrates, who believed that moral principles were objective, transcending personal opinions or particular interests. Quite common today is the opinion that moral principles are entirely relative to the culture or folk pattern in which they are found. This point of view—which we may call *cultural relativism*—derives from a popular interpretation of evidence drawn from anthropology and related studies. In the nineteenth century, brilliant works such as Frazer's *The Golden Bough* and Westermarck's *The Origin and Development of Moral Ideas* marshaled quantities of data which showed how closely the notions of right and wrong were bound up with the customs and beliefs of individual cultures. In our own century, continued study of primitive cultures has thrown much light on the origin and growth of morals and their relation to custom and taboo. From such evidence, cultural relativists argue that moral principles have no objective status. Since moral codes are dependent on the particular culture within which they develop, no one set of moral principles is "better" than any other. Therefore, it is idle to dispute about ethical matters. "It's all relative!"

Unfortunately we cannot here give this type of argument the attention that its popularity warrants. We can only suggest in passing the following criticisms that have been offered against it. First, suppose we grant that morals originated in custom. It does not therefore follow that one set of moral teachings is as good as another, any more than it follows that one custom is as good as another. Second, morality may have *begun* in custom and local practice. But this is not the same as to say that morality is *identical* with custom and local practice. Because religion may have begun with shamans, it does not follow that religion is *nothing but* shamanism. Third, the doctrines of many moral teachers have been conspicuous by their *difference* from the accepted moral teaching of their day, a difference which sometimes resulted in the violent deaths of the moralists in question at the hands of the official representatives of the culture in which they lived. Jesus and Socrates are cases in point.

Perhaps we do not wish to subscribe to the exaggerated form of *ethical absolutism* which asserts the existence, antecedent to experience, of a fixed eternal moral law, externally imposed from above and binding upon all men. But we are not therefore compelled to hold as the only alternative the radical form of *ethical relativism* which states that moral doctrines are entirely subjective and relative, and binding upon no man. The position that one manner of moral behavior is as good as another is no more tenable than the position that one opinion is as good as another.[30] Such

[30] The late Alexander Woollcott was once interrupted in a lecture by

assertions are perhaps logically irrefutable, but only because when we retreat to them we implicitly reject the effectiveness of intelligent discourse and deny the human
power to judge, discriminate, and evaluate.

Might Makes Right; Natural and Conventional Morality

The teaching that ethical principles arise from customs and
folkways is a *genetic* theory of morals, that is, a theory
which talks about morals from the point of view of their
origin and development. A genetic account of morals has
also been offered to support the doctrine that *right* is a
function of superior *power*. Moralists who hold this position frequently distinguish between two kinds of morality
(1) *natural* morality, in which what is right is identical with
what the strong are able to do, and (2) *conventional*
morality, in which a moral system opposed to the first is
constructed by the weak in order to protect themselves.
Various formulations of power morality have appeared at
different stages of the history of Western culture. We find
it in Machiavelli's arguments supporting the power of
Renaissance princes; in some nineteenth-century Darwinists
who drew it as an ethical corollary from the biological
principle of the survival of the fittest; and in the socio-
political theories of the prophets of Fascism. The classic
exposition of the morality of the strong is put into the
mouth of Callicles the Sophist by Plato in the *Gorgias:*

> For the truth is, Socrates, that you who pretend to be en-
> gaged in the pursuit of truth, are appealing now to the popu-
> lar and vulgar notions of right, which are not natural, but only

---

a lady who said "After all, Mr. Woollcott, that's only your opinion."
With a baleful stare, Woollcott replied, "What did you expect, madam?
My hair combings?"

conventional. Convention and nature are generally at variance
with one another . . . the makers of laws are the majority
who are weak; and they make laws and distribute praises and
censures with a view to themselves and to their own interests;
and they terrify the stronger sort of men, and those who are
able to get the better of them, in order that they may not get
the better of them; and they say, that dishonesty is shameful
and unjust; meaning, by the word injustice, the desire of a man
to have more than his neighbors; for knowing their own inferiority, I suspect that they are too glad of equality. And
therefore the endeavor to have more than the many, is conventionally said to be shameful and unjust, and is called injustice, whereas nature herself intimates that it is just for the
better to have more than the worse, the more powerful than
the weaker. [31]

Aristocratic and Slave Morality; Nietzsche

Friedrich Nietzsche accounts for the development of morality in something of the fashion of Callicles. In his *Genealogy of Morals*, the nineteenth-century German philosopher asserts the existence of a primitive aristocratic era in
which morality was identical with the will of the noble.
Conceived thus, natural morality is aristocratic, inseparable
from the will of the superior few which is imposed on the
inferior many. The modern moral tradition of Europe, says
Nietzsche, arose from Christianity, which was originally
a conspiracy of slaves determined to thwart the aristocratic
will of their over lords. Just as sheep, subject to the preda-
tions of wolves, might formally agree that "Eating sheep
is bad," so the Christians devised a moral system in which
weakness and humility were converted into virtues, the
exercise of strength and power into *sin*, their own incompe-

[31] Plato, *Gorgias*, B. Jowett (trans.), 482 483.

tence into immortality: "These weaklings!—they also, forsooth, wish to be strong some time; there is no doubt about it, some time *their* kingdom also must come—"the kingdom of God" is their name for it, as has been mentioned—they are so meek in everything! Yet in order to experience *that* kingdom it is necessary to live long, to live beyond death, yes *eternal* life. . . ."[32] Using their slave morality cunningly as an instrument of social control, says Nietzsche, the Christians were able to overthrow the domination of their noble masters and to introduce to the Western world a morality of inferiority and weakness which has since effectively held in check the aristocratic aspirations of the strong. He looked forward to the day when this traditional morality would be liquidated in a "Transvaluation of All Values." Out of this moral apocalypse, this "Glad Noontide," would emerge a new type of man, the *superman* (*Übermensch*), in whom strength and virtue would again be one.

Summaries of Nietzsche's moral theory, such as the above, are frequently followed by observations to the effect that such a detestable doctrine is self-evidently false, together with pious allusions to Nietzsche's death in a madhouse. This is indeed the less attractive aspect of Nietzsche, his "misunderstood" side, the side which appealed to Hitler (who gave Mussolini an edition of Nietzsche's works as a birthday present) and the Nazi theorists. Nietzsche himself, however, seems *not* to have thought of the superman in the terms in which this questionable concept has so often been interpreted—a "blonde Teuton beast" who would

[32] F. Nietzsche, *Genealogy of Morals*, in *The Complete Works of Friedrich Nietzsche*, O. Levy (ed.), H. B. Samuels (trans.), The Macmillan Company, 1924, pp. 50, 51.

lead a new "master race" to world domination. In order to do justice to the superman, we must observe Nietzsche's distinction between two principles of human nature and human culture: (1) the *Dionysian* principle, which designates the dynamic and infra-rational side of man—impulse, feeling, instinct, power; and (2) the *Apollonian* principle, which refers to man's ethical and rational aspect. The historical effect of the Judaeo-Christian moral tradition, Nietzsche thinks, has been to split the two apart—with the result that we tend to accord to reason and morality a shallow independence, an unreal mastery over the instinctive and dynamic side of human nature. What Nietzsche seems to have in mind when he speaks of the superman is the ideal of an *integration* of the dynamic and instinctive elements of human nature with its rational and ethical components. Thus conceived, the superman is nearer to Goethe than he is to a glorified storm trooper.

Conclusion

Some critics of Nietzsche hold that the trouble with his moral doctrine lies in its assumption that instinct, impulse, the "will to power," and the dynamic, infra-rational side of human nature generally, need to be defended against the encroachments of intellect and morality. True, they say, exaggerated confidence in the power of reason may lead to shallow optimism; complacency in regard to the effectiveness of enlightened moral doctrine may engender a superficial and one-sided view of human nature. But has the instinctive and "natural" side of man ever seriously been threatened by the pretensions of his rational and ethical side? Certainly, we must admit the importance of impulse and subrational drives, agree that they are powerful and rooted deep in man. We should welcome their study so as to understand their nature and effects. But was there ever a time when impulse and "will to power" required *protection* against reason and morals? Do not the actual practices of men and nations plainly show that power morality stands in no danger of losing its popularity?

The world events of the present century have demonstrated (indeed, there was never any need to demonstrate it) that the rational and ethical equipment of man is as yet a thin and fragile instrument, still far outweighed by powerful drives, irrational and amoral, which sleep lightly under the most enlightened humanistic surface and are easily aroused from their slumber. The humane tradition of the West—among whose ingredients are the rationalism of the Greeks, the ethics of the Judaeo-Christian tradition, and the science of the modern world—has been built up slowly and painfully over twenty-five hundred years of time, never at any moment proof against the wildest excesses of human passion and cruelty. From this tradition we have derived a rational and ethical deposit, which is not yet so strong that the need of guarding it is past.

FURTHER READINGS

Aquinas, Thomas, *Summa Contra Gentiles*, Book III, chap. 1–113.

Aristotle, *Nichomachean Ethics*.

Ayer, A. J., *Language, Truth and Logic* (rev. ed.), Victor Gollancz Ltd., London, 1948, chap. 6.

Dewey, John, *Human Nature and Conduct*, The Modern Library, 1930.

Dewey, John, "Moral Reconstruction," in *Reconstruction in Philosophy* (1920), A Mentor Book, The New American Library, 1950.

Hume, David, *An Enquiry into the Principles of Morals*, Clarendon Press, Oxford, 1894.

Jordan, E., *The Good Life*, University of Chicago Press, 1949.

Kant, Immanuel, *Critique of Practical Reason and Other Writings in Moral Philosophy*, L. W. Beck (trans.), University of Chicago Press, 1949.

Kant, Immanuel, *Fundamental Principles of the Metaphysic of Morals*, T. K. Abbott (trans.), The Liberal Arts Press, 1949.

Mill, John Stuart, *Utilitarianism*, The Liberal Arts Press, 1949.

Moore, G. E., *Principia Ethica* (1902), Cambridge University Press, 1951.

Nietzsche, Friedrich, *Genealogy of Morals*, in O. Levy (ed.), *The Complete Works of Friedrich Nietzsche*, H. B. Samuels (trans.), The Macmillan Company, 1924.

Parker, DeWitt H., *Human Values*, Harper & Brothers, 1931.

Plato, *Gorgias*.

Plato, *Protagoras*.

Spinoza, Baruch (Benedict), *Ethics*, R. H. M. Elwes (trans.), Tudor Publishing Co., 1934, Books 3, 4, 5.

Stevenson, C. L., *Ethics and Language*, Yale University Press, 1944.

IO

AESTHETICS

> *It is from Music that the finish is received.*
>
> —Confucius

ETHICS and aesthetics, it is commonly said, are both concerned with "value" or "the good"—the difference between them being that ethics has for its object of study "moral good," while aesthetics deals with "the beautiful." Less broadly taken, aesthetics is identified with "the philosophy of art," that is, the study of the general principles of artistic creation and appreciation. Thus defined, aesthetics is contrasted with *criticism*, whose task is to analyze and appraise particular works of art. As a separate division of philosophy, aesthetics has had a relatively brief history. The word "aesthetics" seems to have been publicly used for the first time in 1735 by the German philosopher A. G. Baumgarten, who afterward published a book titled *Aesthetica*. One of the first influential formal treatments of aesthetics, conceived as a special discipline, was offered by Kant (who studied Baumgarten) in his *Critique of Judgment*. But philosophers did not wait until the eighteenth century to discuss the nature of the beautiful, the function of art, and the role of the artist. Ancients like Plato, Aristotle, and Plotinus had much to say on these topics. Even the medievals, who tended to concentrate on those two plain sisters, the True and the Good, had kind words to spare for the Cinderella of philosophy, the Beautiful—although they sometimes suspected her, metaphysically speaking, of waywardness.

Natural Beauty

If the subject of aesthetic study is taken to be *beauty*, then the province of aesthetics is wider than "the philosophy of art." For there are many other things, beside artistic objects, to which people apply the adjective "beautiful." The beauty of sunsets, landscapes, flowers, and women falls within the realm of *natural* beauty. We moderns seem to find more beauty in Nature than did our classical forebears. What could be more beautiful than sunlight on snow-capped mountain peaks? Yet we have it from Havelock Ellis that, as late as the seventeenth century, persons of considerable sensitivity wrote of "the high and hideous Alps." Indeed, says Ellis, for most travelers before Rousseau's time "The Alps still remained what they had been for Livy and for Amianus, a scene of unmitigated horror which no one could approach for the sake of pleasure."[1]

The natural beauty which the Romans admired was of a tidy and cultivated kind, like that of Horace's garden. Even Plato, archpoet that he was, describes natural scenes in terms of what we would call the pleasant rather than the beautiful. Says his Socrates, sitting down by the bank of the Ilissus with Phaedrus:

By Herè, a fair resting-place, full of summer sounds and scents. Here is this lofty and spreading plane-tree, and the agnus castus high and clustering, in the fullest blossom and the greatest fragrance; and the stream which flows beneath the plane-tree is deliciously cold to the feet. . . . How delightful

[1] H. Ellis, *From Rousseau to Proust*, Houghton Mifflin Co., 1935, p. 78.

is the breeze:—so very sweet; and there is a sound in the air shrill and summerlike which makes answer to the chorus of the cicadas. But the greatest charm of all is the grass, like a pillow gently sloping to the head. My dear Phaedrus, you have been an admirable guide.[2]

It is the comfort of it all—the cold water on his feet, the grass pillowing his head—that seems to make the greatest impression on Socrates. He goes on to observe to his pupil that he rarely goes out to the country. "I am a lover of knowledge," says Socrates, "and the men who dwell in the city are my teachers, and not the trees or the country." How different from Wordsworth:

> One impulse from a vernal wood
> Will teach you more of man
> Of moral evil and of good
> Than all the sages can.

The Arts

Besides natural beauty, there is beauty in art. But what is art? There are the useful arts, and the fine arts, and some which appear to be both. In premodern times the notions of "art" and "craft" were not as widely separated as they are today. It is thought by some that all art originated in the desire of the craftsman to make his object not only useful but pleasing. The plain bowl was adequate for food, but the prehistoric potter added some bright colors in a pleasing design. What visitor to Sardinia or Sicily has not been delighted with those gay paintings with which the peasants, in accord with tradition, decorate their humble carts. A fine Persian or Chinese rug is a pleasure both to walk on and to look at. The Greeks built their temples and the medievals

[2] Plato, *Phaedrus*, B. Jowett (trans.), 220.

their cathedrals for communal worship. In modern America, the finest products of engineering and construction combine beauty with utility. New York City's RCA tower soars into the sky with a grace far surpassing that of its taller rival, the Empire State Building; and the Whitestone Bridge arches over the East River as if it had no weight at all. What a pity it is, say philosophers Santayana and Dewey, that in the modern world we have come to think of art as something divorced from experience, something to be inspected on Sunday afternoons in a special building with the sepulchral name of "*museum.*"

The Fine Arts

The "fine" arts include the spatial and visual arts of architecture, sculpture, painting, and drawing; and the temporal and auditory art of music. The "literary" arts include poetry, drama, and (a latecomer) the novel. The history of art tells us how in the past many of these forms have combined with and served one another. The Greek drama required the accompaniment of music and the dance. The medieval cathedral needed sculptured figures for the exterior, paintings for the altar, and the music of plain chant for the Mass. Drama and poetry were one in the plays of Shakespeare, Racine, and Goethe. In modern times, however, the arts have split apart from one another, each form tending to go its separate and autonomous way. True, music, drama, and even the dance are combined (uneasily, some think) in the modern opera. The old Russian ballet was an admirable synthesis of the dancing of Fokine and Nijinsky, the music of Stravinsky and Ravel, and the scene painting of Bakst. And today there is something of a revival of the poetic drama—notably at the hands of T. S.

Eliot. But, generally speaking, at present the individual art forms are cultivated on separate levels. Too separate for their own good, say many critics.

The conventional classification of the arts gives no indication of historical development. Some art forms have declined, others have risen from lowly state. Our poets no longer write epics, leaving this to the novelists. Indeed, the audience for poetry of any kind today seems to have dwindled. The great ages of sculpture seem to be past. But music, once a humble auxiliary among the arts, is now loved for its own sake. It has been said that music is the art most characteristic of modern Western culture. Schopenhauer pronounced it "the art of arts," and Pater claimed that all art aspires to the condition of music. Some pessimists (and they may be right) tell us that the day of great artistic creation is over for the West, that all that remains for art today is repetition or parody.

There seems to be no reason why "fine" art should be restricted to the conventional categories. In the eighteenth century, hydraulics and landscape gardening were taken quite seriously as art forms, and in our own day, Ernest Hemingway's *Death in the Afternoon* convinced many that bull fighting has its own aesthetic. The motion picture has enormous resources which have from time to time been employed to produce an artistic masterpiece.

Form and Content

The fine arts use a sensuous medium—stone, wood, metal, etc., in the case of architecture and sculpture; color and line in painting and drawing; tones and rhythm in music. The literary arts have no comparable sensuous medium at their disposal; they must use words, which are comparatively conceptual. Hence it is difficult for aesthetic philosophy to formulate principles which apply to both "fine" and "literary" arts. In all works of art, however, it is possible to distinguish between *form* and *content*. A poem is about something. A musical composition is built up out of themes. A painting is a representation of this rather than that. A novel tells a story. All this is content. But in every art the content is disposed in a certain way. The material is handled, ordered, controlled. To borrow a popular cliché, it's not only what the artist says, it's the way that he says it. Corey's line:

They told me, Heracleitus, they told me you were dead.

is poetry. But this is prose:

They told me you were dead, Heracleitus.

It is probably useless to ask which is more important—form or content. Philosophers of art agree that in the finest creative work there is a perfect union between the two elements. But form is essential. It is not something superadded to the content of a work of art. In poetry, imagery or metaphor is not tacked on to the subject matter of a poem to make it read nicely. Form is integral to art, not an embellishment of it. When content gets the upper hand at the expense of form, the value of the work of art is compromised.

Types of Aesthetic Theory

Here is a man looking at a Chinese vase or listening to a Schubert quartet. He says, "That's beautiful." Now, we ask, how do philosophers of art approach the problem of the beautiful? Do they talk about those generic properties which the vase and the music both possess? Or do they talk about the effect produced in the man? In other words, do philosophers of art assume that beauty is something *in the object*, and proceed to analyze those qualities by virtue of which an object is a work of art? Or are they more interested in discussing what happens *in the man* as he sits there enjoying the beautiful thing? Now philosophers of art will hasten to tell us that beauty is a coöperative affair; that it cannot be discussed in terms of either subject or object alone. Both must be taken into account in any discussion of aesthetics, they say, for in the aesthetic experience there is an attunement or rapport between subject and object— something like a sympathetic vibration between two strings. "Art," says DeWitt Parker, "is sympathetic representation; the effort not only to reveal an object to us, but to unite us with it."[3]

Nevertheless, it is possible to distinguish (very roughly) between those theories which approach the problem of art and the beautiful from the side of the *object* and those whose approach is from the side of the *subject*. This contrast is sometimes recognized by dividing aesthetic doctrines into theories of *form* and theories of *expression*. In theories of form the approach is "objective." The philosopher tries to tell us what it is that makes an object beautiful. For example, he may say that the object possesses certain properties, such as unity, wholeness, balance, symmetry, etc. In theories of expression the approach is more "subjective." The philosopher is not so much interested in talking about the formal properties of the beautiful object as he is in discussing the nature of *the aesthetic experience*. He wants to tell us what occurs *in us* when we are enjoying a beautiful

[3] D. H. Parker, *The Principles of Aesthetics* (rev. ed.), Appleton-Century-Crofts, Inc., 1946, p. 82.

thing. A similar (and overlapping) contrast between types of aesthetic theory may be observed if we compare *metaphysical* theories of art—particularly those of the classic Platonic type, which suggest that art reveals the universal in the particular—with *psychological* theories, which stress the emotional state of the appreciator.

Related to theories of the psychological type are *genetic* accounts of art. In this case the philosopher endeavors to explain how art came about in the first place. He explains art through its origins. Art begins in decoration of useful objects; or it begins in play; or in imitation. Or the genetic theorist may suggest that art has biological roots and call our attention to the role of bright and pleasing colors in sexual selection in the animal kingdom, or to the habits of certain birds who collect pretty stones.

In the following pages we shall examine some individual theories of art and see to what extent (if any) the doctrine in question relies on each or all of these basic approaches to the problems of art and the beautiful.

THE METAPHYSICAL APPROACH: ART AND THE UNIVERSAL

Art as Imitation and Vision; Plato

In Plato we find the seeds of a number of subsequent theories of art and the beautiful. His doctrine of art as *imitation* is turned by Aristotle into a genetic account of art. On the psychological side, he suggests in one dialogue that art is *pleasure;* in another he gives a striking description of the *emotional state* of one who experiences a beautiful object. He even foreshadows the romantic notion of the pathological nature of art; the artist is a madman, although it is a divine kind of madness that afflicts him. Most characteristically, he tells us that in the experience of beauty we have an *intuition of a universal form.* This side of the Platonic aesthetic comes to us through a long line of philosophers of art down to Schopenhauer and Croce.

When he is thinking of the artist as imitator, Plato tends to take a dim view of him. His objections are based on both metaphysical and political grounds. What the artist does is to make a representation or copy of a natural object. But, according to the Platonic theory of Ideas, all natural objects are themselves copies of the eternal Forms which alone are real. The artist is one who makes a copy of a copy, and thus art is twice removed from reality. Since he is occupied with shadows of shadows, it is hard for the artist to be a solid citizen. Politically, he is unreliable. Hence, Plato in his capacity of political philosopher reluctantly excludes the artist from his Ideal Republic.

In his capacity as poet-philosopher, however, Plato has more favorable words for the artist. The reason is once more metaphysical. The eternal Forms, which are the sole reality, are invisible. Accessible to reason alone, they cannot be disclosed by the senses. There is one exception, though. One only of the immutable essences is revealed to us, at least partially, by the senses. This is the Form of beauty:

And the essence of beauty, as I have explained, was revealed to us along with the other essences, but in this world it is beauty that we apprehend the most clearly shining through the clearest of our senses. For sight is the sharpest of all our bodily senses. Wisdom cannot be seen; for if wisdom could have afforded any such lively and visible image of herself, we should have been mad with love of her, or any other of the essences that are lovely. But, as it is, beauty alone has this privilege, so that it is the most manifest and lovable of all things.[4]

The lover, says Plato, is inflamed by the beauty of his beloved. He too, like the poet, is visited by a sort of divine madness. And it is well that this should be so. For mortal beauty, if we but follow where it points, can lead us as it were up a ladder which we mount step by step with the indispensable aid of intellectual discipline. At each stage of our ascent we come nearer and nearer to the kingdom of the real, until at last the soul, shot through with a kind of incandescence, no longer knows but *sees* in an all but blinding moment of illumination—the Form of beauty itself.

What is suggestive in Plato's parables of beauty is not only the idea that beautiful objects disclose a universal form but also the notion of the *intuitive* character of aesthetic experience. Since Plato, many philosophers of art have called our attention to the immediacy and directness with which we know the beautiful. Beauty, they tell us, is not reached by syllogisms or demonstrated by theorems; it is something directly apprehended. In Bergson's language, we do not move around the object of art; we do not know it discursively by means of its external relations; we enter into it and find ourselves at one with it. Croce denies to art the character of conceptual knowledge, and makes intuition the key to his entire theory of aesthetic.

Universal and Radiant Form; Aristotle and Aquinas

In Aristotle we find something of each of the standard approaches to philosophy of art. There is the genetic point

[4] Plato, *Phaedrus*, 250, E. F. Carritt (trans.), *Philosophies of Beauty*, Clarendon Press, Oxford, 1931, p. 16.

of view. Art begins in imitation. It is natural in man to imitate others, and it is also natural for him to delight in representative works which successfully imitate things. From
the psychological side, there is the effect of art upon the
emotions which Aristotle calls *catharsis* or purgation—and
of this we shall have a little more to say further on. Finally,
from the "objective" side, art embodies the universal. According to Aristotle, the function of the poet is to describe,
not the particular—the kind of thing that has happened. The
poet's task is to describe the universal—the kind of thing
that might happen. "Hence poetry," says Aristotle, "is
something more philosophic and of graver import than
history, since its statements are of the nature rather of universals, whereas those of history are singulars."

In Aquinas we find the teaching that in the beautiful object the universal is made manifest in the particular—at least
this is how many of his commentators interpret him. According to St. Thomas, there are three formal properties
which beautiful things possess: (1) *integritas* or unity (of
the whole), (2) *consonantia*, the harmony, balance, or
order (of the parts); (3) *claritas*—clarity, brightness, or
radiance.[5] Now the first two properties of the beautiful are
classic in aesthetic tradition. The unity and simplicity of
the admired object (*unus et simplex*) had been noted by
Aristotle. Plotinus had specified the harmony and proportion of the parts. But *claritas* or "radiance"—what is this?
Readers of James Joyce will recall that in his novel *Portrait of the Artist as a Young Man* the hero Stephen De-
dalus ponders this very question. Is the Thomistic *claritas* the universal form made manifest in the sensible object?
Or does *claritas* refer to the instantaneous apprehension of

[5] Aquinas, *Summa Theologica*, Part 1, Q. 39, Art. 8.

the form or character of the object itself? "The radiance of which he [Aquinas] speaks is the scholastic *quidditas*, the *whatness* of a thing. This supreme quality is felt by the artist when the esthetic image is first conceived in his imagination. The mind in that mysterious instant Shelley likened beautifully to a fading coal. The instant wherein that supreme quality of beauty, the clear radiance of the esthetic image, is apprehended luminously by the mind which has been arrested by its wholeness and fascinated by its harmony is the luminous silent stasis of esthetic pleasure. . . ."[6]

E. F. Carritt interprets the Thomistic *claritas* in this way: Aquinas believes that if we knew ultimate reality (God), we would know it, not by conceptual knowledge, but directly and intuitively. Now when we encounter what is beautiful, we are able to grasp its nature in an act of immediate apprehension. This intuitive knowledge of a sensible thing is a small-scale analogue of the apprehension of ultimate reality. In fact, the ultimate reality may be said to appear in or through those sensible objects which are beautiful: "The reason why it thus appears in or through *some* individual sensible objects, is that there is a real difference in these objects, not a difference in man's attitude to them. They are objects where the matter and form or essential character are mutually adequate, so that there is completeness and due proportion of parts, and distinctness like the clarity of colour. Objects which the form thus shines through or illuminates are peculiarly suited to our faculties of perception and are beautiful."[7] In this way, the universal is made manifest in the particular.

[6] J. Joyce, *Portrait of the Artist as a Young Man*, The Modern Library, 1928, p. 250.
[7] E. F. Carritt, *op. cit.*, p. 50.

The Platonic Forms and the Wheel of Ixion; Schopenhauer

According to the nineteenth-century German philosopher Arthur Schopenhauer, we know the world under two aspects—idea and will. Viewed as idea, the world is what Kant said it was—*appearance*, ordered by the mental forms of space, time, and causality. That is to say, from the standpoint of knowledge, the world is but a coherent dream, orderly illusion. But there is also the world as it is *in itself*. This is *will*. Reality is one eternally striving will, blind and amoral, immanent in all individual things. The omnipresence of the indwelling will is revealed to us directly in our own restlessness, passion, and never satisfied desire. The will, which is the sole reality, is one. But seen from our point of view, that is, under the forms of space, time, and causality (idea), the will becomes multiple; it divides into its members or creatures, in each of which it is present like the Godhead in the several hosts of the Eucharist. The infinite will thus *objectifies* itself in its numberless finite parts. The multiplicity of natural objects is no more than the will itself seen from the secondary and derivative level of human knowledge.

On the one hand, then, we have the cosmic will—one, eternal, ever striving. And on the other, there is the multiplicity of finite things into which the will seems to divide. But between the two realms stand the *Platonic Ideas*. These are the universal types of things, the models which Nature seems to strive in vain to copy. These Forms have a kind of demi-existence outside human knowledge and hence are unaffected by time and multiplicity. We may compare the world will to a roaring waterfall—blind and irresistible in its senseless power. The multiple individuals in the world of space and time are the countless fragmentary drops into which the raging torrent shivers in its plunge. Now the rainbow, hovering beautiful and motionless above the boiling torrent, is the realm of the universal Forms, the archetypes of all things. Existing independently of the categories of the mind, the Platonic Forms inhabit, so to speak, a lovely half-world somewhere between the cosmic will, taken as one and undivided, and the crawling multiplicity of the individuals in which the will objectifies itself.

It is these universal Forms—located outside the struggle and compulsion of things, detached from the blind striving of the will—which are the objects of the artist's vision. The artist is a genius, a special man, not like "the common mortal, that manufacture of Nature which she turns out by the thousand every day." He alone among his fellows can contemplate the timeless Form behind the particular object. He alone can understand what Nature, in all its multiplicity and dividedness, is trying unsuccessfully to express: "The true genius . . . recognizes the Idea in the particular thing, and thus, as it were, *understands the half-uttered speech of nature,* and articulates clearly what she only stammered forth. He expresses in the hard marble that beauty of form which in a thousand attempts she failed to produce, he presents it to nature, saying, as it were, to her, 'That is what you wanted to say!' And whoever is able to judge replies, 'Yes, that is it.' "[8]

From this metaphysical account of art in terms of con-

[8] A. Schopenhauer, *The World as Will and Idea*, R. B. Haldane and J. Kemp (trans.), Routledge and Kegan Paul Ltd., London, 1948, vol. 1, p. 287.

templation of Platonic Form, Schopenhauer proceeds to draw a psychological and moral conclusion concerning the function of art. *Art is escape*. Escape from what? Escape from the relentless striving of the will within us; escape from the never-to-be-satisfied longing produced in us by the infinite demands of the will. For we are creatures of the will, tormented by the thirst of a thousand desires. Of these, the most powerful is the sexual, in which the blind and irrational character of the will most nakedly reveals itself. For sex is but the means the will employs to perpetuate itself in other creatures in order to go on striving endlessly. We know from bitter experience that to satisfy one desire is to cause ten others to spring up in its place; to indulge desire is to throw an alms to a beggar—it keeps him alive today so that he may starve tomorrow. We are slaves of *wanting*, bound as prisoners to an endlessly turning wheel as was Ixion of old. But in art we find a real—if temporary —release from the anguish of life. Art is like sweet balm on wounds. For it has the power to detach us from desire, and therefore from suffering. When we behold the beautiful, we slip loose from the will for a blessed moment of respite; we gaze upon the universal in things in pure, objective, will-less contemplation: "Then all at once the peace which we were always seeking, but which always fled from us on the former path of the desires, comes to us of its own accord, and it is well with us. It is the painless state which Epicurus prized as the highest good and as the state of the gods; for we are for the moment set free from the miserable striving of the will; we keep the Sabbath of the penal servitude of willing; the wheel of Ixion stands still."[9]

[9] *Ibid.*, p. 254.

THE PSYCHOLOGICAL APPROACH:
THE NATURE OF AESTHETIC EXPERIENCE

Art as the Expression of Emotion

Here is a tale about the origin of art in terms of expression of feelings. A certain primitive man encountered a strange animal, a buffalo. The huge beast came very close to the man and frightened him. The man hurried back to the shelter of his cave. Safe there, but still aroused, the man seized some soft colored stone and on the wall of the cave traced the outline of the fearsome thing. His drawing finished, he felt calmer. Fellow cave dwellers crowded around the picture, grunting and nodding appreciatively. Art was born.[10]

This little story may not represent an adequate account of the genesis of art. Nevertheless, it is consistent with the widely popular conception of art as the expression of the emotions. Says Clive Bell (best known for his doctrine that "significant form" is the one quality common to all works of visual art): "Created form moves us so profoundly because it expresses the emotion of its creator. . . . No one ever doubted that a Sung pot or a Romanesque church was as much an expression of emotion as any picture that was ever painted."[11] It is usually added that in art the emo-

[10] There is wide agreement among contemporary experts on primitive art that such cave paintings had a primarily *magical* significance. "The best proof," says Arnold Hauser, "that this art was concerned with a magical and not an esthetic effect, at least in its conscious purpose, lies in the fact that the animals in these pictures were often represented as pierced by spears and arrows or were actually shot at with such weapons after the completion of the work." *The Social History of Art*, Alfred A. Knopf, Inc., 1951, vol. 1, p. 28.

[11] C. Bell, *Art* (1914), Chatto and Windus, London, rev. ed., 1949, pp. 49, 58.

tions are expressed in such a way that they are communicated to others. Tolstoy says that the artist hands on to others the feelings he has lived through, and that these others are infected by these feelings and experience them: "To evoke in oneself a feeling one has once experienced and having evoked it in oneself then by means of movements, lines, colours, sounds, or forms expressed in words, so to transmit that feeling that others experience the same feeling—this is the activity of art."[12]

Conflict and Equilibrium of the Emotions

But art is more than just the expression of emotions so as to communicate them. It is the expression of emotions in a particular way. This way, say many philosophers of art, is *harmony* or *balance*. It is interesting to note that the key concept of harmony or balance is found in both formal and "psychological" theories of art. With this difference: In classic theories of the formal or "objective" type, the harmony or balance is located *in the object*. Thus, a beautiful thing is said to possess the properties of symmetry, proportion, harmony of the parts, etc. In modern theories of art which stress the psychological side of it, the concept of harmony or balance is also invoked, but the harmony is located *in the feelings*. It is sometimes said that art begins with a *conflict* among the emotions and that in the aesthetic experience these conflicting feelings are brought into equilibrium or harmonious synthesis. Says Helen Parkhurst: "For those in whom conflicting passions are especially profound and irreconcilable, not even through religion nor through love is there possible without some disturbing re-

---

[12] L. Tolstoy, *What is Art?* A. Maude (trans.), Oxford University Press, London, 1931, p. 123.

pression the perfect synthesis of emotions essentially anti-
thetical. For them, the less integrated, the more tormented
individuals, there is one type of experience, and probably
it is the only one, within which all warring tendencies are
not merely preserved and harmonized but actually made to
serve the ultimate ends of perfection. And this experience
is the esthetic."[13]

Aristotle held that when we view a tragic drama the
emotions of pity and fear are aroused, but in such a way
that these emotions undergo a *catharsis* or purgation. This
puzzling doctrine has been construed in nearly a hundred
different ways, the simplest of which is that a moderate
amount of pleasurable excitement is good for mental health.
A more sophisticated interpretation of *catharsis* is that in
the aesthetic experience the emotions are stirred into life,
but arrested, brought under control in such a way that the
movement of the awakened feelings is self-contained and
balanced. This interpretation of *catharsis* is somewhat
similar to the contemporary aesthetic doctrine of *synaesthesis*, advocated by I. A. Richards and others. According
to the theory of synaesthesis, in aesthetic experience all our
faculties are called into play; our impulses are awakened
and alert. But these aroused impulses are in a state of balance or equilibrium. Supporters of the synaesthesis theory
quote with approval the ancient Confucian doctrine of
equilibrium and harmony as given in the *Chung Yung:*
"When anger, sorrow, joy, pleasure are in being but not
manifested, the mind may be said to be in a state of Equilibrium; when the feelings are stirred and co-operate in due
degree the mind may be said to be in a state of Harmony.
Equilibrium is the great principle. If both Equilibrium and

[13] H. H. Parkhurst, *Beauty,* Harcourt, Brace and Co., 1930, p. 29.

Harmony exist everything will occupy its proper place and all things will be nourished and flourish."[14]

Art and Expression; Croce

One of the most renowned philosophers of art, the Italian Benedetto Croce, defines art as expression. Expression of the emotions? No, just expression. But expression of *what?* Of intuitions. In fact, art *is* intuition. Intuition and expression are correlative. To intuit is to express, and nothing else.

Croce's theory of art is quite difficult to understand, although there is widespread agreement that it is very important. One reason for its difficulty is that Croce is an idealist, holding that everything which exists is mental or spiritual and that there are no such things as physical facts. A work of art has no formal properties; what we find in it is our own spirit smiling at us. Art is intuition, and intuition is imaginative, non-conceptual knowledge which comes from our feelings. "Intuitions are truly such because they represent feeling, and only thence can they arise."[15] Now no one has intuitions without expressing them. To have a genuine intuition of a geometrical figure is inseparable from our ability to draw it. So, in art, to *have* an intuition is to *express* it.

But how does an artistic or aesthetic intuition differ from any other kind of intuition—such as that of a triangle? Croce replies that there is no important difference between the two types of intuition. *All* intuitions are beautiful. This explains why sensitive people can find beauty in every-

[14] I. A. Richards, C. K. Ogden, and J. Wood, *The Foundations of Aesthetics*, Lear Publishers, 1929, p. 14.
[15] B. Croce, *A Breviary of Aesthetics*, E. F. Carritt (trans.), in Carritt, *op. cit.*, p. 241.

thing, even in an old shoe. "One artist is thrown into transports by a smiling landscape, another by a rag shop, another by the pretty face of a young girl, another by the squalid countenance of an old rascal."[16] If there *is* any difference between the ordinary run of intuitions and those of art, it is quantitative only—not qualitative. That is, the intuitions of art are wider and more complex than those we generally experience. The intuition of a popular love song is truly beautiful, but it is beautiful in a limited way compared to the complex intuition of a love song by Leopardi.

In art, intuition (or, if you prefer, imagination) expresses itself in images, and these take form in words, colors, lines, tones. They are neither good nor bad, real nor unreal, useful nor useless. They are beautiful. "Art is vision or intuition. The artist produces an image or a dream; and those who appreciate his art turn their eyes in the direction he has indicated, look through the loophole which he has opened, and reproduce in themselves that image."[17]

Art as Pleasure

Beauty, says Santayana, is pleasure. It is pleasure *objectified* —pleasure regarded as the quality of a thing. Some may object that Santayana stresses the subjectivity of beauty at the expense of its formal qualities. But at least he reminds us that all art is, in some sense, an entertainment and a delight. In the aesthetic experience the emotions are aroused, but the excitement is pleasurable, not painful. Art frequently deals with the painful and the ugly, but in some way—hard to explain—representation of these things produces satisfaction. Is it because, as Aristotle says, successful

[16] B. Croce, *Aesthetics*, D. Ainslie (trans.), Macmillan and Co., London, 1929, p. 99.
[17] B. Croce, *A Breviary of Aesthetics*, cited in Carritt, *op. cit.*, p. 233.

imitation always pleases even when the subject is ugly? Or
is it that in art we never take the painful situation literally,
but only "as if" painful? Perhaps Schopenhauer is right
when he says that in contemplating a representation of the
tragic side of things we find austere satisfaction in the compelling way in which the artist lays hold of the universal
by means of the particular. ("Yes, that is it.") Says Santayana: "We are more thankful for the presentation of the
unlovely truth in a lovely form than for the like presentation of an abstract beauty: what is lost in the purity of the
pleasure is gained in the stimulation of our attention, and
in the relief of viewing with aesthetic detachment the same
things that in practical life hold tyrannous dominion over
our souls. . . ."[18]

The beautiful, says Aquinas, is that which, when beheld,
pleases. (*Pulchra sunt quae visa placent.*) Of course, not
everything which pleases is beautiful. But, say the critics,
if a work of art does not please, it fails. This does not mean
that a work of art must please everybody. Beautiful things
can be difficult, and may not yield us pleasure easily. Art
is not simply an affair of warm-hearted good feeling; Beethoven's *A Minor Quartet* does not wear its beauty on its
sleeve. The peculiar quality of aesthetic pleasure has been
a problem of interest to generations of philosophers of art.
Plato speaks of "unmixed" pleasures, such as the smell of a
rose, and says that the pleasures of art are "pure" pleasures,
since they are not followed by pain. Kant tells us that the
pleasure we take in the beautiful is *disinterested* pleasure.
There is no suggestion of utility or profit in the satisfaction
we derive from the beautiful. The object of art is not re-

[18] G. Santayana, *The Sense of Beauty*, Charles Scribner's Sons, 1896,
pp. 207, 208.

garded as a means or instrument; it pleases us as an end in itself. Thus the aesthetic state is pleasure "without interest" (*interesselos Wohlgefallen*).

Art as Play

Kant's conception of aesthetic experience as enjoyment of an object, not for profit or utility, but for its own sweet sake is related to his suggestion that art is *play*. Work is activity for an end. Play is an activity agreeable in itself. Hence art is more closely related to play than to work.

The poet Friedrich Schiller picked up this notion from Kant and in his *Aesthetic Letters* developed it into a theory of the genesis of art. Art begins in the play impulse, and play is a kind of overflow or discharge of superfluous energy. Man works when motivated by need; he plays when his superabundant vitality overflows and takes form in pleasurable activity which is its own end. The highest form of human play is art. Taking his cue from Schiller, Herbert Spencer finds the origin of aesthetic activity in animal play, which he also interprets as the expression of superfluous energy. In his *Principles of Psychology* he tells us that in animals of higher types the energy not wholly drawn off by the satisfaction of physical needs is expended in play which awakens all kinds of agreeable feelings. In aesthetic experience the faculties of the organism are exercised in such a way that a maximum of activity is combined with a minimum of strain.

To Karl Groos, art is the highest form of the universal game of *make-believe*. The frolicking puppy pretends to attack his master. The little girl treats her doll "as if" it were her child. Adult sport—wrestling, tennis, etc.—provides make-believe fights, conventionalized struggles for supremacy, which are far more pleasurable than the "real thing." The artist, too, desires supremacy; he does not create for pleasure alone. Out of his own "make-believe" he achieves a spiritual ascendancy over his fellow men. "Spiritual supremacy," says Groos, "is the aim of the highest art, and there is no real genius without the desire for it."[19]

Art as Wish Fulfillment; Freud

Groos' notion of the artist's achieving supremacy through make-believe is not unlike the theory of Sigmund Freud, the father of psychoanalysis. According to Freud, art is the projection in fantasy of the heart's desire. The artist (an introverted, almost neurotic type) is motivated—like all men—by deep-rooted, instinctive drives. He wants power, fame, honor, riches, women. But he lacks the means to gratify these longings. So he projects his desires into fantasy. This might lead a person of lesser capacities to preoccupation with unreality and ultimately to neurosis. But not to the artist. He finds his way back to reality because the products of his fantasy bring to him by an indirect route the very things he really wants. The artist is able to create fantasies to which the ordinary man turns with delight—for the ordinary man is not satisfied by his own poor daydreams. Out of his ability to project his fantasies in such a way that other men find pleasure and consolation in them the artist reaps his reward in their gratitude and love. Thus he wins "through his phantasy—what before he could only win in phantasy: honor, power, and the love of women."[20]

[19] K. Groos, *The Play of Animals*, D. Appleton and Co., 1898, p. 295.
[20] S. Freud, *A General Introduction to Psychoanalysis* (1920), Garden City Publishing Co., 1952, pp. 327, 328.

Empathy

In Freud's theory the idea of the projection of the self in art is a rather simple one. The artist has certain basic longings; these are projected in fantasy, which is then objectified in the art work. But among aesthetic theories we find another which involves a concept of self-projection more difficult to grasp. This is the empathy or *Einfühling* ("in-feeling") theory identified with the aesthetic doctrine of Theodor Lipps and his disciple Vernon Lee.

In aesthetic experience there are present in us what the psychologists call "sympathetic motor responses." The conventional illustrations of this are drawn from architecture. The Doric column seems to press down firmly on its foundations; we "read into it" our own unconscious muscular tensions. Faced with a splendid skyscraper, the human organism exhibits sympathetic muscular behavior, as if it were straining for flight. Music seems to induce all kinds of muscular tensions—as those of us can confirm who have ever had the misfortune to sit through a performance of *Tristan* beside a music lover whose impassioned jerkings testify to his kinesthetic unity with the music. Now if the empathy theory of aesthetic enjoyment amounted to nothing beyond calling our attention to the sympathetic postural or muscular attitudes provoked by or projected into art, we should have little difficulty understanding it. But the empathy theory means more than the projection of kinesthetic tension into objects. True, says Lipps, so complete is the unity in aesthetic experience of self and object that we may fall into sympathetic muscular attitudes. But these are only external, behavioristic signs of the "in-feeling." What really brings about the unity of subject and object in art is that we project into the object all kinds of activities and feelings, ranging from simple physical attitudes to the most developed processes of the human spirit. In the enjoyment of the sight of a human figure in motion: "I am now with my feeling of activity entirely and wholly in the moving figure. Even spatially, if we can speak of the spatial extent of the ego, I am in its place. I am transported into it. I am, so far as my consciousness is concerned, entirely and wholly identical with it. Thus feeling myself active in the observed human figure, I feel also in it free, facile, proud. This is esthetic imitation and this imitation is at the same time esthetic empathy."[21]

Lipp's empathy theory suggests that in the aesthetic experience the "ego" is projected into the object admired. Vernon Lee disassociates herself from this "metaphysical" interpretation of empathy and rests content with defining it as the "complex mental process by which we invest objects with the stored up and averaged and essential modes of our activity."[22]

ART AND SOCIETY

Art and Morality

"Morality" in its broad meaning refers to right relations between men; in a narrow meaning, it touches on sex. Art has relation to morality in both senses. Time and again, throughout the ages, moralists have charged that art encourages idleness and stimulates sexual passion. In every era, guardians of public morals have covered up statues, turned paintings to the wall, banned poetry, burned books, halted

[21] T. Lipps, cited in M. M. Rader (ed.), *A Modern Book of Esthetics*, Henry Holt and Co., 1935, p. 298.
[22] V. Lee, *The Beautiful*, Cambridge University Press, 1913, p. 66.

operas, censored plays—all on the ground that the works in question offended moral decency. Renowned philosophers of art have themselves had anxieties on this score. Plato was convinced that music and poetry could soften the sinews of the soul, leading the young to lives of idleness and dreams. Tolstoy feared art's dangerous proclivity for stirring the flesh; he denounced paintings of nude women and novels about adultery; he wrote *The Kreutzer Sonata* to show how music could inflame the passions.

We tend today to pass over the outraged cries of moralists and Philistines with a smile and a shake of the head. Yet, in a way, they are right. If art has the power to awaken all our faculties, we cannot expect the sexual side of our nature to remain unkindled. As Santayana says, "The whole sentimental side of our aesthetic sensibility—without which it would be perceptive and mathematical rather than aesthetic —is due to our sexual organization remotely stirred. . . ."[23] Kant, we remember, said that the pleasure of aesthetic experience is *disinterested*. Schopenhauer interpreted this to mean that in art the faculties are detached from all willing, most particularly from sexual desire. With his doctrine of art as escape from the will, Schopenhauer took the aesthetic state to be a pure will-less contemplation in which sensuality is put out of action. Nietzsche denies this. Art does not calm the will; rather it excites it, even when refining it. For all its capacity to soar in the realm of spirit, art is rooted in sense, even in the sensual. The inspiration found by painters and sculptors of all ages in the nude female body shows that in art something very different from Kantian "disinterest" is involved. (Nietzsche cites the example of Pygmalion.)

Using the word "morality" in a broader sense: it is al-

[23] G. Santayana, *op. cit.*, p. 59.

most a classic thesis in aesthetics that art and morality occupy different spheres. The realm of the moral is the practical, says Croce; morality is an affair of the will. But aesthetic activity is essentially contemplative and, as such, has nothing to do with practical activity:

> Art, in fact, as was long ago observed, is not produced by an act of the will; the good will which makes a good man does not make an artist. And since it is not produced by an act of will, art is exempt from moral distinctions, not by any privilege of immunity, but because moral distinctions simply do not apply. An artist may imaginatively represent an act worthy of moral praise or blame; but his representation, being imagination, is worthy of neither. Not only can no penal code condemn an imaginative representation to death or to prison, but no reasonable man can make it the object of a moral judgement. To judge immoral Dante's Francesca, or moral Shakespeare's Cordelia, whose functions are purely artistic and who are like notes of music from the soul of Dante or Shakespeare, would be no better than to judge a triangle wicked, or a square moral.[24]

But, adds Croce, if art is outside the sphere of morality, the artist is not. "As a man he comes under its laws and never escapes the duties of a man."[25]

Art for Art's Sake

Exaggerated emphasis on the separation of art and morality marks the views of certain critics and literary men of the latter half of the last century. Théophile Gautier, author of the erotic *Mlle de Maupin*, brandished the slogan *"L'art pour l'art"* to confound the Philistine bourgeoisie. Walter

---

[24] B. Croce, *Breviary of Aesthetics*, cited in Carritt, *op. cit.*, p. 236.
[25] *Ibid.*, p. 237.

Pater inspired a generation of budding artists to "burn with a hard gem-like flame," to get into the brief interval of life "as many pulsations as possible": "Only be sure it is passion —that it does yield you this fruit of a quickened, multiplied consciousness. Of this wisdom, the poetic passion, the desire of beauty, the love of art for art's sake, has most. For art comes to you proposing to give nothing but the highest quality to your moments as they pass, and simply for those moments' sake."[26] Oscar Wilde made epigrams: "All art is quite useless. . . . There is no such thing as a moral or immoral book. Books are well written or badly written. That is all. . . . No artist has ethical sympathies. An ethical sympathy in an artist is an unpardonable mannerism of style."[27]

Critics of the "art for art's sake" doctrine admit that the artist should not be expected to concern himself in his work with moral and ethical matters. But they find implicit in *l'art pour l'art* an erroneous belief that aesthetic values are somehow set apart from human values, taken generally. But art is an intensely human affair and, as such, cannot be compartmented away from human good. "Beauty, being a good," says Santayana, "is a moral good; and the practice and enjoyment of art . . . fall within the sphere of morals —at least if by morals we understand moral economy and not moral superstition."[28] And Thomas Mann concurs, "The infinite effort for what is good artistically has the same root as the endeavor for what religion and morality

[26] W. Pater, *The Renaissance* (rev. ed.), Macmillan and Co., London, 1925, pp. 238, 239.
[27] O. Wilde, *The Picture of Dorian Gray*, Preface.
[28] G. Santayana, "A Brief History of My Opinions," in *The Philosophy of Santayana*, Irwin Edman (ed.), The Modern Library, 1936, p. 20.

call 'good.' "[29] But the classic reply to the "art for art's sake" doctrine remains Nietzsche's:

If art is deprived of the purpose of teaching morality and of improving mankind, it does not by any means follow that art is absolutely pointless, purposeless, senseless, in short *l'art pour l'art*—a snake which bites its own tail . . . what does all art do? does it not praise? does it not glorify? does it not select? does it not bring things into prominence? In all this it strengthens or weakens certain valuations. . . . Is his [the artist's] most fundamental instinct concerned with art? Is it not rather concerned with the purpose of art, with life? with a certain desirable kind of life? Art is the great stimulus to life; how can it be regarded as purposeless, as pointless, as *l'art pour l'art?*[30]

Art and the Social

Today, with our emphasis on social and political categories, there is a widespread popular feeling that the value of a work of art can be measured, to some degree at least, in terms of its social significance. Here is an extract from a student paper:

I think that Richard Wright's *Native Son*, with its wonderful portrayal of the social injustice suffered by the Negro people at the present time in the United States is a far better work of art than James Joyce's *Ulysses*. Wright is concerned with moral and social values, and his powerful work makes men aware of evil and injustice, and inspires them to conquer it. Joyce, on the other hand, stands aloof from society. He doesn't

[29] T. Mann, "How to Win the Peace," *Atlantic Monthly*, February, 1942, p. 177.
[30] F. Nietzsche, *Twilight of the Idols*, in *The Complete Works of Frederick Nietzsche*, Oscar Levy (ed.), The Macmillan Company, 1924, pp. 79, 80.

374 The Meaning of Philosophy

seem to care anything about it. He doesn't seem to care even if people can't understand his difficult books. That sort of thing is all right for esthetes and pseudo-intellectuals. But today the artist, if he's worth his keep, has got to descend into the arena, meet practical problems, and help his fellow man by means of his art.

Now Tolstoy says much the same thing in *What Is Art?* To him the purpose of art is to promote the brotherhood of man. If a work of art does not have the power to lift up the hearts of a large number of men, uniting them in a sense of brotherly love, then art has lost its value. The thesis of Tolstoy and the student cited draws strength from the fact that in our time some forms of art have become so specialized and difficult as to be practically inaccessible even to persons of some sensitivity and education. These art forms have become the special province of small cults or coteries, while the majority of people are unaware of their existence. Here art becomes, as Irwin Edman says, "a sporadic little nervous dissipation for a small group rather than the expression of a civilization healthy and general, which flowers in the arts into imaginative appreciation."[31]

From time to time, artists of the first rank turn their talents to social protest. In painting alone, one thinks of Daumier's satires on officialdom, Goya's "Horrors of War," and Picasso's "Guernica." It is questionable, however, whether art should be regarded primarily as a social or political instrument. Thus conceived, art too easily degenerates into storytelling with a moral, or into outright political pamphleteering. Hitler banned "abstract" or "modernist" painting as *Kulturbolshevismus* and encouraged the production of rather obvious nude statuary of Aryan men

[31] I. Edman, *Arts and the Man*, W. W. Norton and Co., 1939, p. 44.

and maidens. But the painters of the Soviet Union are by no means given to "modernism" or "abstract" art. They paint equally obvious tractors, and scenes from Russian revolutionary history which are photographically accurate and politically edifying. This is art as propaganda.

Great works of art have a way of keeping in touch with the moral realm without instruction from moralists or social thinkers. It is not necessary, perhaps it is even harmful, for a work of art to step outside its own frame, and to play upon our prepared responses, social or political. For what happens then is that content is exploited at the expense of form. We may not agree with Aristotle that form is "by nature, prior" to matter. But we can agree that in art, at least, form should not be relegated to a secondary role. Besides, the artist is a stubborn fellow, impatient of conformity and, by virtue of his vocation, somewhat unreliable. For his task is to make beautiful things. And, as Galsworthy says, where beauty is, things never run quite straight.

FURTHER READINGS

Aristotle, *Poetics*, in J. A. Smith and W. D. Ross (eds.), *The Collected Works of Aristotle Translated into English*, Clarendon Press, Oxford, 1908–1931.

Carritt, E. F., *An Introduction to Aesthetics*, Hutchinson's University Library, London, 1949.

Carritt, E. F., *Philosophies of Beauty* (An Anthology), Clarendon Press, Oxford, 1931.

Croce, B., *Aesthetics*, Douglas Ainslie (trans.), Macmillan and Co., London, 1929.

Dewey, John, *Art as Experience*, The Macmillan Company, 1934.

Ducasse, C. J., *Art, the Critics and You*, O. Piest, New York, 1944.

Edman, Irwin, *Arts and the Man*, W. W. Norton and Co., 1939.

Gilbert, K. E., and Kuhn, H., *A History of Esthetics*, The Macmillan Company, 1939.

Kant, I., *Critique of Judgment*, J. H. Bernard (trans.), Macmillan and Co., London, 1892.

Langer, Suzanne K., *Feeling and Form*, Charles Scribner's Sons, 1953.

Lee, Vernon, *The Beautiful*, Cambridge University Press, 1913.

Nietzsche, Friedrich, *The Birth of Tragedy*, in O. Levy (ed.), *The Complete Works of Friedrich Nietzsche*, H. B. Samuels (trans.), The Macmillan Company, 1924.

Parker, DeWitt, H., *The Principles of Aesthetics*, Appleton-Century-Crofts, Inc., 1946.

Parkhurst, H. H., *Beauty: An Interpretation of Art and the Imaginative Life*, Harcourt, Brace and Co., 1930.

Plato, *Phaedrus*, in *The Dialogues of Plato*, B. Jowett (trans.), Oxford, Clarendon Press, 1892.

Plato, *Republic*, 400–402, 597–607.

Plato, *Symposium*, Socrates' Speech, 199–212.

Rader, M. M., *A Modern Book on Esthetics* (An Anthology) (rev. ed.), Henry Holt and Co., 1952.

Richards, I. A., Ogden, C. K., and Wood, J., *The Foundations of Aesthetics*, Lear Publishers, 1929.

Santayana, G., *The Sense of Beauty*, Charles Scribner's Sons, 1896.

Santayana, G., *Reason in Art*, Charles Scribner's Sons, 1934.

Schopenhauer, Arthur, *The World as Will and Idea*, R. B. Haldane and J. Kemp (trans.), Routledge and Kegan Paul Ltd., London, 1948, vol. 1, Book 3.

Tolstoy, Leo, *What Is Art?* A. Maude (trans.), Oxford University Press, London, 1931.

INDEX

INDEX

Index

Index